The Teenager's Guide to the Stock Market

Start Building Wealth Now

Jim Brent

Late Wisdom, Inc.

Library of Congress Control Number 2019938993

Brent, Jim
The teenager's guide to the stock market: start building wealth now /Jim Brent
p. cm.
Includes index.
ISBN 978-1-7339409-0-0

1. Investing in common stocks. 2. Stock market. 3.Investment strategies. 4. Mutual funds. 5. Exchange traded funds. 7. Stock market timing. 8. Passive management. 9. Active management. 10. Factor-based investment management. 11. Long term investing. 12. Emotions and the stock market. 13. Robo investing. 14. Buy-and-hold. 15. Dollar-cost-averaging. 16. Personal finance. 17. Money management. 18. Investment management. 19. Finance. I. Title.

Late Wisdom, Inc.
P.O. Box 12
Flossmoor, IL 60422

Manufactured in the United States of America
10 9 8 7 6 5 4 3 2 1
First Edition

Dedication

To the youth of our country – the future belongs to you. Invest your time and money wisely.

Acknowledgements

I would especially like to thank Beverly Rodgers for her excellent editing skills and for her timely advice. I would also like to thank Heather Augustyn for her skillful help.

About the Author

The author has spent nearly 50 years in investments and investment-related areas. He received his bachelor of science degree from Purdue University and his MBA from the University of Chicago. He has taught investments and corporation finance at the Graduate School of Business at Indiana University NW and has written many articles for various investment trade publications. He is a Chartered Financial Analyst and has been a speaker at numerous investment conferences. As Director of Equity Investments at a major pension fund, he helped oversee the investment of billions of dollars of pension fund money and managed several common stock portfolios. He retired in 1991 at the age of 48. He has written three books, built houses with Habitat for Humanity, and visited over 50 countries. The author writes under a pen name.

CONTENTS

THE TEENAGER'S GUIDE TO THE STOCK MARKET

Introduction

You don't have to be brilliant to make money investing in the stock market, but you do have to know what you are doing. That's why, at age 75, I decided to write this book – to pass on to you the knowledge I wish someone had given me 60 years ago.

Unlike many other investment books, however, you won't find a get-rich-quick formula here. Instead, I'm giving you something of real value: a fact-based, comprehensive, easy-to-read guide that is organized in such a way that you can go into as much depth as desired. Although I will be presenting some sophisticated concepts, I will not talk down to you for I believe if I explain them clearly, without confusing jargon, and in a straight-forward manner you will understand them.

If you stick with it, by the end of this book you will know more about the stock market and common stock investing than many of the investment professionals. The mystery surrounding the market will be cleared away and, with the confidence gained, you should be able to make your own investment decisions, based on your own personality and risk-tolerance.

Remember, right now, while you are young, is the very best time for you to start building serious wealth by investing in common stocks. You only need to have the discipline to start early, invest often, and invest for the long term.

How much money are we talking about if you invest early, often, and for the long term? Neither I nor anyone else can answer that question. We can only look to the past as a less than perfect guide. For example, just a single one-time investment of $5,000 in Microsoft at the beginning of April 1986 would have grown to about $6 million by the beginning of 2019 with splits and dividends reinvested. An investment in Apple? A $5,000 investment at the beginning of 1985 would be worth nearly $2 million by the beginning of 2019 with splits and dividends reinvested[1].

You say I cherry-picked my examples? Well, how about a seemingly stodgy company like Clorox, the bleach people. A $5,000 investment at the beginning of 1985 would have grown to over $550,000 by the beginning of 2019 with splits and dividends reinvested.[2] You say you don't want to take the time to search for individual stocks? Fine. An investment in an index fund that closely tracked the Standard & Poor's 500 index would have returned about $160,000 – an excellent return for a single $5,000 investment made in 1985.[3]

Are you guaranteed this kind of money? Of course not. Nothing in life is guaranteed, whether it's getting the keys to the car, landing that hot date, or making a killing in the stock market. But I believe the odds are in your favor if you start early, invest often, and invest for the long term.

Was it a straight path to this kind of money? Of course not. Microsoft was down -62% in one year and up +125% in another. Apple? It was down -56% one year and up +211% in another. Even Clorox and the S&P 500 index fund had bumpy paths to those long-term returns with Clorox down -29% and up +65%, and the S&P 500 index fund down -38% and up +34%.

Despite all the ups and downs, the long-term success of the products and services provided by these corporations made their common stock investors wealthy. And there is nothing wrong with having lots money if it is gained honestly and spent wisely. Money gives you freedom – freedom from lousy jobs and freedom from being dependent on others. In other words, you become self-sufficient and, to paraphrase the ancient Greek philosopher Aristotle, happiness is having virtuous friends and being self-sufficient. Investing in the stock market should help you with the latter and you're on your own with the former. And don't forget, money also gives you the opportunity to help those less fortunate than you, and that's important for a life well lived.

Stocks like Microsoft, Apple, and even Clorox have had their ups and downs and, as you saw, some of the downs were hard. And while some of the stocks you might pick in the future could be dogs, you don't have to go the individual stock-picking route if you don't want to. There are plenty of index

---

[1] DQYDI.com
[2] TheCloroxCompany.com
[3] DQYDI.com

funds and factor-based investments available for you to pick from. The key to long-term investing is to have faith in our country's economic system of free market capitalism – coupled with an understanding of the stock market, investing for the long-term, and paying attention to what is going on around you economically, politically, and socially. If you do, you should be able to minimize your risk of loss and in time end up with a substantial gain.

Moreover, one of the beauties of investing in the stock market is you don't have to change your life plans. Your plans might be college, vocational school, or maybe you just want to get a job right away because you're tired of school. It's all okay. Just think of investing in the stock market as something that is happening in the background and not getting in the way of you living your life.

You say at your age you have plenty of time to invest in the stock market and, you're right, you do. You have your whole life ahead of you. But as you will learn in this book, now is the best time for you to get started and let the power of compounding work for you as long as you can.

You say you don't want to support certain companies because you don't believe in their policies. Fine. The stock market offers you the stock in more than 4,000 U.S. companies to pick from.

You say you don't want to wait all those years shown in the examples above? Good luck. Investing doesn't work that way. Speculation? Sure, maybe you'll get lucky, but that's not investing. Yes, it might seem like a long time, but remember, investing is happening in the background and is not interfering with your life, and the pay-off in the future could be huge. Besides, if you invest more now, and more often, perhaps the results will come sooner.

You say you don't have any money to invest right now? Well, maybe you can earn some by stocking shelves in the supermarket or bussing tables at the local restaurant. If you're too young to be formally employed, perhaps you can ask your parents, relatives, or neighbors if you can do odd jobs for them such as cutting the grass, washing cars, or shoveling snow. Or maybe you can raise the money by cutting back on expenses. Think of how much money you'll save if you forego those expensive gym shoes, designer yoga clothes, and daily specialty coffee drinks.

You say you're scared to lose your money in the stock market. Perhaps you will. But that's why you have this book in your hands – to learn about investing. We'll cover so many topics that by the end of this book you should have the confidence and the ability to make your own decisions based on your own unique circumstances, and thus hopefully minimize the risk of loss.

You say you'd rather learn about the stock market online. Fine. There are plenty of online resources for you to access. But consider this. While those websites will answer specific questions you might have, this book will answer many of the questions you hadn't even thought of. No clicking from link to link. The scope and breadth of the stock market is here all in one spot, explained in a straightforward manner, and organized in such a way that you can go as deep into the details as you like so you can focus your attention on those areas that interest you most.

So, let's getting started.

> *"Fortune favors the prepared mind." –*
> *Louis Pasteur*

SECTION 1
The Basics

There is a natural tendency to skip any section entitled "the basics." Don't do it. Learning a new skill is like building a new house. A solid foundation needs to be constructed first or eventually the walls will start to crack, the roof will leak, or, worse, the house could collapse. Investing in the stock market is no different. You need a solid foundation on which to build your dream of financial independence. Besides, if you skip this section you won't know what I am talking about in the rest of the book.

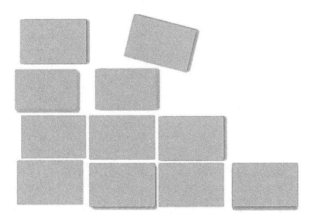

CHAPTER 1

The Power of Youth

Albert Einstein called it the eighth wonder of the world – the power of compounding. It will help you reach your goal of becoming wealthy. I will cover what it is and why it is important in this chapter. I'll also address the myth that the stock market is a casino and will alert you to the games investment sharks play on unsuspecting investors.

But first …

What Is an Investment Anyway?

When you strip everything away, an investment is simply deferred gratification. To explain that further, let's imagine a scenario. What if you were about to become a freshman in high school and you chose to buy Nike's Air Jordan gym shoes when they were first released in 1985? They were a great looking pair of shoes, but shoes wear out. So, let's assume you also bought a new pair in your sophomore, junior, and senior years. Moreover, assume the cost of those shoes was $65 a pair. Granted, you looked cool in them and all your friends admired your good taste. Thus, you got some benefits from your purchases and, if you hung onto them, they might have some value in today's vintage market.

Then imagine if, instead, you took the money you spent on those shoes and invested it in Nike stock? Those four $65 purchases, totaling only $260, with dividends reinvested, would be worth an astounding $200,000 at the beginning of 2019. That's enough for you to buy a beautiful sportscar with plenty left over. And all you did was to defer an immediate gratification of new gym shoes for a deferred gratification of having a sharp looking car.

Deferred gratification also extends beyond the investment of money to how you invest your time. For example, a person can cut classes or ignore homework assignments and spend that time playing video games, heading to the mall, or texting friends. Instead, that person can invest that time in attending classes, studying hard, and doing all the homework assignments. If you take your education seriously and invest the time in it, you will put yourself in a better position to get a great job later. Then, along the way, if you invest as much money from your income as you can, not the 5% to 10% normally recommended by others but absolutely as much as you can, 15% to 20%, you should be on your way later in life to a fortune.

But remember this because it is important: The money you will accumulate through deferred gratification is just stored up fun. It is there to be spent and enjoyed. A person I know went overboard with saving and investing. He spent his entire life working in the hot steel mills in Gary, Indiana. He took few vacations, never helped the community with donations, never got involved in civic organizations – just saved and saved. Then he got brain cancer. Let that be a lesson to you. Enjoy the money you will accumulate. You earned it.

Why Should I Start Now?

As a teenager you probably have many other things on your mind – too many perhaps to even think about the future. There is homework, personal relationships, sports, school activities, and parties to go to.

But time slips by quickly. I know. I didn't believe it when my mom and dad told me that decades ago, but it is true. When I was 5 years old it was a long time until Christmas – and it was. It was one-fifth of my life. With quite a few years under my belt now (75, to be exact), Christmas seems like it was only last month. My perspective of time has changed. The years seem to accelerate the older you get. Sooner than you think, you'll be going off to college or to a job. Then comes marriage, kids, and responsibilities. Soon your kids are off to college and later the first grandkids start appearing.

Yikes – you might say – that's not going to happen to me! Don't bet on it … just ask your parents.

What does all of this have to do with you? Right now, time is on your side and that gives you the opportunity to make maximum use of the power of compounding to increase your wealth. What is compounding and what is its power? Compounding is simply earning interest on your investment and then earning interest on your interest. The power of earning interest on your interest is realized over time and that tends to discourage people because in the beginning the increase in wealth seems to grow at such a slow pace. But wait just a few years – 7 or 8 – and the numbers become very interesting indeed.

Let's make some very straightforward assumptions and see how this works. Referring to Figure 1-1, a single $1,000 investment in year one grows to $5,604.41

> *Put yourself on the path to serious wealth.*

in 20 years when invested at a 9% interest rate. Subtract the initial $1,000 from that amount means $4,604.41 was interest on interest (Column C). In other words, you didn't do a thing except to have the foresight to invest the $1,000 instead of spending it and to kept it invested. For those decisions, you ended up with $4,604.41 more than you started with. Your initial investment, and the power of compounding, did all the work. Had you invested more in year one your results would have been greater.

YEAR	BEGINNING OF THE YEAR (A)	ANNUAL INTEREST EARNED (B)=(A)x9%	ACCUMULATED INTEREST (C)=SUM OF (B)	END OF YEAR (D)=(A) = (B)
1	1000.00	90.00	90.00	1090.00
2	1090.00	98.10	188.10	1188.10
3	1188.10	106.93	295.03	1295.03
4	1295.03	116.55	411.58	1411.58
5	1411.58	127.04	538.62	1538.62
10	2171.89	195.47	1367.36	2367.36
15	3341.73	300.76	2642.48	3642.48
20	5141.66	462.75	4604.41	5604.41

Figure 1-1

Now, let's change the assumptions, and assume you invested $1,000 at the beginning of each year (see Figure 1-2).

In this case, your investment would have grown to $55,764.53. Subtracting the $20,000 you put in means your money earned you $35,764.53 more than you invested.

YEAR	BEGINNING OF THE YEAR (A)	ANNUAL INTEREST EARNED (B)=(A)x9%	ACCUMULATED INTEREST (C)=SUM OF (B)	END OF YEAR (D)=(A) = (B)	ADDED $1,000 EACH YEAR (E)=(D)+1000
1	1000.00	90.00	90.00	1090.00	2090.00
2	2090.00	188.10	278.10	2278.10	3278.10
3	3278.10	295.03	573.13	3573.13	4573.13
4	4573.13	411.58	984.71	4984.71	5984.71
5	5984.71	538.62	1523.33	6523.33	7523.33
10	15192.93	1367.36	6560.29	16560.29	17560.29
15	29360.92	2642.48	17003.40	32003.40	33003.40
20	51160.13	4604.41	35764.53	55764.53	STOPPED

Figure 1-2

So, what does all this have to do with stock investment? Long-term studies have indicated that the average annual return for stocks has been about 9%. Some years more, some years less, and some years even negative. Whether such long-term performance will continue in the future no one knows. But by investing early, investing often, and investing for the long term the odds of realizing impressive returns should be in your favor.

> *"Good habits formed at youth make all the difference." – Aristotle*

And even small amount reinvested wisely can produce excellent returns. In Chapter 3 I will discuss the benefits of reinvesting dividends when received from a dynamic growing company. These seemingly small amounts can grow through the power of compounding.

But Isn't the Stock Market Like a Casino?

Mention the stock market and people will have three immediate reactions: It's a casino, it's a den of thieves, and I sure would like to make some money there. The first two reactions come from ignorance, the third from wishful thinking. Ignorance is not stupidity. Ignorance means lack of knowledge. So being ignorant is not a bad thing. It only becomes so when someone doesn't do anything about it. The third reaction, wishful thinking, can only lead to disaster. But with knowledge and critical thinking skills, you can make a lot of money in the stock market if you're willing to learn.

But are they right? Is the stock market only a casino?

Yes, if you want it to be. There are hundreds if not thousands of get-rich-quick schemes out there and plenty of people ready to sell them to you – *if* you want to gamble. Trust me. I can even take any seemingly solid investment and turn it into a gamble simply by shortening the investment time horizon and borrowing heavily to get the money to make the purchase.

This perception is not the fault of the stock market, however. Many people just want to make as much money as they can as quickly as they can and are willing to gamble in an attempt to become rich. Investing doesn't work that way. Investing involves knowing how the stock market works, picking the right investments that suit you, and waiting for those investments to bear fruit. Someone once said investing should be boring, not exciting, and that person was right.

And what about the stock market just being a den of thieves? Yes, you need to…

Beware of the Sharks

In other words, you also need to be aware of the waters you are swimming in. Simply put, money attracts people whose only goal is to transfer your money into their pockets. I'm sorry, but that is just the way it is.

The schemes these people pull are nothing new. They have burned investors ever since there was a stock market. As the great circus entrepreneur, P.T. Barnum, once said: "There's a sucker born every minute." For the price of admission, one of his hoaxes was to display a dead creature that had the body of a fish and the head of a monkey as if it were once a real live animal. And the crowds lined up with money in hand to see this supposed freak of nature. In the investment world, there are plenty of P.T. Barnums who will try to convince you of a similar impossibility.

Your first line of defense is simply this: If it sounds too good to be true, it generally is, and thus it should be avoided. But just saying that isn't enough, so let's dig deeper and see how some of these scams are put together. Knowing this may help you to avoid them.

Many of the scams will start with a promise of very high returns; others will start with a promise of consistent returns. Those are two really attractive "hooks" used to catch the gullible. Who wouldn't want to have high returns on their investments? Or who wouldn't want to have consistent positive returns even when the market itself was going down?

The desire for high investment returns

Consider penny stocks – stocks whose shares generally have a share price of under five dollars, and many under a dollar, hence their name. Someone – either on TV, in a phone call, or in a spam email – will be telling you how great a particular company is and how they don't want you to miss out. They say they're offering you the opportunity of a lifetime to get in on the ground floor, but you must act right now or you'll lose out. Some might even tell you that these stocks are guaranteed winners.

Make no mistake. You're being *sold* that penny stock, and the salesperson can easily make more money than you ever could from buying those dogs. In the industry, the process is called "pump and dump." The stock's price will be pumped up through an aggressive marketing campaign and through the manipulation of the stock's price and the number of shares traded. When the stock's price hits a certain level, the shares that the marketing firm owns will be dumped onto anyone who was foolish enough to believe the hype. In the process, the marketing firm stands to make millions.

The manipulation occurs when the people within the marketing firm begin selling shares among themselves in order to increase the volume of shares traded and perhaps the stock's price. For an uninformed investor, this appears to be a lot of positive activity. The pitch you'll get is that this phony market action was the result of "someone in the know" accumulating shares before the general public caught on to this great investment. You can hear the words now: "You had better buy now before the break-out occurs." When the marketing campaign and the manipulation stop, the price of the stock you bought will collapse, leaving you with huge losses, and the marketing firm selling these shares will move on to another set of naïve investors.

Another infamous example of the high-return hook was perpetrated by a guy called Charles Ponzi. Remember that name, Ponzi, because you'll hear the term "Ponzi scheme" again and again in your investment career. His approach was to use the cash he received from incoming investors to pay existing investors the promised high returns – after he took a cut out for himself. Some call it "robbing Peter to pay Paul." That phrase started in Merry ol'England centuries ago when land belonging to the Abbey of St. Peter was sold to pay for the construction of a new church, St. Paul. And that's exactly what happens in a Ponzi scheme. One set of investors gets robbed to pay off another set, while the people who originated the scheme rake off plenty for themselves. Eventually these schemes collapse when the supply of incoming investors slows down and there isn't enough money to pay the existing investors.

The desire for consistent returns

This is when someone promises you returns that will be consistent and high even when the market is going down – which is an impossibility, just like the fish with the monkey head. When the market goes down over a long period of time, the vast majority of stocks go down too, some more than others.

A recent example of this hook was perpetrated by Bernie Madoff. Allegedly, Madoff started out straight and slipped into becoming a crook when

> *A problem avoided is always better than a problem solved.*

the market turned down after he had promised consistent no-risk high returns to his investors. Instead of owning up to the losses, he lied. He told his investors the results were still great and then simply changed the client reports. The clients had no idea what was going on. The reports they were given were all rosy.

Eventually, he went the Ponzi route by taking the cash from incoming investors to pay off existing investors in order to maintain the illusion he had created. As expected, the scheme collapsed when the supply of new investors slowed down. Many of his investors were left with huge losses, much misery, and destroyed dreams. Madoff? He got jail time.

I don't want to go too far into the woods, but here's another approach that was used in 1987, and which has been resurrected in various forms today – a promise of no negative returns in exchange for some of the profit should the market go up. For example, if the market goes up, you are entitled to 70% of the gain and the investment manager would collect 30% for its promise that you would not suffer any of the losses should the market go down. It was called "portfolio insurance."

The strategy used a mathematical formula that when the market declined a certain amount, future contracts would be sold to offset that decline. The idea was the money lost in the market would be made up by the increase in the value of the futures that were sold. The problem was the investment managers overestimated the number of futures that could be sold in a severely declining market. These managers were selling but no one was buying which caused the market to go down further which caused more futures to be sold, and down and down went the market in 1987.

The lure of back-tested data

This approach is played using back-tested data to convince potential investors that the investment manager has found the money tree. The manager will go through reams of historical data again and again until a set of trading rules is found that provides an outstanding return. It's called data mining. The manager will then use those back-tested paper results to entice unsuspecting investors into giving the investment manager their money to "invest." The discovered trading rules, however, are unlikely to work in the future because they might have been the result of historical events that are unlikely to ever occur again. I'll get into the topic of back-tested data in more detail in Chapter 10, but I wanted to alert you to this possible scheme now while we are talking about sharks in the investment waters.

Cooking the books

I've already told you about pump and dump, the schemes of Ponzi and Madoff, portfolio insurance, and data mining, but just to make the point hit home, here is one more – cooking the books.

Before computers, the company's accountants would maintain the financial records in large ledge books. They often wore green eye shades to block the overhead light from their eyes. Today, the phrase "green eye shades" is often used to refer to people who are concerned with very detailed financial accounting. The "book" portion of the phrase cooking the books comes from this time period. The word "cook" in the phrase comes from taking something and altering it, for example, taking vegetables and pasta and making or cooking soup. So, cooking the books is a company's management intentionally altering the company's financial records.

This kind of fraud is extremely difficult for individual investors to uncover because it's all happening behind closed doors. The lying, and that is what it is – lying, can come in many forms such as overstating a company's sales, treating expenses as investments, and simply taking money from the company's bank account. Sadly, there are several cases of abuse: Enron (2001), WorldCom (2002), Tyco International (2002), and HealthSouth (2003).

The defenses against this activity are whistle-blowers inside the company, the outside accountants who check the financial statements (see Chapter 14), and investigators from the Securities and Exchange Commission. Most companies are honest. It's only very, very few that cook the books, and those involved generally get caught and sent to jail. If you want more information, I would suggest getting the book *Financial*

Shenanigans: How to Detect Accounting Gimmicks and Fraud in Financial Reports by Howard M. Schilit with Perler and Engelhart.

Proceed with understanding

It's easy for potential investors to get caught up in these scams. Most people might be skeptical at first. Sure, they'll ask questions, but the answers they get are from someone who is very slick. The answers will be wrapped in sophisticated-sounding terms so complex that an inexperienced investor's eyes will glaze over. Then there will be a secret proprietary system the manager uses to select investments – their secret sauce. That's designed to make an investor feel like the manager has some secret knowledge that others don't. Then testimonials from a few high-profile people who might be on the payroll can seal the deal. New investors will think, so-and-so has his or her money with this manager, the manager must be good. It's called the "Halo Effect." Why some people invest their hard-earned money without doing their own homework and relying on so-called celebrities I'll never know. But they do. You shouldn't.

I don't want to leave you with the impression that Wall Street is filled with crooks. It's not. What we are talking about here is just a few bad people taking advantage of the uninformed. It's like saying everyone in high school cheats on tests. It's just a few, and they get noticed. The vast majority of people working on Wall Street are decent, honest, and hard-working people. And hopefully the knowledge you will gain from this book will help you avoid the sharks.

> *"Wealthy people invest first and spend what's left. Broke people spend first and invest what's left." – Unknown*

CHAPTER 2

Free Market Capitalism

The stock market will have down days, and some of them will be hard. What will sustain you during those hard times, as it has for me, is faith in our country and its economic system of free market capitalism – a system that has not only created an incredible amount of prosperity for our citizens, but also gives you the opportunity to become wealthy by investing in an ever-increasing number of dynamic companies.

But economic systems are not fixed. They can change. So when you become of voting age, you're going to have to decide which economic system you want to live under. If you want to invest in commons stocks, I suggest you stick with free market capitalism – it's the best of the alternatives and here's why.

The Wonder of Free Market Capitalism

Remember that lemonade stand or that lawn mowing service you started? Free market capitalism is a system that allows individuals to start, own, and profit from the businesses they create. But it's a free market, so other individuals can also create similar businesses to compete for your customers. In other words, in a free market economy businesses compete against one another to provide you, as a consumer, with the goods and services you want at a price you are willing to pay. Since you are the ultimate decision maker, you get to decide what you want to buy, when, how much, at what price, and from whom. And, through your buying decisions, you decide who stays in business and who doesn't. Sure, the owners of the business might make a profit, but that profit is in exchange for their efforts, and it provides them with an incentive to innovate, thereby expanding the benefits given to you and the rest of society. It's a good deal all the way around – you get the products and services you want you want at a price you are willing to pay, businesses make a profit, and you can participate in those profits by investing in their common stock.

But there's even more to free market capitalism besides ever-improving goods and services and interesting companies to invest in. Consider what Nobel-prize winning economist Milton Friedman had to say[4]:

> The great virtue of a free market system is that it does not care what color people are; it does not care what their religion is; it only cares whether they can produce something you want to buy. It is the most effective system we have discovered to enable people who hate one another to deal with one another and help one another.

But there's another benefit to free market capitalism besides getting people to work together, providing jobs, bringing economic growth to communities, getting wealthy investing in common stocks, and the tax revenues the government receives – and it rarely gets noticed because it happens so smoothly. Free market capitalism is the basis for the efficient allocation of capital among competing interests. I like to think of capital as an economic term for money that is invested for a longer time frame. At any point in time there is a limited amount of capital in comparison to the demands for it among companies who need and want it. In other economic systems, some person, committee, or group makes the allocation decision – who gets what and how much. In free market capitalism, the marketplace (you, me, and other individuals through our collective actions, and motivated by our own self-interests) makes those decisions.

Consider Apple. You like your iPhone, right? Did that smartphone just happen out of the blue? Was it some big government idea? Of course not. Individuals like Steve Jobs and those who worked at Apple created it. And what happened? Capital flowed to Apple, customers bought the iPhone, and (together with its apps) that smartphone made life more productive, more interesting, and more fun for you and a lot of other people. In order to remain in business, Apple has to have access to capital, needs to make a profit, and needs to continually improve its product. In the process, many people are employed by Apple, taxes are paid, the product is improved, and you are

---

[4] *Why Government is the Problem* * Essays in Public Policy, no. 39.

given the opportunity to invest in their stock and thus participate in their success.

But if your products or services are shoddy, priced too high, or someone else has a better idea, capital will flow to other companies, customers will turn away, and your business will eventually cease to exist. Just look at some of the big-named companies that have recently gone under – Sports Authority, Blockbuster, Borders, and Toys-R-Us – to be supplanted by Amazon, Netflix, and others.

Let's be clear, however. Environmental issues and social justice are important. A business has an ethical responsibility to its employees, its customers, its community, and its shareowners. Treat your employees badly and you won't have a stable work force; treat your customers poorly and they will go elsewhere; treat the community badly and it'll reciprocate; and treat your shareowners poorly and they'll sell the stock, thereby depressing its price. You see, a business does not operate in a vacuum. Generating profits over the long term depends on treating all stakeholders fairly. Most businesses get it.

The entire system works as long as you are given the freedom to act in your own self-interest and you and businesses are respectful of the needs of others.

> *"There's no limit to what free men and free women in a free market with free enterprise can accomplish when people are free to follow their dream." – Jack Kemp*

Other Economic Systems

At its ideal, free market capitalism enshrines the *individual* as the decision maker, not governments, kings, or dictators. It allows you to make decisions as to what is in your best interest, and that includes helping others, since it trusts you to do the right thing. Not so with other economic systems – crony capitalism, socialism, communism, and totalitarianism, to name a few. Under these alternative systems, your freedom is limited, and even eliminated under some.

Let's take a critical look at the alternative economic systems.

Crony capitalism

Crony capitalism is often the reason free market capitalism is given a bad rap. It shares many features with free market capitalism, but it's an economic system in which consumers don't determine which businesses get created and stay and which go under. Rather, in crony capitalism the success of the business depends on favoritism that is granted by some government official.

Milton Friedman again[5]:

> Our minds tell us, and history confirms, that the great threat to freedom is the concentration of power. Government is necessary to preserve our freedom, it is an instrument through which we can exercise our freedom; yet by concentrating power in political hands, it is also a threat to freedom. Even though the men who wield this power initially be of good will and even though they be not corrupted by the power they exercise, the power will both attract and form men of a different stamp.

The favors of crony capitalism could be in the form of special tax breaks, government grants, or government business. The politicians and the company each get what they want – the company gets tax breaks, grants, or more business and in exchange the politicians get a favor to call on later, perhaps in the form of increased campaign contributions or a job once they are out of office. It's like an umpire who is a close friend of a coach and who intentionally helps the coach's team win the game.

With crony capitalism merit doesn't count. You don't count. The game becomes who you know and what you can do for them. Someone pays for this, and it is you, through higher taxes, lower product and service quality, and less freedom of choice.

Socialism

With socialism, the companies that produce goods and services are controlled by the government, either through heavy regulation or, in some cases, by government ownership. The government elite say, "We know what's best for society, and we'll protect you from those greedy capitalists. Vote for us. People not profit. We'll decide what goods and services should be produced and what they will cost. We'll decide how to spend your money on which projects and ideas we think are best for society. We'll heavily

---

[5] *Capitalism and Freedom*

regulate and tax the few companies that we allow to be owned by individuals, and if a little crony capitalism creeps in and some of us get rich in the process, so be it. Just leave it to us; 'We're the good guys.'"

Socialism creeps up on society with the start of one idea intended to improve the wellbeing of a country's people. Then another idea, another, and yet another. But all of these ideas lead to more government control, more regulations, higher taxes to pay for them, and less individual freedom. Taxes and more taxes and regulations on top of more regulations eventually reduce productivity and prosperity for all.

A passage from Edith Hamilton's book *The Echo of Greece* illustrates what happened 2,500 years ago in Athens, at the time one of the greatest of ancient Greek city-states, when it slipped into socialism:

> What the people wanted was a government which would provide a comfortable life for them ... Athens was more and more looked on as a co-operative business possessed of great wealth in which all citizens had a right to share. The larger and larger funds demanded made heavier and heavier taxation necessary, but that troubled only the well-to-do, always a minority, and no one gave a thought to the possibility that the source might be taxed out of existence. Politics was now closely connected with money, quite as much as with voting. Indeed, the one meant the other. Votes were for sale as well as officials.

> The whole process was clear to Plato. Athens had reached the point of rejecting independence, and the freedom she now wanted was freedom from responsibility... If men insisted on being free from the burden of a life that was self-dependent and also responsible for the common good, they would cease to be free at all. Responsibility was the price every man must pay for freedom.

Of course we need to pay taxes to support the essential responsibilities of a collective society, but the question is the cost for all these so-called "good" ideas and the accompanying bureaucracy. Eventually the costs add up and the bureaucracies become uncontrollable and dictatorial. What are some of the things our government spent taxpayer money on? Here's a small sample from OpenTheBooks.com:[6]

> $1.2 Trillion – Mistakes & improper payment distribution by 20 Federal Agencies.
>
> $234 Billion – Mistakes & improper Medicaid payments.
>
> $677.4 Million – Colleges of Beauty and Cosmetology.
>
> $753,502 – Virtual shoe-fitting.
>
> $671,522 – Convincing mothers to stop teen girls from using tanning beds.
>
> $114,375 – Cigar taste test.
>
> $11,987 – Historic hobo day.

Some of these might seem funny (the government paying for hobo day), until I tell you that your share of the over $21 trillion of the federal debt (the money our government borrowed that was used to fund these good ideas) is over $65,000, and growing fast. You read that right. Although you're still a teenager, your share of the federal debt is $65,000. You didn't spend the money, you may not have wanted the project, but you are still responsible for your share of the federal debt.

It's difficult to comprehend a trillion of anything, much less 21 trillion which is a 21,000 billion, so let's see if we can first get our minds around how large one billion is. For example, did you know:

> A billion seconds ago … was 1987.
>
> A billion minutes ago … gladiators were fighting in the recently constructed Colosseum in Rome.
>
> A billion hours ago … humans were still using tools made of stone.
>
> A billion dollars ago? That's what the government spent in about the last two hours.

Then there is the power of the bureaucracies that are created to enforce the great ideas. Consider what eighteenth-century philosopher, Herbert Spenser had to say[7]:

---

[6] OpenTheBooks.com, *Wall Street Journal*, September 24, 2018.
[7] *The Man versus the State, with Six Essays on Government, Society, and Freedom.*

> ... we turn to the bureaucracy itself, and ask how it is to be regulated, there is no satisfactory answer ... Under such conditions there must arise a new aristocracy, for the support of which the masses would toil; and which, being consolidated, would wield a power far beyond that of any past aristocracy.

Rampant socialism is incompatible with making money in the stock market because of its negative impact on businesses through unnecessary regulation, the power of the bureaucracies created to enforce regulation, and its dampening of investing enthusiasm through high taxation rates. Simply put: Why bother if your wealth is just going to be taxed away? As Mr. Spenser sums it up:

> ...socialism involves the development of centralization, the extension of governmental power, the decay of initiative, and the subordination of the individual."

Although well-meaning at some level, socialism deadens personal responsibility and restricts the opportunity for individual ownership of businesses and thus your opportunity to better your life by investing in common stock.

Communism

Under communism you can work as hard as you like, but you will receive the same as everyone else. It's called "equality." For example, you're in school and you can study as hard as you like to get an "A," but you'll get the average grade of the class, no more, no less. Or maybe you'll be graded "pass" or "fail," and everyone gets a "pass"

> *While socialism cripples individual freedom, communism obliterates it.*

grade. After all, we need to treat everyone equally. It's only fair. And besides, giving a lettered grade only hurts the self-esteem of those who get Ds and Fs.

Individual ownership of businesses? Forget it. The government will own all of them and will pay individuals a wage according to their needs, not their contribution. We'll decide everything. There will be no rich people or poor people any more. Everyone will be equal – except us, your leaders. We deserve more. Just think what a great society we will build for you. Trust us. We know what's best. Don't mind that history shows that communism morphs into a dictatorship of the elite. Don't mind that communism has been tried in the past and failed. This time everything will be different. All we need is the "right" people in there, and we have them now. Give us another chance. We know what's best.

Totalitarianism

Under totalitarianism the individual is subservient to the dictator. You see, the dictator is more enlightened than you and can quickly put into practice whatever he or she thinks is best for all. Now we'll get things done. No more gridlock. Don't worry. The dictator knows how to work smarter than the common folk.

The Choice Is Yours

As a teenager, someday you will be running this country and will have to decide which economic system you want to live under. Free market capitalism gives you the most freedom – freedom to pursue your own goals, make your own decisions, and live your life the way you want. And you have the opportunity to become wealthy by investing in common stocks over the long term. Not so with other economic systems. But along with freedom comes the responsibility to voluntarily help others and to make the world a better place for all.

Freedom is your birthright, given to you by the Declaration of Independence, the U.S. Constitution, and the Bill of Rights. Many people, perhaps someone in your family, have fought and died to preserve the freedom you now enjoy. But soon, you'll have a decision to make – keep the freedom you now enjoy or lose it.

If you don't believe in free market capitalism, don't go against your beliefs; stop reading this book. Give it to someone who does and who would like to make some money investing in common stocks.

> *Common stocks and free market capitalism*
> *are inextricably linked; belief in one requires*
> *a belief in the other.*

CHAPTER 3

Corporations and You

You need to understand corporations because you'll be part owner of one when you buy a share of common stock. Unfortunately, corporations are often thought of as being big evil entities gobbling up the countryside in search of ever-increasing profits and the environment be damned – Godzilla® on steroids. Since corporations are not well understood, they become easy targets as villains in movies and TV programs and a popular whipping-boy of those with an agenda. Sometimes the criticism is warranted, but most corporations take their responsibilities very seriously. They are made up of people perhaps like your parents, relatives, or neighbors, not some evil-doers. Those who manage the corporation realize that many different groups have a stake in the success of the business – employees, customers, communities, and shareowners – and they take care to balance the needs of all. Those that don't are eventually forced out of business by free market capitalism.

What Is a Corporation?

One of the most important parts of free market capitalism is individual ownership of businesses. Ownership can be as straightforward as your uncle owning the corner store, several of your relatives entering into a partnership to own an apartment building, or thousands of people who don't even know each other banding together to own a stake in something called a corporation to build electric cars, to create alternative energy sources, or to discover life-saving DNA-inspired drugs. Each form of ownership has its own set of legal and tax implications, but all are owned in one way or another by individuals.

We are interested in the corporate form because it offers us the opportunity to participate in the corporation's success though the ownership of its common stock and, after all, that is why you are reading this book.

A legal form of ownership

A corporation is nothing more than a legal form of ownership of a company that, while owned perhaps by thousands of individuals, is legally allowed to act as if it were a single person. Just like a person, the corporation can enter into contracts, hire employees, buy assets, borrow money, sue and be sued, pay taxes, and be subjected to rules and regulations. But it also means that the corporation is the legally responsible party for anything that goes wrong, not its shareowners. It is this last point that makes this form of ownership appealing to individual investors.

This does not mean, however, that a corporation and those in charge of running it can do whatever they want. There still are laws and regulations to be followed, and it is a fine balance between the right amount of laws and regulations necessary to protect the public and the right amount to permit productivity and profitability for the corporation. Also remember that one of the most important constraints on a corporation is the public, not the government. If a majority of the public doesn't like what a corporation is doing, it can just stop buying its products or services and the corporation will either mend its ways or close its doors due to lack of business.

Stocks reflect an ownership position

A share of stock is simply used to indicate an ownership position. The degree of ownership is represented by the number of shares a person or entity owns relative to the total number of shares outstanding. Shares can be either "common" or "preferred." Each has certain rights and benefits. Both common and preferred shares can be further divided into different types based on a further allocation of rights and benefits. In this book we are interested in the common variety of shares, or simply common stock.

A corporation can be "privately" or "publicly" owned

If private, a corporation might be owned by a family, employees, or an investment group. Because its shares are not traded on a stock exchange, the public (you, me, and everyone else) can't own a part of that type of corporation. Some of the largest privately-owned corporations in the United States include Cargill, the maker of some of those Angus Beef® hamburgers you might like; Mars, the maker of M&M® candies; and Albertson, the second largest supermarket chain where you might have bought potato chips.

Private corporations are also subject to various laws and regulations, including the law of the marketplace. That is, if they don't provide the products or services the public wants at a price the public is willing to pay, the corporation goes out of business.

The stock of a publicly owned corporation is traded on a stock exchange, and you and everyone else can buy the stock and become a part owner of that corporation. In addition to the laws and regulations a private corporation must follow, a public one must also follow the rules and regulations of the Securities and Exchange Commission (SEC), a government agency, as well as the regulations specified by the exchange in which its shares are listed for trading.

A private corporation becomes a public one through what is called an "initial public offering" (IPO). I will address that issue in the next chapter because it underscores the need for a stock market to make our economic system work.

Stop and think about it

Perhaps this morning you stopped at Starbucks, shopped at TJ Maxx, had lunch at Panera, or checked your Facebook or Twitter feed on your Apple iPhone. In each of these actions you came in contact with a publicly held corporation and, should you want, you could become a part owner in any of them simply by owning shares of their stock. Or, for that matter, you can become a part owner in any one of over 4,000 other publicly held corporations in the United States.

Stop and think about that. You can own a part of Apple, Inc. Sure, it may be a small part, but it is still an ownership position. That's a big deal. You may not have invented the iPhone, but you can still participate in the financial success of Apple by buying its stock. You don't have to be some super genius who discovered a life-saving DNA-inspired drug that is helping to reduce human misery. You just have to buy the stock of that biotechnology corporation and share in the corporation's success.

Depending on the corporation, they also may send you money every three months in the form of a dividend (your share of the company's profits). Then, when you sell your shares, and if you selected the corporation wisely in the first place, you might be able to sell your shares for more than you paid for them. Free market capitalism, you've got to love it! It gives you the opportunity to buy a part of a corporation, collect a dividend, and possibly sell your shares for more than you paid for them.

When you're buying a stock, just remember that you're buying part of a corporation. Before you invest your hard-earned money, make sure you look long and hard at the business the corporation is in and its long-term prospects. If you have confidence in the corporation and in free market capitalism, you'll be better able to ride through the periods when your stock is not doing very well.

> *"If the business does well the stock eventually follows." –*
> *Warren Buffett*

By now you are probably getting tired of me repeating the word "corporation," so for the rest of the book I will use the more generic term "company."

Who Runs the Company?

The managers. Who selects the managers? The board of directors. And who selects them? You do, as an owner of the company. As a shareowner, you get to vote on who will sit on the board of directors. The board is a very important group of people. It is their responsibility to choose the people who actually run the day-to-day operations of the company. They elect a "Chairman of the Board" and also the "Chief Executive Officer" (CEO). Sometimes the two posts are combined. But more than that, it is the board's responsibility to make sure the people who run the company act in the best interest of the shareowners, and for the long-term profitability of the company, the customers, the employees, and the community as well.

Annual meeting

Once a year a big meeting is held and all shareowners are invited to attend. At this meeting, members of the board and senior management will share their plans for the future and will discuss other issues important to the company's business. If you have any questions or comments, this is the time to speak up. But, remember, be respectful of your other shareowners. If you don't like what the company is doing, sell your shares and move on.

Proxy vote

You will also have various matters on which to vote. Generally, you get one vote for each share you own. However, different classes of stock have different voting rights, so it really depends what class of shares you own (more about classes of shares later). You'll be voting on who gets to sit on the board as well as other important issues. The official vote occurs at the meeting. However, as a practical matter, "proxy" voting actually occurs before the meeting. A proxy is someone or some organization who takes your instructions as to how you want your vote to be cast and does so. This is called "voting by proxy."

Proxy voting is done for two reasons. First, the meeting is often held in a city that is too far away for many shareowners to attend and it is important that all shareowners at least get the opportunity to vote. Second, it solves a logistical problem. Counting votes from hundreds or thousands of shareowners at the annual meeting would be a real hassle, so a decision is made to do it beforehand and have results officially ratified at the meeting.

The company will be controlling the process and your proxy ballot will contain its suggestions on how it would like you to vote. Sometimes other individuals or companies not associated with the company will send you letters requesting your "proxy vote" on matters such as electing a different list of individuals to the board. This is called a "proxy battle," since two groups are battling each other to get your vote – the company and the outside group. You are free to vote any way you choose or not at all.

The reality

Realistically, however, there may be millions of shares outstanding, so your vote may not matter very much. Sometimes a board is also controlled by insiders who directly or indirectly control millions of shares, and hence votes. It might be impossible to displace these entrenched people. You do have choices however. As I mentioned earlier, if you don't like what the company is doing, sell your shares and move on.

How Is the Size of a Company Designated?

If we had a group of people and we wanted to measure their height we would use a tape measure. If we want to measure the size of companies, the most popular way, but not the only way, is by market capitalization. Market capitalization, or simply market-cap, is the company's stock price multiplied by its number of shares outstanding (some other ways are by earnings, sales, and number of employees).

Knowing a company's size is important because it is used in various investment strategies. For example, some money managers specialize in smaller companies, others in medium-sized companies, and still others in large companies. But large, medium, and small are relative terms – large or small as compared to what?

Some investment managers have decided the break-points should be as follows:

Mega-caps – Over $200 billion
Large-caps – $10 billion to $200 billion
Medium-caps – $2 billion to $10 billion
Small-caps – $300 million to $2 billion
Micro-caps – $50 million to $300 million
Nano-caps – Under $50 million

Others will take a group of stocks, say a list of 500 of them, rank them by market capitalization, and divide the list into thirds. The first third would be called large-cap, the next medium-cap, and the last small-cap. Others will expand the list from 500 to 1,000 or more. As you can see, a small-cap stock in one grouping might be a medium-cap stock in another.

This becomes important when you are trying to decide which mutual fund or exchange traded fund you want to invest in because different universes and different breakpoints have different risk and return characteristics.

What Are the Benefits of Owning Common Stocks?

The four primary benefits to you as a shareowner are price appreciation, dividends, ability to buy and sell quickly, and limited liability.

Price appreciation

This is what we're all hoping for when we buy a stock – its price goes up and we make some money. Let's face it, that's often the only reason people buy common stocks. The sad part is they also forget that the price could go down. That's the risk you take (more about risk in Chapter 7).

Dividends

A cash dividend is your share of a company's profits that is distributed to you as a shareholder. Many companies pay a regular cash dividend every three months. Sometimes a company will pay an extra one-time "special dividend." But the dividend doesn't have to be in cash. It can be in the form of additional shares of stock, a "stock dividend." Instead of being quoted in dollars and cents, a stock dividend is quoted as a percentage of a share. The choice of what to distribute (cash or additional shares of stock) and how it is distributed (on a regular basis or one time only) depends on the company's dividend policy, and that depends on what the board believes is in the best interest of shareowners (more about this topic later).

Date of record and ex-dividend date: A dividend will be paid to whomever is listed on the company's books as a shareowner on the "date of record." Therefore, if you want the dividend, you have to be on the company's books on or before the date of record. Recognizing it might take some time after you made your purchase for you to get on the company's books, a date, called the ex-dividend date, is set a few days before the date of record as the cut-off date for inclusion in the dividend payment. The result is, if you buy the stock before the ex-dividend date, you will receive the dividend. If you buy the stock on or after the ex-dividend date, you will not.

Price action on the ex-dividend date: Before trading starts on the ex-dividend date, the exchange will adjust the opening price downward by the amount of the dividend. This is done so that both the owner of the stock before the ex-dividend date and the one who buys the stock on the ex-dividend date are treated fairly.

An example might help. Say a company announces a dividend of $1.00 per share and you own the stock before the ex-dividend date. At the close of trading the day before the ex-dividend date, the stock closed at $25.00. The next day – the day of the ex-dividend date – it opens at $24.00 ($25.00 minus the $1 dividend). The owner of the stock before the ex-dividend date now has a stock worth $24.00 but also has the cash dividend of $1.00, and thus this investor is kept whole. A new investor who buys on the ex-dividend date would pay $24.00, since the company is worth less because the cash used to pay the dividend is no longer in the company's bank account. Both are treated fairly. What happens after the open is up to the investors and speculators in the market.

Liquidity

It is a benefit to be able to buy or sell something quickly when need be. Under normal circumstances, and depending on the stock being traded, you can do that, often within seconds, and with little or no hassle compared to other forms of investment. Contrast that with buying and selling real estate, which might take weeks or months.

The degree of liquidity a stock has depends on many factors such as the amount of tradable stock and who wants to trade and at what price. The first, the amount of tradable stock, is often called the degree of float. A company may have millions of shares outstanding, but many if not most of those shares might be owned by companies or investors who are not likely to trade them.

The second, who wants to trade and in what quantities, depends in large part on the action of the market (more about liquidity in Chapter 22).

Limited liability

Although you are a part owner of the company, no one is going to lay claim to your personal assets if the company is involved in and loses a big lawsuit, or for that matter goes out of business. This is not true with some other forms of investments where the creditors can come after your personal wealth. Your exposure (loss) is limited to the amount you paid for the stock.

It's not all upside

Of course, owning common stock is not all upside. Sometimes the stock's price will move in the wrong direction and continue that way for a very long time. Moreover, while you have a vote in deciding who sits on the board of directors, in reality you have little control over the company. It is in the hands of the board and its managers. Also, if a company goes bankrupt, as a shareowner you are last in line to recover anything from the sale of assets. Chances are good that you will receive nothing and will have lost the entire amount you paid for the stock. These are the risks you take.

What Influences a Company's Dividend Policy?

The choice of whether to pay a cash or stock dividend, or nothing at all, depends on the company's dividend policy, and that depends on what the company's board of directors believes is in the best interest of its shareowners. That's fine. But you should know what that policy is because it can be an important input to your decision as to what stock to buy.

The company's need for cash

A company might say we really need to keep the cash in the business in order to buy the things we need to make the company grow even faster. Not paying a cash dividend is characteristic of so-called "growth" companies. For example, Facebook and Alphabet (the parent of Google) don't pay regular cash dividends.

Avoidance of double taxation

A company might say that by paying a cash dividend we are doing a disservice to you as a shareowner because the cash you receive will have been already taxed once at the corporate level and, depending on your tax bracket and brokerage account, might be taxed again – in other word, taxed twice. Here's how that happens. Dividends are generally paid by the company from after-tax earnings. Thus, any cash the company uses to pay a dividend has already been taxed. Now you receive the dividend. Depending on your tax bracket and the type of brokerage account you established, you have to pay taxes on the cash you received from the dividend payment. That's double taxation: once at the company level and again at the individual level.

The company says, since this is the case, we will keep the cash, figuring you can sell some of your shares if you really need the money. You'll still have to pay taxes on any gains if you sell your shares for a profit, but at least you avoid paying taxes on the dividends; moreover, by keeping the cash in the company, we can reinvest it and perhaps the share price might increase faster.

Tangible proof of success

Other companies choose to pay a cash dividend, as they believe it's important that shareowners receive something from what the company has earned. Indeed, some retirees and others depend on that dividend check and select a company because of its generous and dependable dividend policy. AT&T stock used to be famous for that, and was known as the "widows and orphans" fund for that reason. However, just because a company pays a dividend doesn't mean it is a no-growth company. Some of the companies that have had a long-term record of paying dividends are 3M, Coca-Cola, Johnson & Johnson, McDonalds, and, yes, Apple.

Cash vs. stock dividends

The company also has the option of paying a stock dividend and may do so because of the same reasons cited above: the need to retain cash and the avoidance of double taxation. In addition, the company's management might also think ownership of more stock will psychologically bind the shareowner closer to the company.

Dividend Reinvestment Program

Some investors choose to reinvest the cash dividends back into the company through a dividend reinvestment program; these reinvestments form the basis for the magic of compounding that we discussed in Chapter 1. Although the size of cash dividends might seem small, if they are reinvested in a company's stock and that stock price continues to rise over time, these small dividend payments can add up to big money.

For example, at the beginning of Chapter 1, I said that four $65 investments, a total of $260, starting in 1985 would have grown to an astounding $200,000 with dividends reinvested. That stellar result came from strong and increasing Nike earnings, which resulted in increased share price that in turn prompted stock splits and allowed for an increase in the size of dividend checks, the cash from which was used to buy more Nike shares. The per share dividends paid by Nike were relatively small, around 25 cents a share every three months. Had you not reinvested those dividends, you would have ended up with about $13,000 in cash and a market value of your share, including splits, of about $87,000 for a total of about $100,000 – outstanding for a $260 investment. But had you simply reinvested those dividends in this dynamic and growing company, you would have ended up with about $200,000. Will these results continue in the future? I don't know. This is only an illustration of the power of compounding.

If you do decide to reinvest dividends, you might consider using the company's dividend reinvestment program (DRIP). This is a program that many companies have established to allow shareowners to reinvest dividends in a cost-effective

> *"The serious investor knows that among the many signposts that point to corporate and investment growth, a rising dividend trend is perhaps the most significant." – Geraldine Weiss*

manner. You can check out the rules and the pricing formula by requesting information from the company's investor relations department.

Earnings Announcement

Companies generally report their earnings about the same time every quarter as other companies, in what is often called the "reporting season." Since many investors look at the size and direction of earnings as a sign of the future prospects for a company, this communication is important.

Speculation on size

Not waiting for the announcement, analysts will try to forecast the earnings number. These individual forecasts are collected by other firms who average them and provide a "consensus forecast" along with the range of analysts' expectations for the company. A wide range generally means analysts are not sure what is going on within the company and, therefore, for an investor that means greater investment risk – and possibly a greater reward. Rather than simply averaging the forecasts to come up with a consensus, other firms will give more weight to those analysts who are deemed to have done a good job of forecasting in the past.

Companies even get into the forecasting game by giving their "guidance" as to the range within which the actual results are likely to fall. This is done to dampen speculation, but it is not above some companies to issue low guidance numbers that they fully expect to beat so that their management looks good and possibly their stock price will go up as a result of a positive earnings surprise.

The announcement is made

The speculation ends when the company reports its earnings and new information suddenly comes into the marketplace. If the actual earnings are very different from what was expected, the stock's price will either go up or down depending on the size and direction of the surprise. Generally, the reaction is swift. A large positive surprise suggests that the company's prospects have brightened above expectations and the number of potential sellers will quickly dry up, causing the share price to gap higher. Likewise, if the surprise is negative, the number of potential buyers will quickly dry up. Who wants to buy a company's stock when it appears the company's prospects have darkened? In that case, the stock price is likely to gap down.

The swiftness of the price adjustment does not give an individual investor much of a chance to make some money. But don't despair. Earnings surprises seem to have a lingering component. That is, after the initial adjustment period, prices seem to drift in the direction of the initial surprise. For how long and for how high? For positive surprises, the upward drift might last for up to two months, for investors might think more positive surprises are coming. A string of positive surprises is especially encouraging.

What Happens When a Stock Splits?

A "stock split" sure feels great when it happens. Suddenly you have more shares. In a two for one split, the number of shares you own doubles – 100 shares become 200 shares; in a three for two split, they increase by one-third – 200 shares become 300. But before you get too excited, although you have more shares, the market price of each will go down by the amount of the split and the price of your holdings remains the same, at least initially. For example, if the stock's price is $100 a share before a split, and you own 100 shares, your investment is worth $10,000 ($100 times 100 shares). After a two for one split, however, the stock's price become $50 a share. Now you own 200 shares, so your investment is worth $10,000 ($50 times 200 shares) – the same as it was before the split.

Not every company feels a stock split is necessary, however. For example, at the beginning of 2019, Warren Buffett's Berkshire Hathaway's Class "A" shares traded for about $300,000 per share. Mr. Buffett has said he does not split his shares because the share price helps him attract like-minded investors who invest for the long term. Well, that's fine for someone who invested with him from the beginning or has lots of money to buy the stock now. But even Mr. Buffett realized that he needed to appeal to a larger body of potential investors without disturbing his base of long-term investors. He issued a new class of shares called Class "B." These traded for about $200 per share at the beginning of 2019 (more information about classes of shares later).

On the other hand, a "reverse split" does not feel good at all, for suddenly you have fewer shares. In a 1 for 10 reverse split, 1,000 shares suddenly become 100. But like the regular split, the value of your holdings does not change, at least initially. Generally, however, a reverse split is not a good sign. Often management does it because if they didn't, the stock's price would slip below a certain level and the stock would be delisted from the stock exchange where the shares are traded. If a reverse split happens to the shares you own, you might want to look elsewhere, for most of these stocks continue to underperform. However, someone might still try to interest you in these stocks as turnaround candidates. For example, in 2003 Priceline did a 1 to 6 reverse split, so your holding would have gone from 600 shares to 100 shares; this caused the stock's price to increase to about $25 a share. In early January 2019, Booking Holdings (the company that now owns Priceline and other companies) traded for about $1,700 a share.

Unlike the ex-dividend date, if you bought a stock the day before it splits or reverse splits, you are entitled to the results of the change.

What Are Stock Buybacks?

With buybacks, a company itself goes into the market and buys some of its own shares. It generally starts with an announcement that the company intends to buy shares up to a certain dollar limit. But just because the company makes such an announcement, it doesn't mean the buybacks will happen or will happen anytime soon. It is just an announcement of intentions, not a commitment.

There are four main reasons for a buyback:

Part of the company's dividend policy

Instead of a cash dividend, stock buybacks are often thought of as a way to return cash to shareowners.

The stock is considered to be undervalued

The company thinks its shares are undervalued and it intends to remove (called "retire") the purchased shares from its books, thus reducing the number of shares outstanding. If that is the case, it means that there is another large buyer in the marketplace for the company's shares – the company itself. The more buyers there are the better, especially this one, since management should be in the best position to know if the stock's price reflects value.

Need for shares to fulfill an obligation

The company intends to use the purchased shares to fulfill an obligation made to some of its senior executives. The programs vary from company to company, but essentially the company gives the right to certain employees to purchase shares at a discounted price if certain performance goals are met. If the goals are met, to fulfill the promises, the company can buy the shares in the open market and then give them to the executives who, in turn, are free to do with them as they wish. This buyback doesn't reduce the number of shares outstanding. It only changes their location from the marketplace to the employee's pocket.

Use accounting magic to boost earnings per share

I will discuss this in Chapter 14 under the topic, "How to Make Earnings Look Better Than They Are."

Why Are There Different Classes of Stock?

When it comes to voting rights, not all stock issued by a company is equal. Some shares have more voting rights than others. For example, two companies might have three different classes of stocks, A, B, and C, but the distribution of voting rights might be different. In one company, holders of class A shares might have one vote per share and might be owned by employees. Holders of the B class might have ten votes per share, and be owned by the company's founders. Holders of the C class shares might have no voting rights and are offered to the public.

Another company might also have three classes of stock, A, B, and C, but it decided to distribute the voting rights differently. Class A might have no voting rights and are offered to the public. Class B might be reserved for early investors and executives, and have one vote each. Class C shares might have nearly all of the voting rights, and are held by the company's founders. The point is when you see multiple shares types, generally the voting rights are held to varying degrees by the founders with an intention of increasing their control over the company.

Is this fair? Some say yes, some say no. Yes, it allows founders to focus on the long-term growth of the company, whereas "one share, one vote" investors might favor a quick profit or even a takeover by another company. Others say no. It's unfair to let just a few people hold all the voting power – power that might be abused.

If you are unhappy about having no or limited voting rights, don't buy the stock.

What Are Preferred Stocks?

These hybrid securities have the features of both a common stock and a bond; how much any given preferred stock resembles a common stock and how much a bond varies from preferred stock to preferred stock. Generally, a preferred stock gives up voting rights in exchange for a promise (and it's just a promise) of a fixed-sized dividend each year. Some preferred stocks have a cumulative provision whereby if the preferred dividend payment is missed, it is added to the next payment and must be paid before the common stockholders receive a dividend. Another feature might allow a preferred stock to be convertible to a common stock if certain conditions are met.

What makes a preferred stock different from a bond is that while bonds have a stated maturity date, preferred stocks do not. They are perpetual unless the terms of the issue state otherwise. Moreover, the company can skip a preferred stock dividend, but if a company misses a payment to a bondholder, the bondholder can force the company into bankruptcy. This is one reason why a company might issue preferred stock instead of a bond.

What Are the Pros and Cons of Foreign Stocks?

You might have been told that you should invest in international stocks. The reasons given are many foreign economies are growing faster than the United States economy and, as such, offer a greater opportunity for profit as well as offering diversification benefits. This message comes from a variety of sources, but mainly from investment advisors. Before you rush headlong into foreign stocks, however, I would like you to consider a few things.

Many U.S. companies are internationally oriented already

U.S. companies aren't dumb. If they see an opportunity to compete in international markets or acquire international companies, to the extent that they can, they will. In 2017, 43.6% of the total sales of the companies in the S&P 500 were from overseas.[8] About 30% of the total market-cap of listed companies in the world ($79.2 trillion[9]) are companies in the S&P 500 ($23.9 trillion[10]). How's that for international exposure with supposedly domestic companies?

Currency fluctuations can wipe out any profit

When you buy a foreign stock, you need to use the currency of that country to make the purchase. That means you have to convert U.S. dollars into that country's currency, and that exposes you to exchange rate risk – that is, the price in U.S. dollars you paid to buy the foreign currency may be different when you sell the foreign currency to buy U.S. dollars.

For example, you exchanged your U.S. dollars for the foreign currency at a given rate and you used the foreign currency to buy the foreign stock. Say you made a profit in the foreign stock and now you want to convert the foreign currency into U.S. dollars, but the exchange rate went against you and you lost money in currency the transaction, perhaps more than what you made in the foreign stock. Thus, with foreign investments, you're actually playing in two markets at the same time: the foreign stock market and the currency market. Not only do you have to pick the right foreign stock, but you also have to pick the right time to buy and sell in the currency market.

Political risk can wipe out your entire investment

Some foreign governments can change suddenly and the new government might decide it doesn't like U.S. investors buying and selling shares of its companies on its stock exchange. That government can create many problems including imposing currency restrictions where you can't convert its currency into U.S. dollars or it might even nationalize the company you invested in, in effect confiscating all of your investment.

---

[8] us.spindices.com
[9] The World Bank Group
[10] Siblis Research, Ltd.

Foreign countries don't always play fair

Some countries erect high barriers intended to prevent foreigners from investing in their companies. These barriers can be either explicit or implicit. An explicit barrier might be higher brokerage costs or additional charges such as stamp duties, taxes, clearing fees, and exchange fees. All of these barriers raise the cost of buying and selling foreign stock and cut into any potential profit or compound any loss over and above the impact of the currency risk.

Implicit barriers are ones that are not clearly expressed but are barriers anyway. Depending on the country, many companies can be owned by family members or by a network of interlocking ownership with other companies, groups, or banks. So the "free float," which is the number of shares that are actively traded, can be a fraction of the number of shares outstanding. The reduction in the number of shares available for investment severely restricts trading volume, thus causing share prices to fluctuate widely, which in turn increases the risk of an investment.

Another implicit barrier involves the availability, quality, and timeliness of information about the foreign company. For example, foreign accounting rules can be substantially different from those in the United States, which are generally clear-cut, consistent across companies, readily available, and produced in a timely fashion. That's not necessarily the case with foreign countries, especially for companies in what are called the "emerging markets." Without good quality and timely information, the risk of investing increases dramatically.

When you dig deeper into foreign markets you will find there are a host of restrictions that make buying foreign stock in some countries extremely difficult. Samsung's a good example. Their Galaxy cell phones are popular and you might want to buy Samsung stock because you sense a money-making trend. Samsung is a South Korean company that trades mainly on the South Korean Stock Exchange. It is not listed on any major U.S. stock exchanges. Samsung's website, however, states that you can buy shares directly on the South Korean exchange, but you must first obtain an investor registration certificate from the Korean Financial Supervisory Services and follow a bunch of other complex rules. Good luck with that.

What Are American Depository Receipts (ADRs)

These are certificates that are traded in the United States and represent shares of a foreign company's stock. They are often traded on one of the major stock exchanges. One ADR may represent a fraction of a foreign share or it might represent several foreign shares. ADRs make it easier for you to invest in a foreign company because they are priced in U.S. dollars. But you still have currency risk and the additional costs outlined above.

> *"Stocks aren't lottery tickets. There's a company attached to every share."*
> *– Peter Lynch*

CHAPTER 4

A Place to Trade Stocks

In 1792, twenty-four individuals got together under a Buttonwood tree outside 68 Wall Street in what is now downtown New York City. They set up shop there, and it became the place to go if you wanted to buy or sell securities. They were called "brokers" just like they are today, and for their services they would collect a fee or commission, just as they do now. If the other side of a trade could not be found, or could not be found quickly enough, a broker might take the position for his own account. These individuals were known, then as now, as "market makers" or "dealers."

Time passed and they moved inside – who wants to sit under a tree in winter? More time passed, names changed, the tree came down, and eventually the place where stocks were traded became known as the "New York Stock Exchange." Even more time passed, exchanges in other cities came and went, and the Nasdaq (National Association of Securities Dealers Automated Quotation System) came into existence and remains to this day. Even more time passed and eventually the physical marketplaces evolved and combined with other exchanges to what we have to today – an electronic stock market that spans the globe, and where billions of dollars of trades occur across different trading platforms and countries every day.

Why We Need a Stock Market

Some people will tell that you the stock market is only a place where the fat cats get rich while the poor get shafted. They say it's a den of crooks waiting to steal your money. Do away with it and let's concentrate on working people who make things instead of those who make fortunes trading pieces of paper. Let's occupy Wall Street and tear it down.

Clearly, these folks are misinformed and don't understand the vital role the stock market plays in our economic prosperity. Consider this. Buildings, machinery, and computers are all examples of "hard assets." People get paid to use those hard assets to produce goods and services that are then sold to the public. But hard assets and a person's labor are only part of the story. Companies need money in order to buy those hard assets and to pay wages to employees. This is where investors and "financial assets" come into the picture. Common stocks and bonds are examples of "financial assets." The money from the sale of these financial assets to investors, together with the profit earned by the company from the sale of its goods and services, provides the cash to buy the buildings, machinery, and computers, and to provide jobs.

No investors, no financial assets. No financial assets and profits, no hard assets or jobs. No jobs, no prosperity. It's as simple as that. And the key component in all of this is to have a place where companies can go to raise the money they need and where investors can go to exchange their money for part ownership of a company. And that place is at one of the exchanges that make up the stock market. Eliminating the stock market simply defeats the goal of helping our people and our country's prosperity.

But a stock market also

... provides a price for a share of stock

The price is the result of the opinions of thousands of buyers and sellers making decisions in a free and open marketplace – and is a valuable piece of information. It is the basis for all buy, hold, and sell decisions made by investors. Companies use it when they formulate a decision to sell more stock or to buy back shares. A company's supplier might use it when trying to decide whether to extend credit to the company. Senior management might watch it closely, since their bonuses could be based on it. And other contracts, such as for convertible bonds or convertible preferred stock, might also depend on it as well.

... provides a performance benchmark

The change in price over time is also a very important piece of information provided by the stock market. It can tell you quickly, and sometimes brutally, whether you're making money or not. However, not only does it tell you about the performance of individual stocks that trade in the market, but also how the entire market has performed. Based on the results, you may want to switch to another stock, to an index fund (more about them later), or to another investment manager if you turned your money over to one to invest.

... is an indicator of future economic growth

The stock market's action is a major component of what is called the Index of Leading Economic Indicators (I'll talk more about it in Chapter 24). But briefly, as the name suggests, this index gives policymakers clues as to the future direction of economic growth, which they can then use when making various policy decisions. How the stock market is performing is an important part of that picture.

... stimulates product improvement

As strange as it might seem, you and I get better products and services because of the stock market. Make no mistake: Companies don't operate in a vacuum. Competitors look at the share price of their competition relative to how well their own share price is doing, and that might be a signal that the company should do something differently. For example, look at Apple. They were the first with the iPhone, but eventually the management of other companies saw the money Apple shareowners were making and wanted in. What did those other companies do? They developed similar products and charged a lower price. That in turn spurred Apple to improve its products, which in turn spurred other companies to improve their products, and so on. Who benefits from all this competition? We do. We get better products at a lower price.

What Is a Stock Exchange?

It's simply a place where you can buy and sell shares of stock through a stock broker. In the United States, we have two major stock exchanges: the NYSE (New York Stock Exchange) and the Nasdaq. Combined, these two exchanges are larger than the next eight largest exchanges in the world combined.[11] To be "listed" on either one of these exchanges, a company must meet certain requirements. Because of differing requirements and for historical reasons, the NYSE generally lists larger, more well-established companies, whereas the Nasdaq generally lists smaller, sometimes more technologically-oriented companies.

Although we have these two major exchanges, that doesn't mean that your order will be fully or even partially executed on them. Routing technology will scan all the places where your order can be executed and send your order there and, if it can't be filled completely, move on to another venue. Depending on the liquidity of the stock and the size of your order, all

---

[11] DollarAndSense.com

this happens very quickly – so quickly that you don't even realize it's happening.

The reason I brought up these two exchanges is the distinction between them becomes important when I discuss indices and index funds in future chapters.

Alternatives to Trading on an Exchange

Direct purchase

You don't have to buy and sell stocks through a broker on an exchange if you don't want to. Some companies will sell their stock directly to you. There will be various formulas to determine the price and procedures to follow. Some companies will charge you a fee, while others won't. You might even be able to have the money you want invested taken directly from your checking account on a monthly basis. If there are any dividends, they will be mailed to you or you can reinvest them into more shares of stock. You can ask the company's investor relations department for more information if you're interested. Just make sure you understand the terms and conditions before you go this route.

Sale to another individual

If you own shares and want to sell them, you could also do it the old-fashioned baseball card way – you could seek out a friend, a neighbor, or a stranger to buy your shares. Then, if the deal is agreed to, all you have to do is notify the company's transfer agent of the change in ownership. However, finding a buyer – or seller, if you wanted to buy – could be a hassle. Best to use a broker.

Initial Public Offering (IPO)

Earlier I talked about private and public companies. An IPO is how a private company can become a public one whose shares can then trade on an exchange. For example, say you had a great idea for a new web service. Where would you get the money to buy the necessary computers, servers, and the other stuff you need to get your company going? The answer is initially from savings, parents, loans from your family and friends, and maybe over the internet. In investment lingo, this is called raising money in the "primary market."

Say you got lucky, your idea caught on, and the company grew and grew and you needed more money than you could raise in the primary market. You, like so many other companies in the past, might decide to ask strangers if they would like to buy shares in your company in what is called an "initial public offering" (IPO). It's called "initial" since this is the first time that the public has had an opportunity to buy part of your company. The following will give you a rough idea of the mechanics.

Before the shares can be traded in the open market, your company has to follow all the rules set by the Securities and Exchange Commission (SEC) and by the stock exchange where you wanted your shares to be listed for trading. Next, your company would probably hire an investment banker, or several, to help you with the sale of the initial shares being offered and with other details, especially what the offering price should be.

The next step requires you and your investment banker to find people who want to buy your stock. Generally, target customers would be other investment bankers. Thus, you would go to each potential customer and make your pitch in what is called a "road show." You and your senior management team would explain to these firms why they should buy your stock. If they were interested, you would ask them to "subscribe," or promise to buy, a certain number of shares at a certain price before the stock became public. This is when things get interesting. If you set the stock price too high, they might not subscribe to the offering. If it is too low, your company will not get all the money for expansion you had hoped for.

Eventually an offering price is determined and you have a list of customers willing to subscribe to your offering. Typically, the list would contain several firms who had subscribed to large chunks of stock. These firms in turn would approach their customers and ask if they would like some portion of the offering they committed to. Those firms in turn would offer smaller chunks to any other interested investors.

Finally, the appointed day arrives. It's tradition at the New York Stock Exchange for the executives of a newly listed stock to stand on the podium overlooking the trading floor and have one person, perhaps you, bang the gavel to signal the start (or closing) of the trading day. The other individuals of your team who are standing behind you are all smiling and seem very happy. At that point, your company ceases being a private company and becomes a public one and the shares begin trading in what finance people call the "secondary market."

By this time the people who subscribed to the issue would have made their payments and received the shares they were promised. The money received from all those who subscribed, less pre-agreed-to commissions and fees, would be given to your company to do with as you and your management team wished – pay bills, buy more equipment, and hire more people.

When trading starts, the company's shares are just like any other shares being traded in the stock market – with one big exception. There is a tendency for the share price to start trading at a price much higher than the subscription price, and in some cases, dramatically so. Thus, those who were able to participate in the subscription could make a bundle of money very quickly.

You might ask: "Why can't I buy that hot new stock at the subscription price and sell it later for a big profit when the shares start trading on the exchange?" Good question. This is one area of the market that stinks for small investors. I'll give you the party-line answer first. Many investment bankers don't want to be bothered with small investors who want small quantities of stock – they say to do so is too time consuming and too expensive. Perhaps. But there is also the non-party line, and that is simply this: They might want to curry favor with their best customers by offering them first crack at a hot IPO deal. You scratch my back and I'll scratch yours.

There is still a chance for you to participate, but not a big one. If you learn that your broker is helping the investment banker with the subscription, you can tell him or her that you'd like to buy some at the subscription price. Your chances are slim, but it doesn't hurt to ask.

Another question that often comes up is: How do the founders of the company and others become rich? Some of the stock in the company is not offered for sale to the public and is owned by those who started the company, by employees, and by those who invested in the company when it was private. Now you know why all those people standing on the podium above the stock exchange trading floor are smiling. They suddenly have become very wealthy.

But don't assume that committing to the subscription price and then selling the shares at a higher price when the company starts trading is a sure thing – it isn't. Facebook set the subscription price at $38 a share, the top of a range of estimates. Some thought Facebook would start trading at $80, which would have been a huge windfall if you could get the shares at the subscription price. Others were not so optimistic. After all, Facebook did not have much in earnings at the time. So you had a huge difference of opinion as to what the shares were worth.

On Friday, May 18, 2012, the day trading started, Facebook hit a high of $45 a share and quickly settled down to close at $38.23, a mere 23 cents above its subscription price. Not much money to be made there unless you were very quick. Within a few days its shares were trading at $25.52 and eventually went even lower to $17.55. Eventually it turned around, and at the beginning of 2019 Facebook was trading at $134.87 a share. But there are other IPO stories where returning to the subscription price is still a dream.

Alternatives to a Traditional IPO

I have explained the traditional way companies come to be traded on a stock exchange, but it is not the only way. Here are two alternatives.

Direct listing

With the concurrence of an exchange, a private company just lists their shares for trading. The company, its employees who own shares, and the company's backers can sell their shares to anyone who wants to buy them. Using this route, the company avoids the fees charged for a normal IPO and lets the market place set the price. How many shares that are sold, and thus the amount of capital raised, depends on the demand for the shares.

Dutch auction

This approach allows investors to bid for the number of shares they want at a price they are willing to pay. The company then determines the highest clearing price that sells all the shares that were offered. For example, say the bids were $10 per share for 100 shares, $8.00 for 300 shares, $7 for 600 shares, and $5 for 1,000 shares. The company wants to sell 1,000 shares for the highest amount they can get. The $10 bid will get the company 100 shares, the $8 bid 300 shares and the $7 bid 600 for a total of 1,000 shares. So, the $7 bid is the highest clearing price that will sell all the 1,000 shares. That then sets the price and the $10, $8, and $7 bids all get the shares they bid for at the price of $7. The investor who bid $5 for 1,000 shares will not receive any shares. In my example, the company wanted to sell 1,000 shares but the same process is used if the company wants to raise a certain amount of money instead.

Each of these approaches, IPO, direct listing, and Dutch auction, has its advantages and disadvantages. Facebook used the IPO route, Spotify used the direct listing, and Alphabet (Google at the time) used the Dutch auction. The point, however, is those creative ways to raise money would not have happened were it not for a dynamic stock market.

Ticker Symbols

From the beginning of time people wanted news about something that happened a long distance away. Remember Helen and the Trojan horse?

Well, a chain of signal fires stretching miles and miles from what is now Turkey (the site of Troy) to Greece was lit one after another until the signal reached Greece telling the citizens that the war was won.

Signal fires just didn't seem like such a good idea for transferring information about stock prices. Enter Thomas Edison – yes, the same guy who invented the light bulb, which are now LED circuits. Anyway, in 1871 he invented a telegraph machine that would transmit stock trading information. Someone would sit at one end of the wire typing in the information and it would appear on a thin paper ribbon at the other end. Mr. Edison's machine made a clicking or ticking sound as it punched out symbols representing the characters and numbers of the trade. The machine was nicknamed the "ticker" and the paper ribbon the "ticker tape." You can just imagine someone saying: "Hey Joe, check the 'ticker' and tell me what the 'tape' says about railroad stock prices" (the hot stock of the day).

All kinds of phrases were coined during this era, and many are still used today. Take the phrase "painting the tape." No, it's not changing the color of the paper tape from yellow to red. It's a form of stock manipulation that is illegal and could land someone in jail. It generally takes two forms – intentionally increasing the trading volume of a stock or attempting to manipulate a closing price – both of which are intended to give an advantage to the manipulator. I spoke about this in Chapter 1 in the context of pump and dump.

Another term that still applies today is "fighting the tape." This is when an investor goes against the direction of either an individual stock or of the market itself. An investor is fighting the tape when he or she buys when everyone else is selling, or vice versa. Many traders would say this is a dumb idea, saying, "The trend is your friend," and that you should go with what it is saying. But if you bucked the trend and you're right, you could make lots of money. If you're wrong and the tape is right, you can get creamed.

One more journey down memory lane – the "ticker tape" parade. Everyone loves a parade, and the more festive the better. So, when big shots came to New York City and a parade was held for them, the brokers would gather up all the used ticker tape and, as the big shots went by, they would throw it out the window and the tape would come streaming down in long ribbons. Judging from all the photographs at the time, it was quite a sight. The term is still used today to signify a very special parade.

The ticker tape was a roll of thin paper that was perhaps an inch in width, coiled on a roll. It was expensive, and to type the company's full name was wasteful. Thus, each company was required to select a unique abbreviation or identifier for their company. Most selected an abbreviation for their ticker symbol that was based on a shortened version of the company's name. For example, American Telephone and Telegraph selected the letter "T"; Ford selected "F" and Kellogg selected "K." Single letters were much coveted at that time and still are. Visa wanted and got "V" when Vivendi dropped it.

Other ticker symbols followed the name of the company. International Business Machine's is "IBM," Apple's is "AAPL," and Target's is "TGT." But a company did not have to select a ticker symbol based on its name. For example, Brinker International selected "EAT" as its ticker symbol – yes, it's a restaurant chain. Harley-Davidson's ticker symbol is "HOG" and Southwest Airway is "LUV" as a nod to where its headquarters is located, Love Field in Dallas.

Each exchange had certain rules for what symbols were acceptable. The NYSE had three letters as their limit and Nasdaq had four letters. That changed a bit when one company wanted to move from the NYSE to Nasdaq and was allowed to keep its ticker symbol that was only two letters long.

As time went on life got a bit more complicated and the ticker symbol had to be adjusted. A dot "." extension was added to NYSE symbols and a fifth letter to Nasdaq stocks to provide additional information about the company or the shares. Here are some of the more important extensions:

A	Class "A" shares
B	Class "B" shares
D	New issue
E	Delinquent SEC filings
K	Nonvoting (common)
Q	In bankruptcy

The "." became a bit cumbersome, so when checking prices or placing an order, it is often dropped. In other words, the ticker symbol for Berkshire Hathaway class "A" stock is BRK.A, but depending on where you go on the internet it could be BRKA or BRK-A. Same with their class "B" shares – BRKB or BRK-B

Ticker symbols are unique and are used to identify a specific company and the type of shares you want to buy or sell. You type in a set of letters and press the "buy" key and those are the shares you'll get. So, it's very important to know the exact ticker symbol to use. There are various places where you can find a company's ticker symbol on the internet, but the best place is in the investor's section of the company's website.

How Pricing Is Handled on an Electronic Exchange

This section will give you a rough idea of how electronic stock exchanges work. But first, let's get our terms down correctly. If you want to *buy* a stock, you are going to pay the *ask* price. This is the price the sellers of the stock are *asking* for a share of stock. If you want to *sell* a stock you are going to get the *bid* price. This is the price buyers are *bidding* for a share of stock.

Registered brokers, dealers, market makers, and specialists are allowed to post a statement to the world that they are willing and ready take the other side of the transaction. They will sell when you want to buy and they will buy when you want to sell, but they specify they will do so only at a given price and only for a given number of shares.

For example, one registered broker might say, "I'm willing to sell 100 shares at $25.05 a share." Another dealer might say, "I'm willing to sell 200 shares at $25.10 per share." Another dealer might be willing to sell 500 shares at $26.10 per share. So what we have created is a list of prices and quantities at which registered brokers or dealers are willing to sell you shares.

I'M WILLING TO SELL YOU	AND I'M ASKING
100 SHARES	$25.05
200 SHARES	$25.10
500 SHARES	$26.10

The same thing is true for the registered brokers or dealers who are willing to buy a stock from you:

I'M WILLING TO BUY FROM YOU	AND I'M BIDDING
100 SHARES	$24.95
500 SHARES	$23.00
200 SHARES	$22.00

An "order book" is created from all the bid-ask prices that were offered by the brokers and dealers. In concept it would look like this:

# SHARES	BID PRICE	ASK PRICE	#SHARES
100	$24.95	$25.05	100
500	$23.00	$25.10	200
200	$22.00	$26.10	500

Notice the bid price (the price you would get if you wanted to sell) is below the ask price (the price you must pay if you want to buy). The difference between the bid and ask price is called the "spread."

We will talk about the different types of orders in Chapter 6, but briefly, let's say you want to buy 600 shares "at-the-market." For the first 100 shares, your order would be filled at $25.05. Then your order would move to the next available shares in the "order book" which are priced $25.10, so you would buy 200 shares at that price. Your order is still not completed so it would move down even further for the remaining 300 shares, which you would buy at $26.10. The same process happens when you want to sell, and you would get the bid price. In reality, the bid and ask prices, as well as the quantities, are constantly changing so your order might be filled at or near the $25.05 price. I've found if my order is broken up and gets cheaper if I am buying, I need to exercise caution; It's not a good sign when the market is willing to sell at cheaper and cheaper prices when you're buying.

For illustration, I have presented a static order book. In reality, there are many order books in many different venues and they are all constantly changing, often so fast that only super-fast computers can keep up.

Liquidity

When we discuss liquidity, we really want to know how much stock we can buy or sell at any given point in time without causing a material change from the last sale price.

The answer to that question can be found in the order book for a company's stock. There we can see a stock's "depth" and its "liquidity." Depth is measured by the number of shares that are being offered for trading at the best bid-ask price. If lots of shares are being offered for purchase or sale, the market for that stock is considered deep. In other words, a lot of stock can be traded without causing a material change from the last traded price. On the other hand, liquidity is a function of the number of shares being offered for trading at the next-to-the-best bid-ask price, and the next after that, and so on.

Getting access to a current order book where you can see a stock's depth and liquidity is not easy, and it can change quickly based on new information that constantly flows into the market. However, a quick and rough assessment of relative depth and liquidity can be determined by looking at the number of shares of the stock that are traded each day over a period of time as well as the average size of the bid-ask spread.

Market Participants

If you are going to invest in the stock market, you should at least be aware of your competition. Besides other individuals like yourself, there are a number of large institutions who invest in the stock market in hopes of achieving a good return, just like you. They are pension funds, insurance companies, state and municipal government entities, and foreigners. They make their own investment decisions or, more likely, hire several firms to do it on their behalf. When I was working for a large pension fund, I managed an index fund, a growth portfolio, and a yield portfolio, in addition to hiring several investment advisors including many who managed assets overseas.

Every year the Investment Advisor Association issues a report that gathers and compiles government-required disclosure documents into a report called the "Evolution Revolution: A Profile of the Investment Advisor Profession." In their 2018 report they said nearly 12,500 registered investment advisors were managing $82.5 trillion in assets for 34.0 million clients. These advisors manage money for the large institutions as well mutual funds and exchange traded funds.

You should not be intimidated by these numbers or the competition they represent. Many of the investors and firms have various rules prohibiting them from investing in certain areas of the market. Many have committees that they have to go through for approval to make investments. Many of their jobs are dependent on short-term results. Thus, as an individual, you have significant advantages. First, you can be more flexible: There are no committees to report to, no colleagues to second-guess your decisions, and no meetings to attend. Second, the size of your trades will probably be small, so you won't have the liquidity problems facing large institutions who need to trade hundreds of thousands of shares. Finally, your major advantage is your youth; you have the ability to have a long-term perspective.

The U.S. Securities and Exchange Commission

The Securities and Exchange Commission is the government watchdog organization that oversees the stock market. Their stated mission is to protect investors; maintain fair, orderly, and efficient markets; and facilitate capital formation. They play a vital role in ensuring investors have a level playing field and receive useful information in a timely manner. They also have the legal authority to enforce any violations. For more information on their role in the stock market you can refer to www.investor.gov.

CHAPTER 5

Measuring Stock Market Performance

You might have heard, "The DJIA rose 250 points today," on the evening news or seen it on your smartphone. What they were referring to was an increase in an index – that is, a single number intended to reflect the movement of a collection of different stocks. The index they were referring to was the Dow Jones Industrial Average. But the DJIA is comprised of only 30 stocks, so how can it describe the action of a stock market that contains over 4,000 actively traded stocks? Answer: It can't. It can only describe the performance of a certain important segment of the market – in this case, the stocks of large, well-established companies.

There are many different indices, ranging from the more well-known ones to the exotic ones. In this chapter, I tell you why indices are important, how an index is constructed, and what some of the major indices measure.

Why Are Indices Important?

Each index has a message for you, and the wise investor will listen to what they are saying. For example, paying attention to a market-wide index might give you clues as to the future direction of the market and, therefore, an idea of when to buy or sell stocks. Second, many indices have been constructed to measure the performance of various segments of the market. By tracking these indices, you might identify which segments are expected to perform the best, and thus where to concentrate your stock-selection efforts. Third, an index will give you something against which to measure your stock-picking skills. Maybe you'll find that you aren't all that great at picking individual stocks and you might want to change your strategy. Finally, investment managers have developed portfolios of stocks designed to replicate the performance of various indices. If you are considering investing in one of these index funds, you had better know what's in them and how they are constructed before you invest or you might be in for an unwelcomed surprise.

How Are Indices Constructed?

Indices are constructed through a three-step process. First, a decision needs to be made on which segment of the over 4,000 stocks on which to focus on. Secondly, a decision needs to be made as to whether all companies in the segment should be included or just a representative sample. Finally, the index-maker needs to decide how much weight to give to the performance of each stock in the index so that a single number can be calculated that is intended to represent their collective performance.

Which segment of the market?

Because of the diversity of the companies represented in the stock market, index makers are faced with a huge challenge. Think of the stock market as if it were a sheet of paper. Using scissors, you could cut the paper into any shape you wanted – big pieces, small pieces, shapes such as stars, or even your name. For example, in the stock market you might focus on the stocks of companies over a certain size, all stocks except financial ones, ones determined by a committee, or ones determined by a rule-based computer program. Which segment you pick depends on what you want to measure.

Here are just some of the ways some index makers have divided up the market:

By size of company:

Mega-caps – Over $200 billion

Large-caps – $10 billion to $200 billion

Medium-caps – $2 billion to $10 billion

Small-caps – $300 million to $2 billion

Micro-caps – $50 million to $300 million

Nano-caps – Under $50 million

By sector groups:

Energy

Materials

Industrial

Consumer Discretionary

Consumer Staples

Health Care

Financials

Information Technology

Communication Services

Utilities

Real Estate

The sectors are then divided into industry groups. For example, the Health Care sector is divided into the following, which are then divided even further:

Health Care Equipment & Services

Pharmaceuticals, Biotechnology & Life Sciences

If you want more information, search Wikipedia for the Global Industry Classification Standard. The GICS® groups companies into 11 sectors, 24 industry groups, 69 industries, and 158 subindustries – an ever-changing list, as the economy continues to evolve.

How many and which companies to include?

Sometimes historical precedent had already made these decisions. For example, the DJIA has contained 30 stocks since 1928, and it is doubtful they will change the number any time soon. A committee decides which 30 stocks to include.

Historical precedent also dictates that the Standard & Poor's 500 index has 500 companies in it as it has since 1957. In recent times, however, it has had slightly more than 500 stocks since some companies have issued different classes of common stocks. A committee decides which stocks to include.

The Wilshire 5000 Total Market Index™ was developed in 1974 in an attempt to create an index for the "entire" market, or as their fact sheet reports, "All U.S. equities with readily available prices." The actual number of companies in the index has varied from a high of 7,562 names on July 31, 1998 to 3,486 names on June 30, 2018. The last time it contained at least 5,000 companies was on December 29, 2005. This illustrates both the difficulty of developing a stable index for the entire market and how dynamic the stock market can be with companies entering and leaving the marketplace for various reasons all the time. A committee and an algorithm decide which stocks to include.

Some other number-based indices that are broad-based are the Russell 3000 index (largest 3,000 publicly traded U.S. companies) and the Schwab 1000 index (largest 1,000 publicly traded U.S. companies). Then there are indices that do not have a fixed number of stocks in them – the New York Stock Exchange Composite index that covers the NYSE and the Nasdaq Composite index that covers the Nasdaq exchange. These two indices also include securities other than U.S. common stocks.

How much weight should be given to each stock's performance?

Once the decision has been made as to which companies are included, we get into the nitty-gritty of blending each stock's performance into a single number. This is done by giving each stock's performance a different weight. The choice of a weighting scheme is an important decision since it has a dramatic impact on the resulting index number. These are the weighting schemes used in the major indices.

Price-weighted: The current price of all the shares in the index are added up and divided by the number of companies in the index. A price-weighted index gets tricky, however, when a stock splits, a company in the index acquires another, the committee drops one company and adds another company, or the occurrence other events. When these corporate originated events occur, they should not be allowed to impact the index number. For example, in Chapter 3 we learned that when a stock splits it causes the number of shares to increase and the price of each share to go down, but the value of the holdings remains unchanged. If the new lower split price is used in the calculation of a price-weighted index, the index number would be distorted. To prevent this from happening, a new divisor has to be calculated so that the index number remains unchanged. Once a new divisor has been determined, the calculation is easy – just add up the prices of the stocks in the index and divide by the new divisor (see Appendix B for the math).

Capitalization-weighted (also known as value-weighted): In Chapter 3 we learned that the market capitalization of a company is the company's share price times the number of shares outstanding. Add up all the market capitalizations of the stocks in the index and you basically have the raw index number. To report such a huge number doesn't make much sense, so a second step is required. The current total market capitalization number is divided by a specially constructed divisor that adjusts the index for some corporate actions as well as name changes, and is benchmarked to a starting round number such as 100. It is this second step that makes the index easier to report and understand (see Appendix A for the math).

The major complaint with capitalization-weighted indices is that the largest companies dominate the index's performance. This has an effect of distorting the diversification that a committee might have originally intended.

Float-adjusted, capitalization-weighted: This is the same as capitalization-weighted, except instead of using the number of shares outstanding to calculate capitalization, the shares that are closely held and rarely traded are subtracted from the total number of shares outstanding. This is done to give a truer picture of the shares that are available for trading.

Other weighting schemes

There are many other schemes that factor-based managers use in the development of their benchmarks (see Chapter 13 for the difference between an index and a benchmark). Some of them are:

Equal-weighted: This approach gives equal weight to each company regardless of its size or share price. For example, if we started with $100,000 and with 100 names, each stock would get $1,000 allocated to it, a 1% representation. This degree of representation will be substantially different than for the same stock in any of the other weighting schemes. The major complaint with this weighting scheme is that it requires frequent buying and selling of shares to remain true to its stated objective of equal weights.

Modified capitalization-weighted: This is the same as market capitalization-weighted, except a ceiling is placed on the representation of large, market capitalization companies. This is done to give more performance exposure to the stock of smaller companies.

Open-weighted: This weighting scheme can be anything the factor-based manager wants it to be. They are free to use earnings, sales, number of employees, or anything else and in any combination as weights in constructing the benchmark (more about factors in Chapters 10, 13, and 16).

Major Stock Market Indices

Here are some details about the three major stock indices you often hear reported in the news (refer to their websites if you want more information).

Dow Jones Industrial Average (DJIA)

This is a price-weighted index consisting of 30 large, well-established companies. Although the number has been constant since 1928, the companies within the index have changed over time. The index consists of large corporations that are often referred to as "blue chip." A blue chip is actually the color of a very high-value chip used in casinos. The term was picked up by the stock market as shorthand for a company of high quality.

The decision on which companies to include in the DJIA is made by a committee. The guidelines for inclusion, according to the Dow Jones website, are as follows:

> While there are no rules for component selection, a stock is typically added only if it has an excellent reputation, demonstrates sustained growth, is of interest to a large number of investors and accurately represents the sector(s) covered by the average ... the DJIA is not limited to traditionally defined industrial stocks. Instead, the index serves as a measure of the entire U.S. Market, covering such diverse industries as financial services, technology, retail, entertainment and consumer goods.

The names of the companies in the DJIA are easily recognizable, as you can see:

3M	JP Morgan Chase
American Express	McDonald's
Apple	Merck
Boeing	Microsoft
Caterpillar	Nike
Chevron	Pfizer
Cisco Systems	Procter & Gamble
Coca-Cola	Travelers
DuPont	United Health Group
ExxonMobil	United Technologies
Goldman Sachs	Verizon
The Home Depot	Visa
Intel	Wal-Mart
IBM	Walgreens
Johnson & Johnson	Walt Disney

Standard & Poor's 500 (S&P 500)

This float-adjusted capitalization-weighted index is widely used in investment research and is an important component in the Leading Economic Indicators (see Chapter 24). It contains stock of the leading companies in the leading industries. It represents about 80% of all U.S. publicly traded companies by market-capitalization. From 1957, the index contained 500 companies, but recently, because some companies have issued different types of shares, it has contained more than 500 stocks.

The decision on which companies to include is made by a committee. The guidelines for inclusion, according to SPDJI website are as follows:

> Company count of 500 (currently slightly over due to multiple share classes), U.S. companies, $6.1 billion market-cap or greater, at least 50% of shares outstanding available for trading, positive as-reported earnings over the most recent quarter, as well as over the most recent four quarters (summed together), adequate liquidity and reasonable price - highly tradable common stocks, with active and deep markets. Sector balance is also considered in the selection of companies.

Nasdaq Composite Index

This market-capitalization-weighted index contains approximately 3,300 domestic and international based stocks listed on the Nasdaq exchange. According to the Nasdaq website:

> To be eligible for inclusion in the Composite the security's U.S. listing must be exclusively on the Nasdaq Stock Market (unless the security was dually listed on another U.S. market prior to January 1, 2004 and has continuously maintained such listing), and have a security type of either: American Depositary Receipts (ADRs), common stock, limited partnership interests, ordinary shares, real estate investment trusts (REITs), shares of beneficial interest (SBIs), and tracking stocks. Security types not included in the Index are closed-end funds, convertible debentures, exchange traded funds, preferred stock, rights, warrant, units and other derivative securities.

Wilshire 5000 Total Market Index^{SM}

This full (and available floated-adjusted) market capitalization index attempts to measure "...the performance of all U.S. equity securities with readily available price data." According to the Wilshire website:

> To be included in the Wilshire 5000 Index, an issue must – Be the primary equity issue; a common stock, REIT or limited partnership; Have its primary market listing in the United States; and Not be a bulletin-board issue – these issues are not included because they generally do not have consistently readily-available prices.
>
> The company's primary issue for index valuation is determined based on the following criteria: Market capitalization; Trading volume; Institutional holdings; and Conversion rules (for companies with multiple share classes).

An index is a single number intended to reflect the movement of a collection of stocks.

APPENDIX A
How an Index Number is Computed

This appendix is intended to provide general information on how an index number is computed for a capitalization-weighted index. Rather than reporting the total market capitalization, it is referenced back to an earlier market capitalization and then benchmarked to some round number such as 100. This makes it much easier to report and understand rather than using the total market capitalization number.

Say an index was started in 1957 and the stock prices and number of shares outstanding were as follows:

COMPANY (A)	PRICE PER SHARE (B)	SHARES OUTSTANDING (C)	MARKET-CAP (D)=(B)X(C)
W	50.00	1000	50000
X	15.00	1500	22500
Y	45.00	2000	90000
Z	10.00	3000	30000
			192500

A year later stock prices have changed:

COMPANY (A)	PRICE PER SHARE (B)	SHARES OUTSTANDING (C)	MARKET-CAP (D)=(B)X(C)
W	54.00	1000	54000
X	20.00	1500	30000
Y	47.00	2000	94000
Z	11.00	3000	33000
			211000

Market capitalization increased from $192,500 to $211,000 which are awkward numbers to report. If we benchmark the starting point at 100, and using a ratio analysis, we can compute the change and have a much easily understandable number to report.

$$211000 \div 192500 = X \div 100$$

$$X = (211000 \text{ x } 100) \div 192500$$

$$X = 109.61$$

Therefore, our index of four stocks increased from 100 to 109.61 and we can report the new index value of 109.61, or an increase of 9.61%.

APPENDIX B
How Corporate Events Are Handled

Often company-initiated actions such as stock splits, reverse splits, spin-offs, acquisitions, mergers, and stock dividends, if left untreated, could cause a major distortion in the index number. Here's an example of how an index-maker deals with the situation for a price-weighted index.

Assume there are four stocks in our index and Stock A had a 2 for 1 stock split. What divisor should we use so that the value of the index does not change because of the split?

STOCK	PRICE BEFORE SPLIT	PRICE AFTER SPLIT
A	40.00	20.00
B	15.00	15.00
C	45.00	45.00
D	60.00	60.00
TOTAL	160.00	140.00
DIVISOR	4	?
INDEX	40	40

To compute a new divisor so that our price-weighted index value of 40 doesn't change, we solve the following equation:

$$40 = 140 \div X$$
$$X = 3.5 \text{ (new divisor)}$$

So, dividing 140 by 3.5 (our new divisor) the index's value remains 40.

CHAPTER 6

Establishing and Using a Brokerage Account

The easiest way to trade stock is through a stock broker. They have the systems in place to make it simple, easy, and efficient. They will take care of all the nitty-gritty paper work, including year-end income tax information, thus allowing you to focus on what to buy and sell.

But first you have to establish a brokerage account – that includes finding a broker that suits your personality, evaluating the types of accounts you can open, and identifying the types of orders you can use to buy and sell shares as well as identifying alternative ways of holding your stock. These are the topics covered in this chapter.

However, if you are under the age of 18 (or 21 in some states), you are considered too young to open a brokerage account by yourself. You will need to find a custodian. This could be a parent, a grandparent, or someone else you trust who will listen to your input. The account will be in your name, but the custodian will be making all the trades on your behalf.

Finding a Broker Who Suits Your Personality

There are two major categories of brokers: discount and full-service.

Discount broker

If you are a "do-it-yourself" kind of a person, you might consider using a discount broker. Among the biggest are Schwab, Fidelity, TD Ameritrade, E-Trade, and Interactive Brokers. All have mobile trading apps, but be careful, because having readily available access might result in too much in-and-out trading, and that could result in poor returns.

With a discount broker you'll be making all of the decisions yourself – what to buy, when, and how much. Ditto for when it comes time to sell. By shifting the investment decisions to you, the discount broker saves money on staff and the savings are passed on to you in the form of lower transaction costs, generally under $10 for an internet-placed order, with the major firms offering trades at $4.95 or lower. Sometimes a discount broker will give you free trades as an inducement to sign up. If not offered, ask. It never hurts. A discount broker might charge you for some services such as limit orders, mutual fund orders, broker-assisted orders, and other services. Some will also offer what's called "wealth management services," a form of investment consulting – for a fee. Best to get a schedule of the price for all service offerings so you won't be surprised by an unexpected fee.

Many discount brokers will give you free access to some very sophisticated online investment research tools and training material. Take advantage of it. Some will even give you their opinion about a particular stock. But before you take their advice, check out their decision-making track record. Also, remember that their advice is generally based on what they expect to happen over a 12-month investment time horizon. As a result, if you follow their advice you might find yourself trading more often that you probably should.

Full-service broker

Full-service brokers come in two varieties: human and computer driven. I will discuss the computer-driven ones, which are often called "robo-advisors," in Chapter 21. Human full-service brokers, such as Edward Jones, Merrill Lynch, and Raymond James, to name a few, can give you investment advice. It's up to you if you want to act on those recommendations. You can also turn over all investment decisions to them and they will tell you later what has been done on your behalf. Again, check their track record.

The advantage of a human full-service broker is that it gives you someone to talk with and bounce ideas off of. Sometimes that is a valuable service. Realistically, however, your account is going to be relatively small, at least to start with. Some brokers might give full-service to a small account because they are hoping it will grow over time. Others just see small accounts as time wasters. Sorry, that is just a reality. Remember, this is how a broker earns a living; there are only so many hours in the day, and more income can be derived from larger accounts. Fees for a full-service broker vary, but will generally be around $50 per trade or some percentage of money under management.

Some Things to Look for When Hiring a Broker

What is the reputation of the firm?

Are they financially sound? Have they been around for a while? Do they offer good customer service? Can you get service during times of peak volume? Although I think it's rare that a difference of opinion between you and the broker as to what was said or done cannot be resolved quickly, it is good to know that they have a reasonable dispute-resolution process in place just in case. Tip: The firm's stock performance and a research report on them can tell you a lot about what investors think about the brokerage firm.

Does the online broker have a physical office nearby?

I'm probably old-fashioned in this regard, but if I have a problem, I really want a face-to-face conversation, rather than trying to talk with someone on the phone in a distant location or by email.

What services do they offer?

Clearly, online brokers have online access, but what else do they have to offer? Is there an interest-bearing account for the cash you might have in your account? Do they have online access to mutual funds and any other investment vehicles you might want? Can you get free access to their research, and is it any good?

How much cash do you need to open an account?

Clearly this is important, because the money you have to invest will be small to start with. Understand the fees. How much will each trade cost you, as well as the cost to trade mutual funds (which is generally higher than for stocks)? Are there any ongoing account maintenance fees? Any other fees such as small account fees?

Looking to the future, what other services do they have?

Do they have access to global trading on foreign exchanges, options, futures, and bonds? Do they have traditional banking services such as check writing, credit cards, and direct deposit?

What happens if the brokerage firm goes bankrupt?

Does the firm have additional insurance beyond what is provided by the Securities Investor Protection Corporation (SIPC)?

All this may take some time to sort through. You can always search the internet for lists such as "Who are the top ten brokerage firms?" and you can see what others think. But like all similar opinions on the internet, carefully consider the source.

Hiring a broker is not a once-in-a-lifetime event. You are paying the firm, and if you're not happy with their services, you don't have to continue with them. Switching brokerage firms is easy. Just tell the new one that you want your account transferred and they'll be only too happy to do it for you. You don't even have to explain your decision to the old broker. No tears, no hard feeling. Both firms realize it's just business. There might be a termination fee however. If that's the case, then ask the new broker if they will compensate you for that amount with free trades – it doesn't hurt to ask.

Type of Accounts

Once you have selected a brokerage firm, you need to open an account. But what type of account to open? You have two primary alternatives: taxable and tax-exempt. I would recommend that you have a parent or your guardian help you to sort through the alternatives.

Taxable

Taxable accounts can be further grouped into regular accounts and margin accounts. As a minor, you can't open a margin account or engage in short selling, but some day you will become an adult in the eyes of the government. Therefore, in Appendix A to this chapter you'll find an explanation of margin accounts and in Appendix B an explanation of short selling.

But, as a minor, your custodian can open a regular taxable custodial account on your behalf. In this type of account, all your sales and any dividends you might receive are subject to a so-called "kiddy-tax." You need to consult with your parents, your custodian, or an accountant to learn the finer points of the taxes on investment income.

Tax-exempt

You might also have the option of opening a retirement account, either a traditional one or a Roth. I know, it's a long way off, but retirement accounts provide very favorable tax treatments if you qualify, follow the rules, and don't need the money you put aside.

Traditional IRA: A Traditional Individual Retirement Account allows you to deduct from your taxable income the amount of money you put into the account (up to a certain limit) and you pay the taxes when you take money out. As a minor, you are probably not making enough money where a tax deduction will be much of a benefit to you. Therefore, you might want to consider the alternative: The Roth Individual Retirement Account (Roth IRA).

Roth IRA: Senator William Roth of Delaware sponsored this law in Congress in 1997. It presents a wonderful opportunity for you. Within certain rules, you pay taxes on your money before it goes into the Roth account and, if you make wise investment decisions, it will grow year after year tax free. There are restrictions on a Roth, and you need to thoroughly understand them before you establish such an account. For a long-term investor, it can be a great strategy.

Whether you decide to open a regular taxable custodial account, a Traditional IRA, a Roth IRA, or some combination of the three, you must have sufficient money in your account to pay for any stock you want to buy, so get busy earning some.

Types of Orders

Your custodial account has been opened and funded. A decision has been made on what stock to buy. You've identified the ticker symbol and decided how many shares to buy. Now what? Talk it over with your custodian and, if that person agrees, have your custodian place the order with the stock broker. But what type of order? Each one has a different impact on the price you will pay and how long your order will be in effect. In addition, special qualifiers can also be placed on some orders.

Market order

If you place this type of order, you are telling your broker to buy or sell the stock as quickly as possible at the best available price.

Like all other orders, a market order has risks and benefits. The benefit is you will get the action – buy or sell – you want in the quantities you want right now. Bang, you're done. The risk is you won't know the price you paid for a purchase or received from a sale until the transaction is completed. In most cases, except for very illiquid stocks or in extremely stressed market conditions, that's okay. I have found myself debating over the "right" price only to miss an excellent trading opportunity by placing a different type of order.

Words of caution:

(1) The last price you saw on your computer screen is just that – the last price at which a trade was consummated. That trade could have occurred seconds, minutes, or even hours ago. The price of the next trade could be similar to the last one or could be wildly different, depending on market conditions and the liquidity of the stock being traded.

(2) Placing a market order when the market is closed is risky because a lot of things can impact a stock's price before the market reopens. Thus, the price you pay or the price you will get if you're selling could be significantly different than the price you were expecting.

(3) Market orders are filled quickly, so it is doubtful that you can cancel one once it is placed. So, before you push that button on the computer to trade, double-check the direction of the trade (buy or sell), the stock's ticker symbol, and the number of shares you want in the trade.

(4) When the market is moving and prices are rapidly changing, your order might be filled at different prices and quantities.

Limit order

With a limit order you can specify the price at which you are willing to trade. Like all other orders, a limit order has risks and benefits. Depending on the market, the benefit is that you might get the price and quantities you want and you might even get a better price. The risk is that your trade might not be fully executed or even executed at all.

By better price I mean one that gives you more – more proceeds if you are selling (a limit-sell order) and less to pay if you are buying (a limit-buy order). This occurs when the market quickly moves away from your limit price in a direction that is favorable to you. For example, say the shares you want to buy are currently selling for $42, and you placed a limit-buy order for 100 shares at $40. Then, say the company reports earnings that are way below expectation and the stock instantly gaps down to $35. You probably will get the quantity of shares you wanted at $35. Why? Because $35 is a "better" price (cheaper) than the $40 you said you were willing to pay. A similar thing happens when you place a limit-sell order above the current market price and the market gaps up above your price. You are likely to get the higher price.

This explains why you can't place a limit-buy order at a price above the current market price. The market price is "better" (cheaper) than the price you were willing to pay. Likewise, you can't place a limit-sell order below the current market price because the current market price is "better" (gives you more money) than you were willing to accept with your order.

The risk of a limit order is that your trade might not be executed fully or even at all – the market may never hit your price. In other words, no one is willing to trade at the price you specified. But if it does hit your price, your order might get filled, but maybe not. It depends on what direction and how quickly the market is moving around that price and your place in a line that is determined by exchange rules. And you may or may not get the quantities you want.

Stop order

This type of order is similar to the limit order, except that when it hits the price you specified it becomes a market order. For example, let's say you bought a stock and have a nice profit in it and are nervous that the market might go down. You can place a stop-sell order (often referred to as a "stop-loss" order) below the current market price. Should the market reach your price, your order becomes a market order with all the risks and benefits associated with that type of order.

Likewise, you can place a stop-buy order above the current market price, and if the stock's price rises and hits that price it will become a market order. A stop-buy order might seem strange. Why place an order to buy that is above the current price? The answer is simple: You are waiting for the stock to break out of a down trend, and if it does, you want to participate (another reason is to close out a short position, but as a minor this type of account is not available to you).

Stop-limit order

This type of order is a combination of a stop order and a limit order. Remember a stop order becomes a market order when the specified price is hit. However, with a stop-limit order, once the stop price is hit the order becomes a limit order. The stop price can be the same as the limit price but doesn't have to be. For example, a stop price can be $40 and the limit price $35. Should the stock decline and hit the $40 price, the order becomes a limit order with a price of $35 with all the risks and benefits of a limit order.

Trailing stop order

This order is similar to a stop-sell order set below the current market price, except that instead of entering a price you enter a percentage of the current market price

> *"The whole secret to winning and losing in the stock market is to lose the least amount possible when you're not right." – William J. O'Neil*

or a dollar amount. The percentage or dollar amount shadows the stock price as it goes up. If the stock goes down and hits the specified trailing stop amount, the order becomes a market order.

Like all orders, there are risks and benefits to the trailing stop order. If you set the percentage or dollar amount too tight, you might get sold out of what later might be a profitable position. On the other hand, if you set it too loose, you might give up too much. The benefit is you don't have to cancel and re-enter a stop-sell order every time the stock's price changes.

Other features of an order of which to be aware of

How long do you want your order to be in effect? A market order gets executed right away, but with the other orders you can specify how long you want your order to remain in effect. That is, you can say you want a "day only" order, which means it will be effective for only the current trading day. Perhaps that is too short a time period. In that case you can say you want a "good until cancelled (GTC)" order. Depending on your broker, the order could remain in effect for as long as six months. But check with your broker first as to the time frame.

With respect to time and quantities, there are other qualifiers that can be placed on the trade such as "on-the-open," "on-the-close", "all or none," as well as specialized ones. If you're curious, ask your broker to explain them.

Settling Trades

Trades settle in two business days after the day of the trade. You might hear your broker use the term T+2 which refers to the trade date (the "T") plus two days. Thus, when you buy a stock on Monday, you must have the funds in the account on Wednesday. The reverse is true as well. When you sell on Monday the money will be in your account on Wednesday. Settlement for custodial accounts, tax-exempt accounts, and mutual fund trades can be different. Double-check with your broker about the rules.

Trading Restrictions

Trading restrictions on when and how much money must be in your account before you can buy a stock might apply. For example, the most frequent occurrence is in a cash account when you try to buy before there is sufficient money to cover the trade in the account. This can occur when the account has not been fully funded or when an attempt to buy is made before the cash from a sale has settled. Check with your broker for the rules.

How to Hold Your Stocks

When you buy a stock, you have some options on how to hold your stock.

Street name

The most common way is to let the broker hold it for you in something called "street name" registration. Although it's held in the broker's name, not yours, the broker keeps a record showing that you are the beneficial owner of x number shares of that particular stock and keeps your shares separate from the broker's own account.

Many brokers will just automatically hold your stock this way unless you tell them otherwise. They will collect and deposit dividends, provide statements to help you at income tax time, and forward to you any communication that comes from the company, such as annual reports, notices of annual meetings, and proxy statements, as well as send you, at least quarterly, a summary of your positions and the activity that occurred in your account.

This method of holding the stock allows you to trade without any hassle.

Direct registration

Another way of holding stock is called "direct registration." In this instance, the company registers the stock in your name, not the broker's name, in the company's books. With direct registration, confirm with your broker that there is an electronic system that allows the broker to move your stock from the company's books to the broker's book where they can be sold if you so order. The broker should have access to this system and should be able to complete a transfer for you relatively quickly, but may charge you for the service. Check with your broker or with the investor relations department of the company whose stock you want to purchase.

APPENDIX A
Margin Accounts

Once you are no longer a minor you too can open what is called a margin account. A margin account is when an investor can borrow money from the broker up to a certain limit and use that money to pay for the purchase of stock (or if stock is already owned in the account for personal reasons). Since it is a loan, the broker will charge you interest. The amount of money that can be borrowed is a certain percentage of the value of the account. If the account falls below that value, the broker will call and demand more money to bring the account up to the required level. Should that happen, it is termed a "margin call." The investor either comes up with the additional money or the stock is sold to satisfy the loan.

Borrowing money is a form of leverage that can work for an investor if the stock that was purchased goes up, or the investor can be wiped out if the stock goes down. Here's an example:

ASSUMPTIONS

Purchase price of stock = $50
Cash you used to buy stock = $25
Margin loan from the broker = $25

SCENARIO:	STOCK UP	STOCK DOWN
Sale price of stock	$75	$25
Less margin loan	(25)	(25)
Less cash used	(25)	(25)
Profit or loss	$25	($25) loss

APPENDIX B
Short Selling

Once you are no longer a minor you can participate in short sales. A short sale starts when you enter into an agreement to borrow stock from your broker. The agreement has certain terms and conditions including a "rental" fee and the obligation to pay any dividends that might come due. Once the borrowed shares appear in your account, you sell them (go short) and collect the proceeds. Now you wait and hope the price of the shares will go down. If it does, you buy the shares back at the lower price and give them back to the broker, thus closing out the agreement. Your profit is the difference between what you sold the borrowed shares for and the price you paid to buy them back.

Were it so easy to make money! Like everything else in investing, there are risks and rewards. Clearly, if you guessed right and the stock did go down and you "covered" (the term used to describe the fact that you bought back the borrowed shares), you will make money. However, you might be wrong, and the stock's price goes up instead. Then you have to buy back the borrowed shares at a higher price than what you sold them for.

You might even get caught in what is called a "short squeeze." This is where large investors buy the shorted stock thus pushing up its price. They keep buying and force short-position holders into losses, at which time some of them decide to cover their positions. This additional buying drives the price even higher and makes the losses even greater for those who did not cover. Eventually more short-position holders cover, thus driving the stock's price even higher still. At some point the investors who started the squeeze sell the stock they bought and collect a profit.

The risk of getting caught in a short squeeze increases as the liquidity of the stock decreases. Small-cap and ultra-small cap stocks are particularly venerable.

CHAPTER 7

The Risks

When you invest in the stock market expecting a gain, you also have to accept the fact that you might incur a loss. Sorry, that's just the nature of the market. The question then becomes how to minimize the risk of loss while maximizing the expected return so that the chance is worth taking – for you. Notice I said "for you," because everyone has a different comfort level and that level will also vary during different times in your life.

But when it comes to risk, there is one small problem – risk is difficult to explain, hard to quantify, and impossible to forecast with precision. It is only after the fact, when we don't like the outcome, that we realize the magnitude of risk we have taken. But if we want to invest in the stock market, and if we can't eliminate risk, maybe we can understand it, accept it, and work around it to the extent we can.

In this chapter I will discuss the potential sources of stock risk, methods that are used today to measure risk, common-sense ways of reducing risk, and perhaps the scariest risk of all, the collapse of the entire market system.

An Intuitive Look at Risk vs. Return

Smart risk involves understanding how much risk you need to take in order to achieve a given expected return. Figure 7-1 gives you a feel for how the risk vs. return trade-off might appear. But remember, just because you are taking more risk and thus expecting a higher return, doesn't mean that you will necessarily get it. There is a wide range of possible outcomes around an expected return – that is, your return might be better or worse than what you expected.

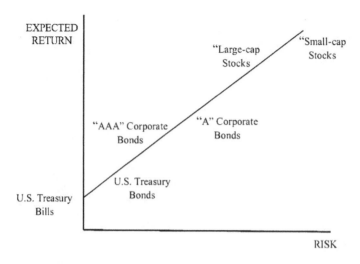

Figure 7-1

One way to look at the risk vs. return trade-off is shown in Figure 7-1. If you don't want to take any investment risk, you should invest in short-term U.S. Treasury bills. You'll get a fixed return and your money back after a short period of time. By keeping the maturity short, you shouldn't have to worry too much about "inflation risk," that is, the risk your purchasing power will be reduced because of inflation. Moreover, since you're lending money to the U.S. government, you don't have to worry about "credit risk," that is the risk that you won't be paid back. The government can always print more money. However, if you do go this route, you're not going to get much of a return.

Moving up the risk vs. return trade-off line, some would say that U.S. Treasury bonds are riskier than U.S. Treasury bills because they have a longer maturity date. In other words, there is a longer period of time for inflation to reduce your purchasing power. To be compensated for that risk, you would expect a higher return. Continuing up the line are corporate bonds, and within that category of securities there are different grades of bonds. Since "A" rated corporate bonds are considered to have more credit risk than "AAA" corporate bonds, you would expect them to have greater return. Moving up further, we get into stocks. Large-cap stocks are thought to be less risky than small-cap stocks because small-cap stocks might have more difficulty surviving an economic downturn, thus a greater expected return for small-cap stocks.

That is an easy way to explain the concept of risk vs. return because it makes intuitive sense. With U.S. Treasury bills you take little risk and you get a little return, whereas with small-cap stocks you take a lot of risk and you expect (but don't necessarily get) a greater return.

Sources of Stock Risk

Conceptually, the risk of a share of stock can be divided into market risk and non-market risk. Non-market risk can be further sub-divided into company risk, sector-industry risk, and factor risk. This is depicted in Figure 7-2. Each element has an expected return associated with it.

Market risk

When the stock market is going up, there is a tendency for most stocks to go up too. Likewise, when the stock market is going down, there is a tendency for most stocks to go down. In other words, there is a component of a stock's risk that is attributable to movements in the overall market. This is called "market risk." If you buy a stock, market risk comes with the purchase. You can't avoid it.

Non-market risk

Decomposing non-market risk is a bit tricky, since it can be divided in so many different ways, and recent studies have indicated some of those "slices" might really be market risk in disguise. Rather than listing all the ways non-market risk can be sliced and diced, for illustrative purposes I am going to give you three ways: by company risk, by sector-industry risk, and by factor risk.

Company risk: A major component of non-market risk can be attributed to the specifics of a company itself with all the peculiarities that implies, the biggest of which is the difference in management teams. Some companies have great managers who run their companies very well, others not so much. Therefore, some companies will shine while others will not, even if they are in the same sector-industry and factor groupings. So you would expect the variability of each company's stock performance to have a large component of risk simply because of how well the company is managed.

Sector-industry risk: I combined these together for ease of explanation. A sector defines a large segment of the economy such as transportation, consumer services, and health care, whereas an industry is simply a subgroup of similar companies that are within a sector group. For example, within the transportation sector there are these industry groups: airfreight and logistics, airlines, marine, road and rail, and transportation infrastructure. These sector-

81

industry groups tend to react in a similar way to economic events. For example, the transportation sector is impacted to some extent by an increase in the cost of fuel. Therefore, a component of risk for an individual airline stock can be attributed to its inclusion in the airline industry group, which is part of the transportation sector, which, in this example, is influenced by economic events one of which is the price of fuel. If fuel costs go up you would expect airline stocks to go down, all else being equal.

Factor risk: This is just a way of grouping stocks that tend to act together because of some characteristic that is different than sector-industry grouping. For example, company size. Say two stocks are in the health care sector. Both would have an element of risk because they are in the same sector. However, one company might be very large while another very small, and that feature has a component of risk associated with it. More about factors appears in Chapters 10, 13, and 16.

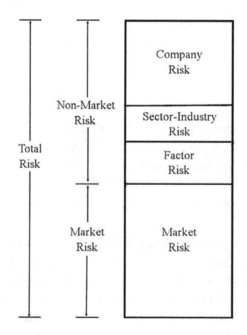

Figure 7-2

Dividing the total risk of a stock into market and non-market risk, and further dividing non-market risk into company, sector-industry, and factor risk makes intuitive sense. But are these divisions the correct ones? As we learned in the study of logic, how we define things influences our actions and thus our results.

Ways to Measure Risk

Now comes the hard part, measuring risk. Nothing is settled here and the debates as to which is the best way are heated. Some of the ways of measuring risk in use today are mean-standard deviation, beta, and so-called smart beta. Beta is a measure of the variability of a stock's return compared to a market return. Smart beta is a measure of a stock's variability with respect to various components of total risk.

Let's start with mean-standard deviation. To understand it, I must go into the statistical weeds and discuss the concept of variability of returns and probability analysis.

Ground work leading to standard deviation of returns

Variability of historical return: I already said that the stock's risk and hence its return can be divided into market and non-market risk and return. For this section, assume we removed market risk and return out of the analysis to focus exclusively on non-market risk and return.

One way to measure risk is to look at how variable a stock's return has been over some period of time. For example, if Stock A's return bounces around more than Stock B's return, academics would say Stock A is riskier than Stock B.

It is easier to understand this with a picture. In Figures 7-3 and 7-4, I have constructed something called histograms, which are just a plot of data that shows the frequency of occurrence of certain historical

> *"Learn every day, but especially from the experience of others. It's cheaper." – John Bogle*

performance numbers. To construct a histogram, you would first need to calculate a stock's return at regular intervals over a study period. For example, your study period might be from the year 1957 to 2018, and intervals could be quarterly returns. Next, you need to establish intervals called "bins" in which you would sort the quarterly returns. In the figures, I used 5% as the width of the bins just to illustrate the concept. Then you would go through the list of quarterly returns and put all those that were from 0% to 4.99% into the first bin, 5% to 9.99% into the second bin, and so forth. You would then count the number in each bin (the frequency of occurrences) and then plot the graphs you see in the figures.

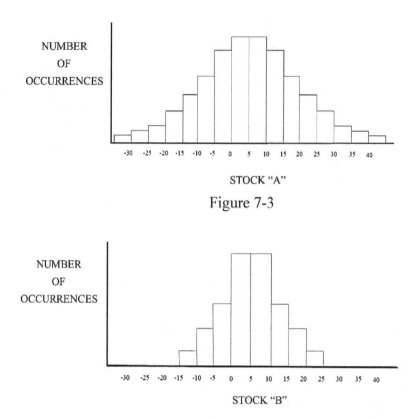

STOCK "A"

Figure 7-3

STOCK "B"

Figure 7-4

Fair enough, so what's the debate all about? First, historical returns are used to identify variability, which may be interesting, but in the stock market we are interested in future risk, not past risk. History may repeat itself, but then again it might not. Second, how far back in time should we go to collect data – one year, 15 years, or as far back as we can? Third, should we use monthly, weekly, or even daily returns in our calculations? The decisions we make here will influence the results we get. Fourth, the variability in returns is not the same as volatility in returns. Variability describes the change in return around the mean (average), whereas volatility describes how much a stock's return changes from one time period to the next, and that is important to investors as well. Finally, we have the risk of over 4,000 stocks to consider. How many combinations of one-on-one comparisons would we have to do to accomplish that? No, we need to construct a standard measurement so we can compare all stocks with one another in an efficient manner. Enter probability and its cousin, standard deviation.

Probability of return: About the year 1650, Blaise Pascal, a gifted mathematician and philosopher, was asked by a friend for help in determining the odds of a dice game that involved two dice and a substantial amount of money. The bet was whether a person could get double sixes within 24 rolls of the dice. On the surface, calculating the odds seems like a pretty easy task. But was it?

It's easy to work out the odds of rolling double sixes with one roll. Visually we can do that by rolling the two dice many times, keep track of the numbers, and draw a histogram. We could also do it mathematically. Since there are 36 different combinations of two dice but only one double six, the odds of getting double sixes with one roll is one out of 36, or 2.78%. But how can we determine the odds of rolling at least one double six within 24 tries?

Mr. Pascal took up the challenge and, in an exchange of letters with a colleague, Pierre de Fermat, the theory of probability was born. Through the years it has been expanded and refined to what we have today, a method of measuring risk. Now I won't go through the logic and mathematics Mr. Pascal went through to get the answer to the question that was posed to him, but for those of you who might be interested, he said given 24 rolls of two dice, double sixes should appear in 49 games out of 100.

So, what does probability have to do with the common stocks? It's a way of assessing risk. Although we cannot have certainty, we can give a probability of an outcome falling within a certain range of possible outcomes based on past experience. For example, we might say 68% of the time the outcome might fall within a range that is plus or minus a certain distance from the mean (average) return.

Standard deviation of returns: The "standard" part of standard deviation is a calculation that tells us how far away 68% of the stock returns have "deviated" from the mean. In other words, if the returns in the histogram are tightly bunched together like Stock B, 68% of them will be close to the mean return and the number for standard deviation will be small. If the returns in the histogram are really spread out like Stock A, the number for standard deviation will be large. The larger the standard deviation, the riskier the stock.

Probability and outcome: Mr. Pascal also went on to say that you should not make a decision based only on the probability of the outcome; you should also consider the consequences of the outcome. To illustrate this, he posed a simple statement to his friends that he framed as a 50-50 probability: God either exists or does not exist. If you assume that God exists and you live a good life, and God does exist, your afterlife will be good. If you assume that God exists and you live a good life, and God does not exist, what have you really given up? On the other hand, if you believe God does not exist and you live a bad life, and God does exist, your afterlife will be pure hell. Mr. Pascal concludes that while the odds are even at 50-50, the outcomes are not the same.

How does this apply to investing in stocks? Assume there is a 50-50 chance that the stock will go either up or down. If it goes up, you might make $10 a share. However, if it goes down, you might lose everything. So, while the odds are the same, the outcomes are wildly different.

Recap: I started by calculating historical returns for two stocks over a period of time. From that data, I constructed two histograms and we saw the one with the greater spread was considered to be the riskier of the two. Then I introduced the concepts of probability and its cousin, standard deviation. The greater the spread, the greater the standard deviation, and thus the greater the risk; the smaller the spread, the smaller the standard deviation, and thus the less risk. In other words, calculating a standard deviation of returns for an individual stock provides us with a number that is an indication of the degree of risk and, using that number, we can easily compare the riskiness of over 4,000 stocks with one another. At least that's the theory. Figures 7-5 and 7-6 might help to visualize this. I connected the tops of both histograms and drew a curve for each. You can see the standard deviation is larger for Stock A than it is for Stock B, thus Stock A is deemed to be risker than Stock B using this measure of risk. Finally, an investor should consider the outcome of an investment in addition to its riskiness to see if the risk is worth taking.

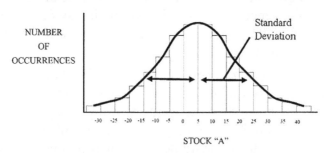

Figure 7-5

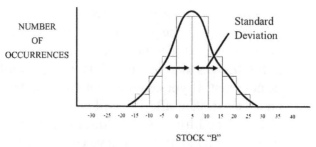

Figure 7-6

Mean-standard deviation

Would it be so easy to determine which investment in the future provides us with the greatest risk using the stock's standard deviation as our guide. First, as I said earlier, but it bears repeating, these calculations are based on historical data. There is nothing that says the same or a similar distribution of returns will occur in the future. Things change.

But there is another issue that is more technical. Calculation of standard deviations requires a normal or somewhat normal distribution of returns. If the stacks of the histogram are of equal sizes on either side, a shape will appear that resembles a bell – hence a "bell-shaped" or normal curve (see Figures 7-5 and 7-6). The problem is a histogram of historical stock returns may not resemble a bell-shape curve. The shape is more likely to be tilted to one side or the other (skewed), may have extremely long tails, or may even have "bumps" near the extremes (fat-tails). Therefore, the actual non-bell shape of the curve presents serious problems for the "mean-standard deviation" approach to measuring historical risk. However, academics continue to work on ways to get around these concerns using some sophisticated equations.

Beta

Beta is a useful tool for measuring a stock's sensitivity to past market movements. Some very smart people took all the historical return data for individual companies and worked out a scheme in which the variability for a single stock could be related to the variability of the market. That is, if the market was up or down by some amount, through their calculations they estimated how much more or less an individual stock's return would be up or down. In other words, how sensitive the stock's price is to market movements. Since they were looking for the slope of the line created by plotting the return for a stock against the return of the market, beta was a natural choice (the letter B, or beta in Greek, is the commonly used designation for the slope of a line).

Through some nifty mathematics, the academics were able to benchmark the market's volatility to 1.0 and have all the stocks assigned numbers relative to that. For example, if a stock had a beta of 1.2 and the market went up 20%, one would expect that stock to go up 1.2 times the 20%, or 24%. On the other hand, if the market went down -30%, one would expect that the stock would go down 1.2 times the -30%, or -36%. At least, that was the idea.

You should be able to get betas from a wide variety of sources. In addition to all the other caveats about using historical data, you need to know what proxy was used for "the" market. Many calculations use the S&P 500 index but, as you learned in Chapter 5, there are other possibilities.

Smart beta

There also are other betas, so-called smart betas. The choice of the word "smart" is a marketing term used to differentiate it from the plain old beta that measures a stock's price sensitivity to the market's movements. Smart betas try to incorporate a stock's price sensitivity not only to market movements but also to sensitivity to non-market factors as well as economic data.

Useful, not definitive

Using mathematical certainty on historical data can often give the impression of accuracy. Just because Stock A was calculated to be riskier than Stock B in the past doesn't necessarily mean that it will be in the future. Remember, the management of those companies has something to say about that. I am not suggesting that these mathematical ways of measuring risk are worthless. They are useful, not definitive.

> *"If past history was all there was to the game, the richest people would be librarians." – Warren Buffett*

Common-Sense Ways of Reducing Risk

Reducing risk through diversification

Diversification is simply adding certain stocks to a portfolio in such a way that the risk of the portfolio is less than the risk of a single stock. I will explain this in two ways: intuitively and mathematically.

Intuitively: Earlier I said the total risk associated with a stock can be divided into two parts – market risk and non-market risk – and non-market risk can be company risk, sector-industry risk, and factor risk. When you start adding stocks to create a portfolio, since the companies have different management teams and different ways of doing things, the risk associated with company risk in the portfolio goes down.

Likewise, if you add companies that are in different sectors and industries, and have different factor exposure, the risks in the portfolio will go down even further. If you add enough stocks and add them in a certain way, you will eventually have a portfolio that resembles the market, and you are left with only market risk to contend with (see Figure 7-7). In other words, you have diversified away company, sector-industry, and factor risk.

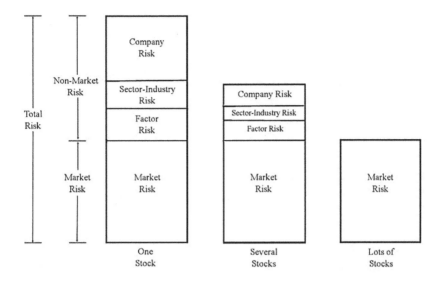

Figure 7-7

But that happens only if you have enough different types of stocks in your portfolio. If you have two stocks in your portfolio and they are from the same sector-industry and the same factor group, then all you are doing is averaging your company risk (see Figure 7-8).

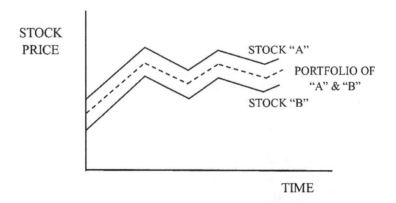

Figure 7-8

You need to have stocks that are different in your portfolio in order to diversify non-market risk (see Figure 7-9).

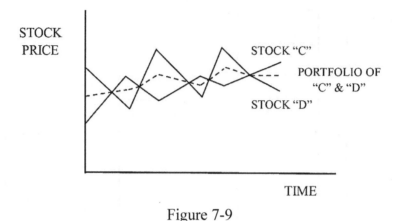

Figure 7-9

Mathematically: There is a statistical technique called correlation of return. I will leave to you to explore how it is computed; however, the results of the calculations will tell you the degree to which the return of one stock is different from the return of another stock. In other words, the extent to which they move together (are positively correlated) or move opposite from each other (are negatively correlated). A positive correlation is between 1 and 0. If a correlation of 1 has been calculated, it means the return from the two stocks move in lock-step together in the same direction just like a precision drill team. When one is up, the other is up; when one is down, the other is down, similar to Figure 7-8. As the correlation of return approaches 0, the movement together is still positive, but less so. At 0 there is no correlation. Their returns are independent.

A negative correlation is between 0 and -1. If a number of -1 has been calculated, it means the returns from the two stocks move in exactly opposite directions, similar to Figure 7-9. When one is up, the other is down. The closer they get to 0, the less the negative correlation. That does not mean, however, that when one stock has a positive return that the other must have a negative return in order to be negatively correlated. Why would anyone put stocks that they think would go down into a portfolio just to reduce risk? That doesn't make any sense. Both stocks might have positive returns but one is moving below its long-term return while the other is moving above its long-term return. These correlation numbers are often used to create a portfolio of stocks that optimizes the risk vs. return trade-off when presented with a very large list of potential stocks. In other words, it would help you determine where in between an investment in one stock and an investment in an index fund lies an optimal portfolio for a given level of risk or expected return. But remember, the idea may be great, but the correlation numbers are calculated using historical return data, and those correlation numbers may or may not hold in the future.

Reducing risk over time

Time is a great friend to have when investing in stocks, and as a teenager it is on your side. Recognize it, appreciate it, and let that friend help you with your investments. To illustrate, let's see what happens when you extend the holding period of an investment in the S&P 500 from a one-year time horizon to rolling five-, 15-, 20-, and 25-year time horizons.

> *"I never attempt to make money on the stock market. I buy on the assumption that they could close the market the next day and not reopen it for five years." – Warren Buffett*

Referring to Appendix A, if your investment time horizon was only 1 year, your returns would have ranged between a high of +37.58% and a low of -37.00% during the study period. As you extend your holding period to 15 years, your highest annualized return would have gone down, but so would your lowest annualized return. Indeed, had you held your investment for 25 years, your highest annualized return over rolling 25-year periods would have been 17.25% and your lowest 9.07%. In other words, there were no losses over rolling 25-year periods. Yes, year-to-year there would have been losses, but those would have been offset by the gains so that your annualized return over the 25 years would have been positive.

Will history repeat itself if you held an investment that closely tracked the S&P 500 for the next 25 years? I don't know. All I know is a lot happened to our country in the past and we survived, and if free market capitalism survives, you should do just fine.

Reducing risk through analysis

A practical and straightforward way of reducing the risk of loss is to be smart when you buy a stock in the first place. In other words, you can reduce your risk by buying stocks that are below their true or intrinsic value. That would give you a cushion should the market go down and great upside potential when other investors recognize the stock you bought is a bargain and therefore is likely to increase in value.

But what is the true or intrinsic value of a company and hence its stock's intrinsic value? That's an easy question to ask but a tough one to answer. Perhaps Chapter 14 might help. Also, buying quality companies during times of market panic could be a good strategy for buying below intrinsic value. The issue becomes how do you identify those quality companies?

Systemic Risk

I have been advocating that you start investing early, invest often, and invest for the long term. That opinion is based on two assumptions: (1) that free market capitalism will be around in the future; and (2) that the massive amount of debt our government has accumulated will not cause hyperinflation. Neither of those assumptions is a certainty. They are game-changers or, as some people would call, systemic risks.

The first systemic risk is a change in our economic system of free market capitalism. Depending on who our electorate (you in a few years) votes into office, our country could slide quickly into socialism. As I outlined to you in Chapter 2, and as history has repeatedly demonstrated, socialism is not a good friend to prosperity, the stock market, or your long-term investments.

The second systemic risk is the country's debt load. Currently our country owes $21 trillion dollars, or $64,000 for every man, woman, and child (actually much, much more when other debt is included) – and is growing fast. The interest alone on this amount, together with the power of compounding, could destroy the value of our currency in a few years. As we have seen in history, many great countries have been brought down by hyperinflation caused by excessive debt.

APPENDIX A
Annual Returns for Different Holding Periods

Year	Held for one year	Held for 5 years	Held for 10 years	Held for 15 years	Held for 20 years	Held for 25 years
1994	1.32%	8.70%	14.38%	14.52%	14.58%	10.98%
1995	37.58%	16.59%	14.88%	14.81%	14.60%	12.22%
1996	22.96%	15.22%	15.29%	16.80%	14.56%	12.55%
1997	33.36%	20.27%	18.05%	17.52%	16.65%	13.07%
1998	28.58%	24.06%	19.21%	17.90%	17.75%	14.94%
1999	21.04%	28.56%	18.21%	18.93%	17.88%	17.25%
2000	−9.10%	18.33%	17.46%	16.02%	15.68%	15.34%
2001	−11.89%	10.70%	12.94%	13.74%	15.24%	13.78%
2002	−22.10%	−0.59%	9.34%	11.48%	12.71%	12.98%
2003	28.68%	−0.57%	11.07%	12.22%	12.98%	13.84%
2004	10.88%	−2.30%	12.07%	10.94%	13.22%	13.54%
2005	4.91%	0.54%	9.07%	11.52%	11.94%	12.48%
2006	15.79%	6.19%	8.42%	10.64%	11.80%	13.37%
2007	5.49%	12.83%	5.91%	10.49%	11.82%	12.73%
2008	−37.00%	−2.19%	−1.38%	6.46%	8.43%	9.77%
2009	26.46%	0.42%	−0.95%	8.04%	8.21%	10.54%
2010	15.06%	2.29%	1.41%	6.76%	9.14%	9.94%
2011	2.11%	−0.25%	2.92%	5.45%	7.81%	9.28%
2012	16.00%	1.66%	7.10%	4.47%	8.22%	9.71%
2013	32.39%	17.94%	7.40%	4.68%	9.22%	10.26%
2014	13.69%	15.45%	7.67%	4.24%	9.85%	9.62%
2015	1.38%	12.57%	7.30%	5.00%	8.19%	9.82%
2016	11.96%	14.66%	6.94%	6.69%	7.68%	9.15%
2017	21.83%	15.79%	8.49%	9.92%	7.19%	9.69%
2018	−4.38%	8.49%	13.12%	7.77%	5.62%	9.07%
High	**37.58%**	**28.56%**	**19.21%**	**18.93%**	**17.88%**	**17.25%**
Low	**−37.00%**	**−2.35%**	**−1.38%**	**4.24%**	**5.62%**	**9.07%**

Source: Wikipedia, S&P 500 index

SECTION 2
Inside the Stock Market Tent

Have you ever heard someone say, "This is like a three-ring-circus"? Well, the phrase got its start from observing a circus in which various acts were being performed simultaneously in three rings lined up in a row. In one ring, there might be jugglers, in the center ring there might be a lion act, and in the far one there might be clowns coming out of a small car. All this activity was used by the owners of the circus to hold the customers' attention on what was going on immediately in front of where they were seated. However, when viewed from the entrance of the tent, it appeared to be mass confusion.

Mass confusion? If that doesn't describe the investment tent that you, as an investor, are entering today, I don't know what does. Investment managers in each of their respective rings – active, passive, and factor-based – are yelling out with their multimillion-dollar advertising campaigns, "We are the best, choose us!" With all this noise going on, how do you know where to sit?

In this section I'm going to start with an overview of each of these rings. In Section 3 I will give you more details, and in Section 4 I will take you inside the respective investment firms for a nitty-gritty look at how the professionals go about their jobs. I intentionally structured the explanation of active, passive, and factor-based investing this way so you can go into as much depth as you want – overview, more details, or nitty-gritty.

You might want to consider one of these alternatives as the center piece of your investment strategy – center piece, not all-or-nothing – because if you have a strategy that suits your personality and risk preferences, you might be able to reduce the tendency to bounce from what seems to be one good idea to the next, which is a sure way to not achieve your goals.

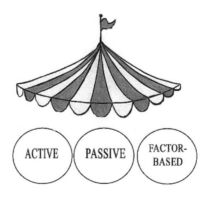

CHAPTER 8

Active Investing – Overview

Active investing is rooted in the belief that through hard work, insights, and skill an individual can buy and sell stocks so that the return achieved, adjusted for risk, is greater than what could have been achieved by investing in the alternatives – passive or factor-based.

Active investing can be implemented in an almost endless number of ways. For example, a speculator can buy and sell stocks during the day and then close out all positions before the end of the trading day. This is called "day trading." Or an investor can invest like Warren Buffett, who buys stocks and holds them for decades. Active investing also includes being entirely in or out of the market, which is called "market timing." And the list of alternatives goes on and on.

In this book, however, I will focus on individual stock selection, for I believe this is a useful way to understand the key concepts of active investing. Individual stock selection involves the search for a stock's intrinsic value and then comparing that discovered value with the stock's price in order to make buy and sell decisions. You can actively manage the process yourself or hire an active investment manager to do it for you. Regardless of which path you take, these are the steps you and the active investment manager would take, and the corresponding parts of this book that provide pertinent information about those steps.

> **Step one:** Develop a list of potential candidates. Chapter 11 is intended to provide ideas on how to do this yourself as well as give you some insights into how active investment managers might go about it.

Step two: Narrow the list to the ones to invest in. This can be done through fundamental analysis or technical analysis. Fundamental analysis (Chapter 14) focuses on the company's earnings potential, and technical analysis (Chapter 23) focuses on the price and volume history of the company's stock.

Step three: Identify the optimal time to invest. Section 6 is devoted to this topic.

Step four: Decide how much to invest. Chapter 7 provides several approaches to the evaluation of risk.

Step five: Decide when to sell. Chapter 14 and Section 6 might help in making the timing decision.

If you choose to hire someone to make the active investing decisions, you have two choices: Actively managed mutual funds or actively managed exchange traded funds (ETFs). Chapters 17 and 18 will help you understand what they are, and Chapter 19 will summarize the pros and cons of each. These managers go through the same five steps I have outlined above.

Appendix A provides a flowchart of the process.

> *With active investing you are betting on your, or the investment manager's ability to select money-making stocks.*

APPENDIX A

Flowchart

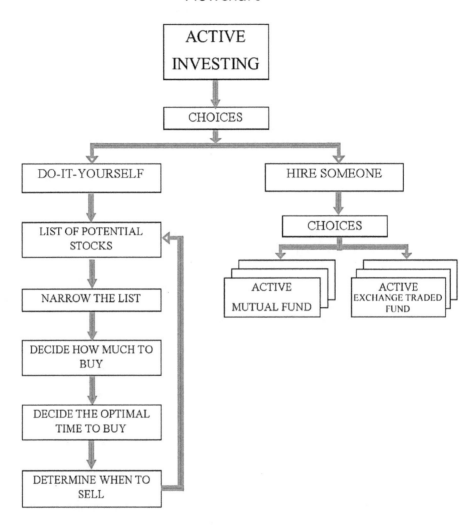

CHAPTER 9

Passive Investing – Overview

Passive investing is rooted in the belief that the stock market is efficient, and thus an index fund designed to replicate the risk and return of the market will outperform active or factor-based strategies over time and adjusted for risk. "Efficient" in this context means that stock prices already reflect available information, and hence it is a waste of time and money for investors to attempt to search for that one winning stock or investment manager.

The stocks in a market index, as well as their quantities, are the result of pre-established rules made by the committee that maintains the index. These market indices were originally created by newspapers and other organizations to give the investing public an idea of how the stock market was performing. The approach is called "passive" because an index fund investment manager willingly and passively accepts without question the decisions made by the committee.

These are the steps you would take to implement a passive investing strategy, and where in the book you will find help with them.

> **Step one:** Decide which market index to invest in. Refer back to Chapter 5 to review how indices are constructed and to tell you how the committees of the major indices make their stock-selection and weighting decisions. Chapter 12 will give you the rationale behind passive investing, and Chapter 15 will open the door to a passive management firm so you can have a look inside.

> **Step two:** Select an index fund manager. Most indices contain hundreds and in some cases thousands of stocks, far too many for an individual investor to buy. Thus, you have two options:

Invest in a passive mutual fund or in a passive exchange traded fund. Chapters 17 and 18 will help you understand what mutual funds and ETFs are, and Chapter 19 will summarize the pros and cons of each.

Step three: Identify the optimal time to invest. Section 6 is devoted to this topic.

Step four: Decide how much to invest. Chapter 7 provides several approaches to the evaluation of risk.

Step five: Decide when to sell. Chapter 14 and Section 6 might help in making the timing decision.

Appendix A provides a flowchart of the process.

> *With passive investing you are betting on the success of a portfolio of stock designed to replicate the stock market.*

APPENDIX A
Flowchart

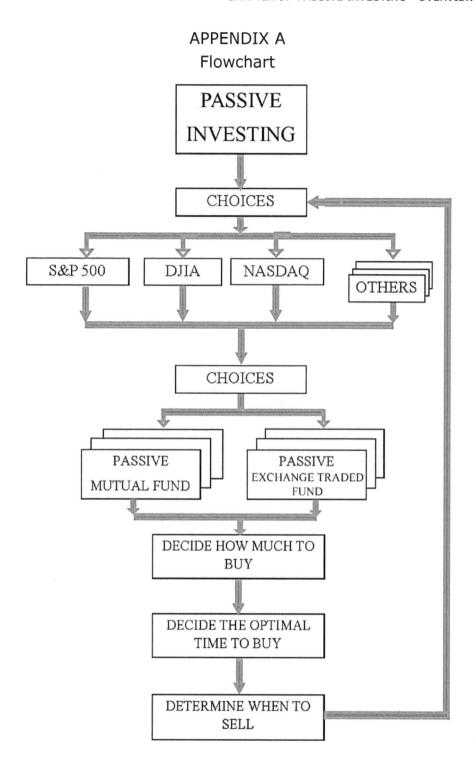

CHAPTER 10

Factor-Based Investing – Overview

The efficient market is a great theory, and for a lot of people it makes sense to act as if it were true. That is, invest in a broad-based index fund instead of taking the time and money to search for that one perfect stock to buy or to find that one great investment manager to make the decisions for you.

However, professors at some universities decided to test the theory. Surprise, surprise: These researchers found pockets of opportunity where investors could have made more money than investing in an index fund. This set off an academic Easter egg hunt for more pockets – a hunt that continues to this day. These little pockets were initially called anomalies because, if the efficient market theory was correct, they weren't supposed to exist. Later the name was changed to another academic term, "factor," which Merriam-Webster defines as "one that actively contributes to the production of a result." To me that means a feature or component that is inherent in stocks that, if emphasized in a portfolio of stocks, would result in that portfolio providing a greater-than-market return.

In other words, rather than search for the intrinsic value of an individual stock or toss your hands up and invest in an index fund, the "factor people" decided to search groups of stocks for a common factor that, if emphasized in a portfolio, was likely to result in a greater than market return adjusted for risk.

Factors are generally named for their motivating theory. For example, investing in small-cap stocks is a factor that is motivated by the theory that small-cap stocks outperform large-cap stocks over the long term. That theory is brought to life by a set of buy and sell rules that were uncovered through a study of historical financial, economic, and market related data. In other words, at its best, you can think of a factor as a set of rules that, if followed, promises to provide greater than market return for a given level of risk over the long term.

These are the steps you would take to implement a factor-based investing strategy, and where in the book you'll find help with each of them.

> **Step one:** Decide which factor to invest in. An investment could be in one factor, in many factors, or in exotic factors. Chapters 13 and 16 are intended to provide more detailed information about factors and to help you understand how they are identified.

> **Step two:** Select a factor-based manager. Many factor-based strategies contain hundreds of stocks, far too many for an individual investor to buy. Thus, you have two options: Invest in a factor-based mutual fund or in a factor-based exchange traded fund. Chapters 17 and 18 will help you understand what mutual funds and ETFs are, and Chapter 19 will summarize the pros and cons of each.

> **Step three:** Identify the optimal time to invest. Section 6 is devoted to this topic.

> **Step four:** Decide how much to invest. Chapter 7 provides several approaches to the evaluation of risk.

> **Step five:** Decide when to sell. Section 6 might help in making the timing decision

Appendix A provides a flowchart of the process.

> *With factor-based investing you're betting on the skill of an investment researcher.*

APPENDIX A
Flowchart

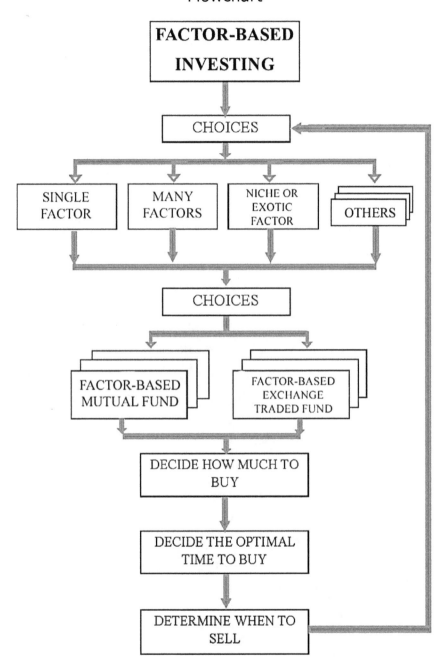

SECTION 3
A Closer Look

In this section we are going to take a much closer look at each of the investment strategies.

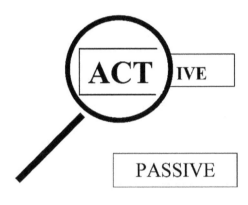

CHAPTER 11

Active Investing

I divided this chapter into two parts. The first centers on how you might develop a list of potential investment candidates. The second part centers on how investment managers develop their list and how well they have performed. In addition, I will provide some insights into selecting an active manager as well as explaining closet indexing and window dressing.

Not all individuals or investment managers use the approaches I have outlined in this chapter. However, this will at least give you a general idea and might help you if you decide to go the do-it-yourself route. But make no mistake: Active investing is tough business. Even investment managers who do this for a living and have a lot of resources at their disposal have a difficult time beating a passive index fund. But you do have some advantages that they don't, the major one of which is your investment time horizon.

Generating Investment Ideas Yourself

If you decide to become your own active manager buying and selling stock, and many investors have done so successfully, here are some ideas on how to generate a list of potential candidates.

Be observant

Investment ideas can come from your classmates. Businesses want to cater to your age group's needs and wants. You and your classmates represent a prime market for their goods and services. How do you identify these companies? By keeping your eyes open for trends that are going on around you. For example, what are you and your friends buying? Is it a specific type of clothing? Is there a favorite restaurant or place of entertainment that you go to? Is there an advancement in technology that you and your classmates particularly like? Anything that you see is increasing in popularity, has a competitive edge, and has a potentially large market for its products or services is a potential investment idea.

Investment ideas can also come from observing your family members and relatives. What are they interested in? What are they buying? How about your grandparents or older relatives? With the aging of America, people are living longer. What are they doing in retirement? Do you see an increase in healthcare, travel, or assisted living? Are they making use of biotechnology? Joint replacement?

Investment ideas can also come from other sources as well, such as seeing products that have been around for years in a different light.

> *When you buy a stock, you are buying part of a company.*

For example, how many times have you asked "Where's the Scotch® tape?" Or maybe you wanted to pin some log-in information to the screen of your computer and you reached for a Post-it® note. Or maybe you cut yourself and needed a Band-Aid®? Or maybe your stomach was upset and you took a Rolaid®? These are everyday products that are made by large companies who have had a long history of innovation and pay healthy dividends – the 3M company for the first two products and Johnson & Johnson for the other two. Granted, those everyday products might represent a very small percentage of the company's business, but associating them with a specific company might be the catalyst for further analysis of that company.

Investment ideas can also come from secondary sources. For example, when a rock is thrown into a quiet pond it creates ripples that expand across the pond. Think of an initial investment idea as the splash created when the rock hits the water, and the secondary idea as a ripple created by the initial splash. For example, the initial idea might be the iPhone; the secondary idea might be the companies that make the parts that go into the iPhone, or even the apps made possible by the iPhone. Or the initial idea might be that more and more people seem to be buying new cars; the secondary idea is the company that makes the heated seats that go into a car. Or people might be remodeling houses more; the secondary idea is the company that makes decking material. In other words, a good investment idea might be companies that supply things to other businesses or a company that depends in some way on the initial idea.

Then you need to identify the company that is supplying these goods or services. Sometimes all you know is the brand name, not who is manufacturing the product. How do you find out who is really making it? Use the internet. For example, if you google, "Who makes Dockers® jeans," you'll find out it is Levi Strauss & Co.

The point is simply this: Be observant. Make a serious effort to increase your awareness of what is going on around you, then ask yourself whether that might be a good investment idea. Be curious. Curiosity is one of the greatest gifts you can have in life, as well as in investments specifically. After you've changed your mindset and look at the world differently, you'll be surprised how many investment ideas you'll find. But remember, some of these might be short-term trends while others may persist. That is for you to decide as you evaluate what you have uncovered.

Devour newsletters, magazines, and newspapers

Another good source of investment idea can be found in reading material, either on the internet or in the print version. What are you looking for? Trends. New products. New services. The reading material could be popular or business related such as *The Wall Street Journal, Barron's, Investor's Business Daily, Forbes, Bloomberg, Businessweek, Kiplinger's Personal Finance, Money, Business Week, Inc., Fortune, Fast Company,* and *The Economist.* These, as well as a host of other magazines, such as *Popular Science, Popular Mechanics, MIT Technology Review,* and *Scientific American,* often focus on new ideas. Most are available in many libraries. Spending a few hours in a library looking through their magazine rack could be enlightening.

Use the web

There are also plenty of sources of ideas on the web. Just search for "future investment trends" and you'll get about 495,000,000 results in 0.49 seconds! You obviously won't get through all of them, but at least the ones you do will give you a feel for what others are thinking about the future.

For-fee services

A good place to start your research is the *Value Line Investment Survey®.* The print version comes in two parts: the first gives you access to about 1,700 of the most actively traded stocks, and the second, *Small-Cap Investor,* gives you access to 1,800 companies with market values under $5 billion. *Value Line* provides a full-page analyst-generated report on each of the 1700 stocks as well as its opinion of a stock's timeliness and safety. Then they sort the stocks into various categories such as stocks projected to have the highest annual total returns over the next three to five years, the highest dividend-yielding stocks, and the biggest "free flow" cash generators. Warren Buffett once said of *Value Line*:

> I don't know of any other system that's as good … The snapshot it presents is an enormously efficient way for us to garner information about various businesses … I have yet to see a better way, including fooling around on the internet, that gives me the information as quickly.

Copies of both of *Value Line*'s publications can be found in many libraries. Although their service is on the internet for a fee, there is something to be said for thumbing through the hard-copy reports. I think sitting down with a copy of both surveys and going through them page by page is one of the best ways to get a feel for the companies that populate the stock market.

Other services are also available to individual investors for a fee. One such source is the American Association of Individual Investors (AAII). Join. They have a wealth of information in their publications including a list of "Investor's Best of the Web 2018" that appeared in the September 2018 *AAII Journal* (see Appendix A).

What others are doing or saying

If you are curious about what stocks Warren Buffett or other investors have in their portfolio, just google "guru investing." In addition to the one listed in Appendix A, GuruFocus, there are plenty of other firms on the internet that will tell you what the more famous investors are investing in. But double-check the guru's track record.

In addition to *Value Line*, your stockbroker's research database might offer its opinion on the investment potential of a company's stock or will share with you the opinions of others. But be careful, for these are often 12-month price change predictions. And of course, before you do anything, you need to check the opinionmakers' performance track record.

Database screening

You can use your stockbroker's research database to screen stocks based on profitability and valuation ratios (more about those ratios in Chapter 14). Screening in this context means reducing a large list of companies to a smaller list by eliminating those companies that don't pass certain pre-established criteria. Your broker is likely to have software programs whereby you can easily screen hundreds if not thousands of companies down to just a few that you can then research further.

Depending on the database, you might be able to screen for financially solid companies with a history of long-term growth, those with a history of ever-increasing dividends, those buying back their shares, those that have been spun off from larger companies, and insiders buying the stock of their company.

Identification Is Only the First Step

Identifying potential investment candidates is only part of the task. You still must do your homework because, although it might be a great company, it still might not be a good investment. I cannot stress this strongly enough. Just because a potential candidate looks good is no reason for you to invest in it. You have to take a detailed look at a company's financials in relationship to its stock price (more about this in Chapter 14).

> *All you need is one or two good ideas in a five-year period to make your mark.*

And if you can't find any great candidates, then what? Wait. Continue to keep your eyes open. Potential candidates will come along. All you need is one or two good ideas in a five-year period to make your mark. Don't feel that you have to invest because you might be missing out. You need to have patience, not a quick trigger finger.

The above is not meant to be an exhaustive list of how to generate investment ideas, but just enough to get you going. Warren Buffett started out small and he's an active investor who recognized the value of investing for the long-term. Perhaps with a long-term perspective and the right tools you too might have similar success. Well, maybe not as successful as his, but still excellent. Remember this: Play to your strength, which is your investment time horizon. Invest early, invest often, and invest for the long-term.

The Ways Active Managers Generate Investment Ideas

Here I will discuss some of the different routes active managers take to identify investment ideas. If you have an inclination, you can do the same thing.

Top-down

This approach starts with the "big picture" – an economic outlook for the global environment. Next comes the economic outlook for the United States. Here active managers look at a wide variety of reports and measures to determine if it is a good time to invest in the stock market. Some stop here and become market timers. They will shift assets into and out of the market based on their perception of the market's direction. Others drill down further and analyze the relative performance of the sector-industry groups. As you learned in Chapter 5, sector-industry groups are segments of the market whose companies or industries respond to similar economic events. For example, if interest rates are expected to decline, the top-down manager might focus attention on those groups that would benefit the most in that type of environment, for example, the housing sector. When interest rates are expected to rise, they might shift into defensive sectors of the market such as health care and food manufacturing. The approach is called "sector-industry rotation."

Other top-down active managers engage in factor rotation such as switching between growth and value stocks based on economic conditions.

Still other active managers drill even further down and attempt to pick the best stock in the selected sector-industry or factor groupings, and that's when their analysis bumps into the bottom-up approach.

Bottom-up

The bottom-up approach can start in a variety of ways. Some investment managers will focus exclusively on a group of stocks in which they believe they have some expertise, such as technology stocks, small-cap stocks, or growth stocks. In fact, many of these active managers were at one time employed in the industry or sector that they now analyze. Other active managers start with the universe of 4,000 or so stocks and screen them down to a "manageable" list using various financial ratios. Still other active managers are keen observers and generate ideas for individual stocks from nontraditional sources such as trade magazines and news reports. Often many of them will make periodic visits to the company's headquarters and factories.

How Do You Find That "Golden-Touch" Active Manager?

When it comes to finding an active manager, you have two options: Hire an investment consulting service to assist you or conduct the search yourself. The task of sorting through all the alternatives by yourself is not impossible, just challenging and time consuming, but it can be educational There are plenty of resources available on the internet and in subscription newsletters that can help you in your quest. But even if you don't pick an active manager who can walk on water, it still might be a worthwhile exercise if you select the right area of the stock market to be in. Yes, the active manager you picked might not be the sharpest tool in the box, but the area of the manager's specialization might outperform all the others over the long term.

Active managers play in a competitive market, so they try to differentiate themselves from the pack by touting their specialization in certain areas of the market. These areas of specialization are limited only by the creativity of the active managers and the names the marketing department chooses to describe their specialty. They also like to claim they have a secret sauce they add to their investment approach, like McDonalds does for its Big Macs®.

Since there are hundreds of different variations of active managers, some consulting services have tried to minimize investor confusion by placing active managers into a specialization-grid. These services have come up with various major categories that are closely related to the factor market theory such as value, growth, and blend that are further subdivided by the size of the company the manager specializes in, such as large-cap, medium-cap, and small-cap (more about what these groupings are in Chapters 13 and 16).

Figure 11-1 is an example of a grid that is often used. Each of these groupings has different risks and expected return profiles so that investors can match their risk tolerance to one of them. For example, the lower right-hand box contains small-cap growth stock managers, and that box is often considered to be the riskiest on the grid. The upper left-hand box contains large-cap value managers and is often considered the least risky. This is only one of dozens of other grids that are used in an attempt to categorize active managers so that an investor can narrow the search.

	VALUE	BLEND	GROWTH
LARGE CAP			
MEDIUM CAP			
SMALL CAP			

Figure 11-1

Some active managers think being pigeonholed in this way is misleading, counterproductive, and unnecessary. They believe it constrains good investment managers from seeking opportunity wherever it exists, because these factors come into and go out of existence depending on economic conditions and investor interest. It is an ongoing battle between these types of managers and the consulting services who construct the grids. A pigeonhole is a small area or hole where pigeons nest and, to many investment managers, resembles the grid in Figure 11-1. Merriam-Webster defines its usage in speech as "…a neat category which usually fails to reflect actual complexities".

On Average, How Have Active Managers Performed?

Performance measurement can be tricky. Take your grades as an example. Are you graded on a curve or according to some level of achievement? If you're graded on a curve, your performance depends on your peer group. If they are brilliant and you are less so, your grades will be substantially below theirs. If you're graded according to some level of achievement, while they might get As, your level of achievement might warrant a B, much better than a C or D if you had been graded on a curve. Finally, over what time period should your performance be measured? When you got that low grade, you might have had a very bad cold for the final exam and couldn't think straight. Longer-term, your grades have been excellent.

All of the points I just made are also true when grading an active manager's performance. In other words, do you grade an active manager according to their peer group or according to some level of achievement? But what if the peer group is really diverse? If a manager is measured by level of achievement, what level is appropriate? Then there is the question of time. Over what time period should performance be measured? These are tough questions, but they need to be answered to get a fair picture of an active manager's ability.

Academic studies

Many academic studies have shown that most active managers cannot beat the return from a predetermined index such as the S&P 500 or a relevant benchmark, and those who do, often fail to repeat their stellar performance in subsequent years. The reason often given include: (1) good luck in the earlier period and bad luck in subsequent periods; (2) good performing stocks in the earlier period and those stocks becoming overvalued in subsequent periods and then regress to the mean; and (3) the construction of the index against which they are measure (for a further discussion of the last point, see Chapter 12).

Still others believe poor active manager performance is due to an emotionally driven market that in its contortions decides which manager succeeds, which fails, and when. In other words, good performance is as random as poor performance.

Active managers' response to performance criticism

As you might expect, active managers are not very happy with the poor grades they get from academic studies. They have several responses to those results.

Wrong index. They claim the academic studies used the wrong index for performance comparisons. An example would be using the S&P 500 index, which is oriented towards large-cap stocks, to measure the performance of a small-cap manager. Those two sectors have wildly different risk and return characteristics.

Wrong peer group. They claim their investment style is different than the peer group they were measured against. An example would be comparing a small-cap manager whose focus is on financial stocks with one that focuses on small-cap technology stocks.

Wrong time period. They claim the academicians used the wrong time-frame over which to measure performance. Active managers say they should be judged over a complete market cycle, not the commonly used yardsticks of one-, three- and five-year periods. They argue that some active managers do better in down markets but lag in up markets, while others perform brilliantly in up markets but poorly in down market, but over the entire market cycle both of these types of managers do an excellent job.

Stock-selection ability is overlooked. They claim that they received no credit for the good job they do in picking stocks. This is the weakest of their arguments because it doesn't matter if a few stocks in the portfolio did well if the entire portfolio did poorly.

Good performance is on the way. They claim that the growth of ETFs has presented a wonderful opportunity for active managers. In Chapter 18 you'll learn that an ETF manager must buy and sell slices of the ETF's underlying portfolio in order to maintain the ETF's price parity with its net asset value. This buying and selling occurs for reasons other than intrinsic value. And in the case of a sale, an active manager might be able to pick up some bargains among the stocks the ETF needs to discard.

In the case of a purchase, an active manager might be able to front-run the transaction since an ETF manager tells the market beforehand what stocks it needs to buy. Front-running is buying something before another investor in hope of selling it to them at a higher price. Front-running is illegal if the information is privileged. For example, if a broker receives a large purchase order from a client and decides to buy some of the same stock for himself or herself before placing the client's buy order, that's trading on privileged information and is cause for dismissal and jail time. But the information as to what stocks the ETF holds and may want to buy is not privileged. It's public information that has been disclosed by the ETF manager itself.

Often the same stock is held by many ETFs. If the ETFs are growing in size because of investor demand, that means these popular stocks will also be in demand. If that's the case, all an active manager has to do is to buy these popular stocks too and let the demand generated by the ETFs carry the stocks higher. There is also a downside to the crossholdings that I will discuss later in the book. But briefly, the crossholdings could trigger a general market panic should all the ETFs simultaneously start selling the same stock.

We provide a service to investors beyond returns. Finally, they claim they provide a service to investors beyond performance. In my opinion, this might be the most compelling reason. That is, they might be able to get a nervous investor to invest in the market in the first place and might be able to keep them invested through the rough patches. And even if the portfolio's return is lower than the benchmark, it still might be higher than if the investor didn't invest in the market at all.

Can Frequent Buying and Selling Impact Performance?

Yes, and this applies to you as well if you decide to go the do-it-yourself route. Every time a purchase or a sale occurs, a transaction cost is incurred. A brokerage commission needs to be paid, the bid-ask spread must be considered, and accounting and administrative costs are incurred. The more an active manager trades, the more transaction cost that are accumulated, and thus the greater the drag on performance.

Turnover rate

This is a measure of how frequently an active manager buys and sells stock. One method of calculating turnover is to divide the total value of shares purchased (or sold, whichever is less) by the total market value of the portfolio over a period of time (usually 12 months).

A high-turnover rate of 80% to 90%, and the accompanying turnover costs, isn't necessarily bad. It only becomes so if the manager's net performance isn't good enough to provide a better-than-index fund return, adjusted for risk.

Holding period

Often it is useful to construct a histogram of how long stocks are held (see Chapter 7 for how to construct a histogram).

What Is Closet Indexing?

Since an active manager's performance is often measured relative to the S&P 500 index, and since they enjoy their jobs and the income it provides, some active managers might be tempted to change their stock holdings in such a way that the resulting composition closely resembles the type of shares held in the index. If the compositions are reasonably similar, so should the returns. Presto, the manager is not likely to get fired for performance results, and will continue to collect active management fees for doing passive management work. They won't tell you what they are doing and hence are called "closet indexers."

Giving active managers the benefit of the doubt, closet indexing can also occur unintentionally. Based on an excellent performance record, an active manager can attract more and more assets. As the assets under management grow larger and larger it becomes harder and harder to find good stocks in which to invest in the quantities required to have an impact on performance. Thus, an active manager might be putting more names into the portfolio, and, when they do that, they might be becoming a closet indexer by default. But how closet indexing occurs – either intentionally or by default – does not matter to an investor. An investor is still paying high active management fees for basically passive performance.

What Is Window Dressing?

Department stores like to dress up their street-side windows in an attempt to lure shoppers inside. During seasonal changes and holidays the windows are made especially appealing.

Before reporting quarterly results and sharing their holdings with existing and prospective investors, some active managers like to engage in a form of window dressing themselves by selling their losers and adding recent hot stocks to make their portfolio look more appealing.

APPENDIX A
Some Internet Sites

STOCK SCREENING

Finviz.com
GuruFocus.com
Morningstar.com
Portfolio123.com
Profitspi.com
Stockrover.com

STOCK VALUATION

Finbox.io
Oldschoolvalue.com
Valuengine.com

STOCK RESEARCH & DATA

EDGAR.shtml
Morningstar.com
Reuters.com
Seekingalpha.com
Stockrover.com
Tipranks.com

CHARTING & TECHNICAL

Freestockcharts.com
Stockcharts.com
Tradingview.com

FUNDS

Csfconnect.com
Etf.com
Ici.org
Morningstar.com
Reuters.com
Zacks.com

ONES I WOULD ADD

Investors.com
Fool.com
Etfdb.com
Mutualfunds.com
Nasdaq.com
Dividend.com

Source: "Investor's Best of the Web 2018," *AAII Journal,* September 2018

CHAPTER 12

Passive Investing

In 1970, a University of Chicago professor, Eugene F. Fama, coined the term "efficient market" in a paper he wrote entitled "Efficient Capital Markets: A Review of Theory and Empirical Work" – a big title with wide-ranging impact. He used the word "efficient" in a way used by academic researchers that is somewhat different than how Merriam-Webster defines it. To quote his paper: "A market in which prices always 'fully reflect' available information is called 'efficient.'" His paper and subsequent work were so important and so widely read that the term "efficient market" is still very much in use today. This paper, and his subsequent work, earned him a Nobel Prize in 2013.

It wasn't long after his paper before the efficient market theory morphed into the passive market theory, which states that if the markets are efficient, why bother spending the time and money searching for that one special winning stock or that one special winning investment manager? Why not just invest in the entire market? That notion resulted in the creation of index funds, which are simply portfolios of stocks designed to track or mimic the risk and return of market indices.

In this chapter I will discuss the basic idea behind the efficient market theory, some requirements that are necessary in order to have an efficient market, and the reasons given that some say prove its existence. Then I will reinforce the point that when picking a passive index fund, you are really making an active decision. I will conclude with a discussion of ways to measure a passive manager's performance.

The Basic Idea of the Efficient Market

Say in the morning before the markets opened, you read on your smartphone that last night XYZ Company announced it had discovered the cure for cancer. Also, let's say the day before, XYZ's stock closed at $30 per share. That was a fair price – then. But do you think that once the market opens in the morning the price will be $30? Of course not. The supply of people who might have been willing to sell the day before would say, "Sell at $30 a share? You've got to be kidding." At the same time, other people who also heard the news might now want to buy the stock. With this new information the demand will increase, and the supply will dry up, and the stock's price will gap up when trading starts the next morning. The new price will be the price at which sellers will be willing to sell and buyers would be willing to buy. Therefore, the new price will reflect the new information.

Now consider this example. Say another company, ABC, has just announced its intention to purchase WXY for $75 a share cash. Not more than five minutes before, WXY was selling for $50 a share. Once the announcement is made, do you think anyone would be willing to sell their shares at $50? Again, of course not. The new price for WXY stock will reflect the new information.

One more example. Company ACB was expected to earn $2.50 a share for the quarter. Based on these expectations, the stock was trading at $140 a share. ACB instead reports 50 cents a share in earnings, which was a big negative surprise. Evidently, something bad must have happened to cause earnings to drop that much – something investors didn't anticipate. What happens almost immediately after the announcement? Of course, the stock's price gaps down and will eventually settle at a price that will reflect this new information.

In all these examples, the consensus of opinion of buyers and sellers prior to the new information was that the stock was worth X. But immediately after the announcement, they rapidly changed their collective minds. Now they consider it to be worth Y, and that becomes the new price you see on your computer screen.

The Efficient Market Theory

New and unexpected information constantly comes into the marketplace, perhaps not as dramatic as my examples, but information that can still move stock prices up or down. And rational buyers and sellers who want to make money or avoid losses will bid the price of the stock either up or down until it reaches an equilibrium and the new price reflects the available information. In other words, the market is "efficient."

Well, maybe yes and maybe no. Exactly how much and how quickly information is reflected in a stock's price has been hotly debated.

Some requirements to have an efficient market

Potential buyers and sellers: You need a large number of people who are motivated by the prospect of making money and are willing to take the time and effort to analyze and value stocks. Why is that important? Because the more people you have involved, the more likely it is that available information will be reflected in the stock's price.

Flow of information: Market participants need to have access to information and it needs to be delivered in a timely fashion. Why is that important? If people can't afford the price of obtaining the information or it doesn't come in a timely fashion, it won't be reflected in the stock's price.

The ability and willingness to act on that information: No matter how good or timely the information is, it is worthless if people do not act on it, and sometimes there are barriers that prevent them from acting, such as the inability or desire to engage in short selling when a stock appears to be overvalued.

Rational investors: Market participants need to evaluate the information in a sensible, logical, profit-seeking way. However, as you will see in Chapter 22 when I talk about emotions in the stock market, purely rational investors at times might be hard to find.

What information is really reflected in the stock's price?

This topic, which is at the heart of the efficient market theory, has also been hotly debated. Academics say there are three levels of efficiency – strong, semi-strong, and weak. The strong form says all information is reflected in the stock's price. That is, all of the requirements that make a market efficient are met to the fullest extent. Thus, there is absolutely nothing you can do to pick stocks that will give you an advantage. The semi-strong form says all publicly available information is reflected in the stock's price. Thus, analyzing financial statements will not give you an advantage in picking stocks. The weak form says the use of historical stock prices and trading volume won't help you in predicting future stock prices. Thus, technical analysis such as charting past trends won't help you in predicting future stock prices.

Nice Theory. Where Is the Proof?

The proof comes in the form of two arguments: Past performance of active managers has been poor, and the index has built-in advantages that make it hard to beat.

Past performance

If active managers who have all the research and technical skills at their disposal cannot consistently and over a reasonable period of time beat the market as defined by the S&P 500 index, then the market by default must be efficient. Many different studies back this up. They show active managers generally cannot consistently beat the relevant index, either before or especially after fees and transaction costs. And the ones who do often do not repeat their stellar performance. These trends have held relatively consistent over long periods of time. Refer back to Chapter 11 for a further discussion of active manager performance.

The index has built-in advantages

The second argument is that the structure of an index, such as the S&P 500, stacks the odds against an active manager. There are three major elements to this argument. The first is that the S&P 500 is capitalization-weighted. Thus, the performance of the largest companies in the index have the greatest impact on the index's return. If just a few of them, perhaps five or ten, are having a good year, and if an active manager is not invested in them, too bad. The active manager will underperform the index. The second element is that from time to time, certain factors such as value stocks are having a good year and account for much of the index's return. If an active manager is not invested in them, too bad. The active manager will underperform the index. The third element is that sectors or industries can account for much of the index's return as well. For example, from time to time individual sector or industry groups such as health care or technology are having a good year and account for much of the index's return. If an active manager is not invested in those sectors or industry groups, too bad. The active manager will underperform the index. Going forward then, an active manager must be able to consistently predict over a long period of time which of the 500 stocks, sectors, or industries in the S&P 500 are going to do well. What are the odds of an active manager doing that? Some suggest very low especially if they are pigeonholed in a specialization grid.

Thinking critically, you should remember that the arguments above are based on inductive reasoning. Inductive reasoning involves going from observations and odds to a general conclusion that is *likely* to be true. But while it is likely to be true, inductive reasoning can't tell you it is *irrefutably* true, hence the hope of outperformance by active managers continues.

Which Index Should I Invest In?

You may think that passive investing absolves you of having to pick stocks and determining how much of each to hold, and you are partially right. It does. But it doesn't absolve you of having to decide which index to select, and that means by default you are picking a certain group of stocks that are weighted in a certain way. In other words, when picking an index fund, you are making an active decision. Each index, and hence each index fund that is based on that index, has its own risk and return characteristics – and the differences can be huge.

Consider this. The DJIA index was up about 240% including dividends over the past 10 years. That's a great number. But the Nasdaq-100 index was up about 473% during the same time period. Looking just at those two returns you might jump to the conclusion that you're going to invest in a Nasdaq-100 index fund. Perhaps that will turn out to be a good decision. But maybe it won't. If you dig deeper into the construction of the two indices, you'll learn that over those years the Nasdaq-100 was up one year +53% and down another -42%, substantially higher than the DIJA. Can you emotionally stand that much volatility? Right now, you might think you can. But as the index slides downward week after week after week, perhaps your conviction will change (see Chapter 22).

If you dig even deeper into the construction of the two indices, you'll find that the Nasdaq-100 contains companies that are smaller and more technology-oriented such as Autodesk, Biogen, and Illumina, whereas the DJIA contains larger, more established companies such as Boeing, Wal-Mart, and IBM. Just looking at the performance numbers you wouldn't know that. Digging still deeper you'll find that these two indices are constructed entirely differently. One is a price-weighted index where the change in price is most important, whereas the other is a modified capitalization-weighted index where the size of the company is most important. All of those factors contributed to the huge difference in return.

Thus, before you invest in an index fund you should know what you're investing in. If you are considering passive management, as a start I would suggest reviewing Chapter 5.

Do I Have to Hire a Passive Manager?

Passive index funds contain hundreds if not thousands of stocks. With limited resources, it is a nearly impossible task for individual investors to fully replicate an index fund. So yes, you need to hire a passive manager. But your strategy doesn't have to be an all-or-nothing approach. You can invest most of your money with a passive manager and the balance either by being your own active manager, hiring an active manager, or hiring a factor-based manager.

You have plenty of alternatives on how to split your investment money. But, in my opinion, one of these approaches – active, passive, or factor-based – should be the main focus of your investments and, if you don't have the time or interest in the stock market, that's where passive management can play an important role.

How Have Passive Managers Performed?

Passive managers tend to come close, but generally underperform the return of the index they are attempting to track. How much they underperform is called tracking error. But not only do you get close to index performance, depending on the index, you also get broad-based diversification, generally lower management fees, and, according to academic studies, higher long-term risk-adjusted returns than many of the alternatives.

What Is Tracking Error?

Tracking error is simply the difference between the performance of an index fund and the paper index it was designed to track. In most time periods, a passive portfolio will have a negative tracking error because a passive manager is trying to create a portfolio of stocks to match an index that is created on paper. In other words, the real world intrudes

> *Tracking error is simply the difference between the performance of an index fund and the index it was designed to track.*

on the perfect world. The performance difference can come from many sources such as the frequency of rebalancing, cash drag, fees, and expense. I will address those issues as we go into more depth on passive management in Chapter 15.

Before you invest you will want to know the magnitude of the tracking error you might expect in the future based on the fund's past performance. Tracking error is especially important when you are trying to decide which passive manager you want to hire when both are trying to track the same index. It involves the manager calculating tracking error on a weekly, monthly, or quarterly basis and then calculating the standard deviation of the differences (Chapter 7 discusses standard deviation, if you need a reminder). The larger the standard deviation, the poorer the job the manager is doing in tracking the index. So instead of the prospective passive manager stating that their tracking error *averages* -0.5% (which might contain large swings), you'll be able to determine the probability of the manager's future tracking error falling within a range of outcomes based on the manager's past performance. The smaller the standard deviation, the better job that manager is doing and the more money in your pocket. The passive manager should make this information available to you. Just ask for the standard deviation of historical tracking error.

Hiring a Passive Manager

Passive managers can be found among the ranks of companies selling mutual funds and ETFs, so you have your choice of which investment delivery system to use to implement your investment strategy (see Section 5). With passive management, no one is seeking to uncover undervalued stock, only to match a pre-established index.

> *"Don't look for the needle in the haystack. Just buy the haystack." – Jack Bogle*

CHAPTER 13

Factor-Based Investing

In this chapter I will discuss where factors come from and the need to exercise caution when investing in factor-based portfolios because of data mining and the bandwagon effect. In addition, I will provide some examples of factor-based strategies and will outline the difficulties of performance comparisons. Finally, I will discuss why you can't pick a single stock from a factor-based portfolio and expect that stock to provide factor-based returns.

Where Do These Factors Come From?

Although these factors offer a glimmer of hope of better-than-index returns, don't get too excited. I said a glimmer, not the bright lights of Broadway. And there is much debate about their existence. Some say these pockets of money-making opportunities are really just pockets of risk: You get the opportunity for greater than index returns only by taking greater than index risk. Others say these pockets are really just short-term fads that shine brightly for a period of time and then go away like fireflies in the summer night, either because investment managers have moved in and eliminated the extra profit, or the market, in its various moods and contortions, decides which factor to favor and when. Others say they are very small pockets, too small or too difficult for someone to make much money exploiting. Still others say it is just fool's gold because the research was faulty.

Does it matter where these factors came from as long as you can make some money? Yes. If one of these factors gets its extra return from an investor taking more risk, then as long as you are willing to assume that risk, the factor is likely (but not guaranteed) to provide you excess return over the long term (assuming, as usual, that history repeats itself, because all these factors are based on historical data). On the other hand, if the excess return is due to changing fads, then you have to keep a very close eye on your investments because the returns might be here today and gone tomorrow. And if it's fool's gold because the research was faulty, you'll want to know how to protect yourself from a mistake. And one way to do that is to understand how good research is done so you can ask the right questions to see if the manager followed proper study protocol.

The Introduction of Computerized Databases

Many factors have been around for a long time and have been used by active investors either instinctively or through experience. However, academic researchers were held back from studying the market in a structured way due to the lack of reliable and easily accessible data. The stock market is incredibly complex; the number of stocks trading in the marketplace is huge; and the companies represented vary widely with respect to size, industry focus, and profitability, to mention just a few dimensions. This makes it an impossible task to analyze this all manually. It wasn't until the University of Chicago, with a grant from Merrill Lynch, formed the Center for Research in Security Prices, or CRSP (pronounced "crisp") when things changed. Its computerized database now contains monthly stock returns going back to 1926 as well as a lot of other information. This, and other extensive computerized databases, have made it easier to study the stock market in a rigorous way.

The Need to Exercise Caution

Why? Consider what Campbell Harvey, professor Duke University, and Yan Liu, assistant professor at Texas A&M University, had to say[12]:

> Most of the empirical research in finance, whether published in academic journals or put into production as an active trading strategy by an investment manager, is likely false. This implies that half of the financial products (promising outperformance) that companies are selling to clients are false.

It's doubtful that things have changed since 2014 so here are some things to watch out for.

---

[12] *The Journal of Portfolio Management*, Special 40th Anniversary Issue 2014.

Data mining

Along with the ease of doing computerized research comes the downside: data mining. Data mining occurs when you have a lot of data and you keep digging and digging until you find a golden nugget that provides greater-than-market return. This is very easy to do when the data is computerized because in a short period of time you can run thousands of complex stock-selection rules, and in that mass of results you might identify one set of rules that would have made you rich in the past had you known about it then. The problem is that this newly discovered golden nugget is more likely to be a result of a random combination of historical events that occurred only once and only during the study time period. As someone once told me, "If you torture the data long enough, it will confess to anything." Sadly, some investment managers will sell this fool's gold to unsuspecting investors touting their "research" as the basis for you to invest with them.

How do you avoid the potential hazards of data mining? One way is to look at how these researchers conducted their studies (see Chapter 16).

Bandwagon effect

There are a lot of really bright investment managers out there, and if one of them sees another manager making money from a factor, you can bet the others will try to replicate that factor too. And as more money pours into the factor, its excess return will go away, leaving no excess return or even cause a negative return. There is an old Wall Street saying, "When the ducks are quacking, feed them." And if the public is buying, you can bet the investment community will do the selling. So, if you decide to make a career in investments and you discover a money-making factor, best to keep it to yourself or you'll have everyone else hopping on your bandwagon.

Use of historical data

Factors are discovered using back-tested historical data and, even though the results might be favorable longer term, there were periods of time when they weren't. Given the sheer number of newly discovered factors and the fact that their returns can fluctuate, you as a potential factor investor has to have confidence that the factor will perform as expected well into the future. That confidence should not only be based on a study that was done to the highest standards but, more importantly, on whether the factor itself makes intuitive sense.

Relative performance

Relative performance is comparing one thing to another. In factor-based studies, that means comparing the performance of a portfolio that has the greatest exposure to a factor with the performance of a portfolio that has the least exposure. Since the researchers are making comparisons between two portfolios, it doesn't matter if the performance of the portfolio with the greatest exposure was negative as long as it was less negative than the portfolio with the least exposure. That's fine when trying to isolate a factor, but just because you lost less money than the alternative doesn't mean you're on your way to serious wealth.

In order to precisely replicate the results of most factor-based studies, you have to buy (in stock market terms, go long) those stocks in the portfolio with the greatest exposure to the factor and sell short those stocks in the portfolio with the least exposure. But for various reasons, an investment manager might not want to engage in short selling and will offer to the investing public only portfolios that had the greatest exposure to the factor. "What's wrong with that?" you ask. Only this – you might not get anywhere near the return the factor study promised you since you are dealing with only half of the study. Some have countered that by arguing if you have greater exposure to the factor than the market you will be creating a situation where you will approximate the long-short results of the factor study. At least that's the argument.

Index or Benchmark?

Before I provide some examples of factors, I want to make a distinction between an index (which relates to passive investing) and a benchmark (which relates to factor-based investing). An index represents the performance of a long-established description of the market, whereas a benchmark represents what an investment manager *thinks* will provide greater than market return adjusted for risk. One finds its roots in the previously established market indices; the other finds its roots in the investment manager's brain.

For example, the S&P 500 index represents a certain segment of the entire stock market, has been around since 1957, and is capitalization-weighted. A factor-based manager might say, "I don't like the S&P 500 index because it gives too much weight to large-cap stocks. I like small-cap stocks." Therefore, the manager's idea is to change the index and create a benchmark that weights the stocks in the S&P 500 index equally, thus tilting the index towards small-cap stocks. But in marketing the idea, the factor-based manager will call the benchmark an index and then claim to be a passive manager. In reality, a factor-based manager is not a passive manager but instead is an active manager who uses passive techniques to implement his or her active idea.

The indiscriminate use of the word "index" muddles the distinctions between passive and factor-based management and creates confusion in the minds of many investors. Therefore, in this book, a factor-based manager tracks a benchmark, that is, a set of rules that were created by the factor-based manager in an attempt to access greater than market returns, whereas a passive manager tracks an index, that is, a long-established description of the performance of the market.

What Are Examples of a Factor-Based Strategy?

The number of benchmarks in this space is huge and growing. Referring to Figure 13-1, the usual approach to creating one is easy. First, pick a universe of stocks from the first column, then pick one or several factors from the second column (see Chapter 16 for definitions), and finally pick a weighting scheme from the third column.

UNIVERSE OF STOCKS	FACTORS	WEIGHTING SCHEME
S&P 500	Size	Market-cap
DIJA	Book value	Price
Nasdaq	PE ratio	Equal
11 Sectors	Volatility	Float-adjusted
24 Industry groups	Momentum	Modified-cap
68 Industries	Quality	Manager-determined
158 Subindustries	Liquidity	
Entire market	Manager-determined	
Manager-determined		

Figure 13-1

For example, the benchmark could consist of the stocks in the S&P 500 index (the universe of stocks) that are large-cap growth stocks (two factors) that are then capitalization-weighted (the weighting scheme). Given the number of possible combinations, I hope you can see there are hundreds, if not thousands, of possible factor-based benchmarks that can be created.

In reality, anything goes in factor-based management, and you **must** exercise caution and fully understand what is being offered to you. Investment management is a business, and anything the factor-based manager

> *"Beware of geeks bearing formulas." – Warren Buffett*

thinks will sell will be provided. For example, cybersecurity is a hot topic now. Thus, cybersecurity stocks form the first column (the Universe of Stocks). Then the manager would select from the other two columns and, voila, a benchmark is created. Do you think Warren Buffett's idea of investing in companies that protect their turf by building a moat around their business by being the low-cost producer, having a technological edge, or promoting brand loyalty is a good idea? Well, that then would constitute stocks from the first and second columns, and all the manager needs to do is to pick from the last column and a benchmark has been created.

Finding That "Golden-Touch" Factor-Based Manager

Since the factor-based manager's only promise to you is to match the benchmark they created, the burden of active management has been shifted to you. You have to decide whether the idea behind the factor that resulted in the benchmark makes sense. You have to decide whether the idea has been adequately vetted. You have to have the conviction the idea will work in the future. Sure, you might be presented with plenty of back-tested results, but that's all history. In some cases, you might not even have the research to rely on, and data mining is always a lingering question mark. To make your search more difficult, many factor-based managers offer exotic ideas using complex implementation strategies that are extremely complex to understand.

Like active management, you can hire someone to help or you can conduct the search for a factor-based manager by yourself. The grid offered in Chapter 11 might help narrow the search, but most factor-based managers defy pigeonholing, that is, their investment style does not lend itself to being placed in a single rigid category.

How Have Factor-Based Managers Performed?

As I said in Chapter 11, performance measurement can be tricky, and that is especially true for factor-based managers. There are two areas to consider: the performance of the benchmark and the performance of the portfolio constructed to track the benchmark. The most important of these is the performance of the benchmark, since it constitutes the majority of any return. However, although the factor-based manager constructed the benchmark, we are actually measuring your investment skills, because you picked that particular benchmark from the hundreds available to you.

Performance benchmark

The standard approaches to measurement are peer comparisons (grading on the curve) and index comparisons (grading according to some level of achievement).

Peer comparisons: This might seem easy. Just collect the performance results of all those managers whose factor-based strategies are similar and compare the manager you are interested in to them. The problem is that while they might all be investing within the same factor, the benchmarks that are created can be widely different. Some might start with the S&P 500 universe of stocks to tease out the factor, while others might use a small-cap universe. Some might use an equal-weighting scheme, while others use a cap-weighted scheme. Still others might construct their own universe and weighting scheme. This degree of diversity makes valid peer comparisons extremely difficult.

Index comparisons: This involves comparing the factor-based return with the return from an index, such as the S&P 500. This comparison might be valid because often those who are marketing these factor-based strategies are generally doing so as a better performing alternative to a passive index fund. However, complicating this comparison is the fact that many factor-based managers often plead for a very long measurement time-frame (in many cases longer than for active managers who are often judged on one-, two-, and five-year periods) because these factors seem to come into and out of prominence over long periods of time.

Benchmark tracking error

Calculating the tracking error for a factor-based manager is similar to that for a passive manager. Since I discussed the concepts in Chapter 12, see that chapter.

Do I Have to Hire a Factor-Based Manager?

Yes. Similar to passive management, the portfolios created by factor-based managers can contain hundreds, if not thousands, of stocks. Investing in that number of stocks is an impossible task for individual investors. But, like other approaches, your strategy doesn't have to be all-or-nothing. You can invest the bulk of your money with a factor-based manager and the rest in other strategies – active or passive.

Factor-based managers can be found in the mutual fund universe, but most appear in a pure form among the ranks of ETFs. Generally, the fee for factor-based management will be lower than active management but substantially higher than for passive management. However, some factor-based managers charge as much, and some even more, than active managers for a comparable product. So, it depends.

Picking a Stock from a Factor-Based Portfolio

If you are undertaking a do-it-yourself active management strategy you might be tempted to go fishing in a factor-based manager's portfolio for investment ideas. However, just understand the return you might receive from the one or two stocks you pick might be better or worse than what was achieved by the entire portfolio. How can that be? The far-left column in Figure 13-2 breaks the risk for one stock into its component parts. As more and more stocks are added in a specific way, a portfolio was created where company and sector-industry risk are diversified away, leaving factor and market risk. That is shown by the middle column. This is the factor-based portfolio that you are fishing in.

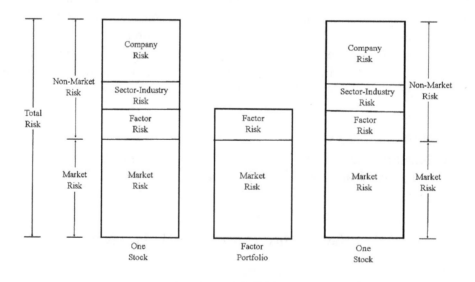

Figure 13-2

However, if you now pick just one stock from that pool, you become exposed again to that which was diversified away – company and sector-industry risk. It is from these sources of risk where you might get a better or a worse return than that which was achieved from the factor-based portfolio.

> *A factor-based manager is not a passive manager, but an active manager who uses a passive technique to implement his or her active idea.*

Inside an Investment Management Firm

Now we really get into the nitty-gritty of active, passive, and factor-based investing. I am going to take you inside investment management firms to give you an inside look at how they go about making investment decisions so that you will have more information to base your decision as to which investment strategy is right for you. If you decide the active do-it-yourself strategy is the way you want to go, the chapter on active management will give you ways on how to evaluate a company and how to assess its stock's intrinsic value.

CHAPTER 14

Active Management

This chapter will focus on one of the foundations of active management, fundamental analysis (the others are technical analysis and emotional analysis. I will address them in the context of market timing in Section 6). For the sake of clarity, I have divided the chapter into two parts on the premise that while you might find a wonderful company (part 1), its stock might not be a good investment (part 2).

In the first part, I will begin with a company's annual report – why it's an important, what's in it, and what to look for. Then, I'll discuss various ways to measure a company's profitability and what is perhaps the single most important determinant of company's future profitability: the company's management. Finally, I

> *"The worst thing you can do is invest in companies you know nothing about." – Peter Lynch*

will identify some management-initiated actions that might be signaling future profitability.

In the second part of this chapter, I will focus on the stock's intrinsic value as opposed to what it is selling for. The results of that calculation would then be used to determine if the stock is a candidate for a purchase or should be sold if it's already owned. I will explain several valuation models, including the dividend discount model, and will conclude the chapter by listing several valuation ratios that are useful in the identification of intrinsic value.

Not all fundamental managers approach active investment in this manner, but at least this will give you an idea how some go about it. The chapter also contains important information if you are considering a do-it-yourself approach to active management.

An Introduction to a Company's Annual Report

The company's annual report to shareowners is the best place for an investor to start his or her understanding of a company, and its potential as an investment opportunity. Get copies for at least the three previous years because you will be looking for trends. Copies can be obtained by requesting them from the company's investor relations department, by downloading them from the company's website, by asking your stock broker for copies, or the SEC website: sec.gov/Edgar/searchedgar/companysearch.html.

Areas of Importance

There are three areas in the annual report to pay special attention to: the reports of the CEO and the chairman of the board, the company's financial statements, and the footnotes to the financial statements.

The reports of the CEO and the chairman of the board

These are often marketing pieces in which the company's deficiencies are glossed over and its achievements, no matter how minor, are glorified. No management wants to present a gloomy picture of their past performance. When you read these reports, be prepared for spin. However, that doesn't mean they are useless. Compare what was said in the past to see if management had a logical plan for the future and if they are actually achieving their goals. Management flexibility in a changing environment is okay, but you would not want to invest in a company whose management can't make up its mind where to lead the company.

The company's financial statements

The financial statements are the company's report card of how well its management has done in the past. These statements consist of the company's balance sheet, income statement, and cash flow statement. I have provided

> *"Never invest in a company without understanding its finances. The biggest losses in stocks come from companies with poor balance sheets." – Peter Lynch*

examples of them in the Appendices (if you are considering the do-it-yourself route, you really need to understand financial statements, and there are plenty of online resources to help you).

Don't be confused when comparing one company's financial statements with another. Different companies often use different terms and ways of presenting the data, but the general categories will be similar. Also, very large companies that have many divisions or own other companies will consolidate the financial reports of these entities. It is the consolidated reports that you will see first. The details of the consolidation are in the annual report; they just require a bit of digging.

Balance sheet: The balance sheet gives investors a "snapshot" view of what the company owns (its assets), what it owes (its liabilities), and the stake shareowners have in the company (its shareowners' equity) at a specific point in time, such as at the end of the year.

The term "balance sheet" comes from the fact that assets are always equal to – or in balance with – liabilities plus shareowners' equity. For example, the money you saved (retained earnings) plus the money you borrowed (liabilities) equals the price you paid for something (assets). While assets, liabilities, and shareowners' equity are the major heading there are many subcategories within each as you can see in Appendix A.

When someone asks, "What's the book value of the company," they are asking for an indication of a company's net worth in accounting terms on a given date. "Book value" is just another name for shareowners' equity as shown on the balance sheet. I bring that up now because you will find the term "book value" cropping up all over the place in investments. But, remember, book value is not the same as intrinsic value. These are two different terms. Book value is an accounting term that is based on the past; intrinsic value is an economic term that results from looking into the future (more on intrinsic value later in this chapter).

Income statement: This statement tells investors how profitable a company was during a given time period, such as quarterly or yearly. It shows what came into the company from the sales of its products or services (the company's net sales, which is total sales minus returns, allowances, and discounts), its out-go (its expenses), and what's left over (its net income). An example is shown in Appendix B.

When someone tells you to pay attention to a company's *top line,* they are telling you to watch the company's growth in net sales, which is at the top or the first section of the income statement. If that figure is increasing without mergers or acquisitions, it means the company is enjoying *organic growth.* Organic growth means the company is expanding through increased sales of existing and/or new products rather than expanding through merging with or acquiring other companies. Therefore, if the company's top line is growing organically and if management keeps innovating and keeps expenses under control, the *bottom line* (net income) will also be growing organically – a good thing.

Cash flow statement: This statement shows how much cash came in, how much went out, and what's left over during a given time period, such as quarterly or annually. In other words, this is the amount of cash the company is able to generate after all the cash expenses have been paid. It differs from the income statement, which recognizes revenues and expenses even though no cash has changed hands. The cash flow statement is generally divided into three parts: (1) cash from operating activities, (2) cash from investing activities, and (3) cash from financing activities. An example is shown in Appendix C.

Auditor's opinion: An outside auditor is hired by the company to express an opinion on whether the financial statements meet generally accepted accounting principles. That opinion is in the form of a letter that is included in the annual report. If an auditor offers a "qualified" opinion you had better dig deeper and find out why. Generally, that is not a good sign because the auditor's opinion should be "unqualified." Note: There is also a movement to have auditors give more information than just a thumbs-up (unqualified) or a thumbs-down (qualified) opinion.

Also recognize that while the financial statements conform to generally accepted accounting principles and have been reviewed by an outside auditor, the accounting principles themselves contain plenty of grey areas where a company can report aggressive or conservative numbers. In other words, there are fudge factors in the accounting standards big enough to swing earnings one way or another. Not by a lot, but enough.

Footnotes

It is also important for you to read the footnotes that accompany the financial statements in the annual report. In these notes the company might tuck things that they really wanted to ignore but are required to report. If you don't understand what the notes are saying, ask the company's investor relations department or your stockbroker to explain what they mean. If you're not happy with the explanation, you might want to move on to another stock – and if the stockbroker has no clue what the footnote meant, to a more knowledgeable stockbroker. Some of the things to look for are how the company accounts for revenues, looming legal cases, hidden debt such as long-term operating leases, uncovered pension liabilities, and self-dealing between management and their family members.

Per Share Basis

One final point before we move on. Companies vary in size from very large to very small. To make them comparable, the raw accounting numbers are divided by the number of shares outstanding to get them on a per share basis. This makes comparisons both through time and across similar companies easier.

Identifying a Company's Profitability

If I had to pick just one thing that drives long-term stock prices it would be the company's ability to earn a profit into the future. What else could drive a stock price besides its company's future profitability? Its price-earnings ratio since it is a measure of how investors feel about the company's prospects (the price-earnings ratio is the stock's price divided by the company's earnings on a per share basis. The higher this number the more willing investors are to pay for a given amount of current earnings because they think future earnings will be even greater).

How a company has performed in the past might give you clues about the company's future. There are many ways and variations how to measure a company's past performance – reported earnings, diluted earnings, operating earnings, core earnings, pro forma earnings, free cash flow, and return on equity to name a few.

Reported earnings

This is simply what's left over from income after all bills have been paid and the accruals, depreciation, interest on debt, and taxes have been accounted for (in other words, net income) divided by the number of shares outstanding to obtain an earnings per share number (EPS).

Accruals reflect an income or an expense that needs to be recognized even though cash has not been received or an expense has been incurred but not paid. An example is electric service that is paid after it has been supplied. For the electric company, it needs to reflect the fact that income was earned when the electricity was supplied to match the expense it incurred in providing it. For the owner of a business who uses the electric service, the owner needs to reflect the service that has been received but has not as yet been paid. Depreciation is similar, except it is the recognition that things like machinery, equipment, and buildings wear out over time, and the rate at which they wear out is considered a business expense that can be deducted from earnings.

EPS appears on the company's income statement and is reported to the U.S. Securities and Exchange Commission and to shareowners. You can find the history of a company's reported EPS in your stockbroker's research database or from the company's annual reports.

Diluted earnings

EPS is not the only version of earnings that can be reported. There is also something called *diluted earnings per share.* For this calculation, the earnings are divided by the number of shares outstanding plus the number of shares that have been promised to others but not yet delivered. Anytime you hear the word "dilution," it is not a good thing for existing shareowners because a fixed amount of earnings will be divided by an increased number of shares, which then reduces or dilutes the reported EPS. It's like sharing a single pizza with two friends, then suddenly having to share it with ten more who suddenly show up.

Digging Deeper into Profitability

Some would argue that reported earnings do not capture the true performance of the operations of the company. For example, the revenue number used in the calculation of reported earnings might include income from things not even related to the underlying operations of the company, such as the sale of assets, interest from investments, or income from rentals. The same is true with expenses. The expense number used in the calculation of reported earnings might include losses on the sale of long-term assets or penalties and fines. Then there is the issue of restructuring costs, legal expenses, gains from mergers and acquisitions, pension plan investment gains or losses, and on and on. What do they have to do with the underlying operations of the company?

Out of this confusion come five additional measures of profitability: operating earnings, core earnings, pro forma earnings, cash flow, and one that takes a different approach, return on equity. I won't drag you too far into the accounting weeds, because it is easy to get lost there. Just remember, these alternatives center on different ideas as to what to include and what to exclude from revenues and expenses when attempting to isolate a company's "true" performance. If you want more details than this overview, just search the internet.

Earnings before interest and taxes (EBIT)

This is what is left over after subtracting from total revenue recurring expenses that are directly related to the operation of the business such as cost of goods sold, labor, depreciation and accruals, and overhead expense. Since it focuses on recurring revenues and expenses, it excludes any unusual or one-time events. It also excludes interest paid on debt and tax liabilities. Overhead expenses are those that do not directly relate to the generation of profits, but are still necessary for a company to stay in business. Examples are administrative salaries, rent, and accounting fees. EBIT is frequently used in academic studies and can be found in your stockbroker's research database. It is also known as operating earnings or operating profit.

Core earnings

This after-tax measure was developed by Standard and Poor's and tries to isolate a company's earning potential by excluding revenues and expenses that are not related to the company's core or primary business operations. For example, it would exclude unusual sources of income from asset sales, pension fund gains, hedging activities, merger and acquisition expenses, and litigation settlements. It would include expenses related to employee stock option grants, pensions, and restructuring of present operations.

Pro forma earnings

In this calculation, anything the company wants to include or exclude is pretty much fair game. Companies provide this type of analysis to give investors an indication of what the financial statements might look like after an anticipated merger, acquisition, or some other important change. Sure, the company might have reasons for what is in the pro forma statement, but an investor really needs to be skeptical because the reasons might be self-serving. These earnings can't be compared to the company's past earnings or, for that matter, to the earnings of any other company.

Free cash flow

Some analysts think instead of focusing on a company's earnings, which might be subjected to fudging, a better approach is to focus on the company's free cash flow. Cash is cash and is not subjected to opinions about the size of accruals, what to include in revenues, or what to add to expenses. Free cash flow is the amount of cash that a company generates during a given time period that is available to make dividend payments, buyback shares, pay down liabilities, and develop new products. There are many ways to calculate the number, but one way is to subtract capital expenditures (capex) from the cash flow from operating activities. Capital expenditures are cash spent to maintain and upgrade plant and equipment needed to produce the company's good or services.

Although it might a good way to measure the underlying profitability, free cash flow must be used with caution and should not be the only measure used. As you can see from the formula, capital expenditures are subtracted from the cash flow from operating activities. Some companies have a very great need to spend cash on plants, factories, and equipment in order to generate income. In other words, their capital expenditures can be great and variable, which in turn makes their free cash flow figure low and variable. Think of a manufacturer who needs a factory in order to make things versus a company that uses brain power to provide a service. The two have different needs to make capital expenditures and thus will have different free cash flow numbers. But that doesn't necessarily make one company a better investment than the other.

The free cash flow number should also be in your broker's research database. Some like to compare the cash from operating earnings to net income to evaluate management's skill at converting net income into cash. If the cash figure is greater than the net income figure over a period of time earning are often thought to be of "high quality."

Return on equity

The underlying profitability of a company depends on the skill of its management. One measure of that skill is return on equity. I will get into how management can influence this number later, but since the title of this section is "Digging Deeper into Profitability," I would be remiss if I didn't add this perspective here.

Return on equity is equal to net income divided by shareowners' equity. If you look at the balance sheet in Appendix A, you'll see that shareowners' equity includes something called retained earnings. This is the accumulated part of net income that wasn't paid out in dividends over the years. Since the balance sheet must "balance," this accumulative portion of net income shows up on the asset side of the balance sheet in such things as short-term investments; in property, plant and equipment; or in other categories (or in a reduction of liabilities). A company's management decides how this accumulated capital should be invested. If it's put into short-term investments such as government treasury bills and the income reinvested, it will generate income and continue to do so in ever-increasing amounts due to the power of compounding that you learned about in Chapter 1. But anyone can invest in treasury bills. Management's job is to invest the money in new ideas or projects in order to earn more, substantially more, than the treasury bill rate. That's their job, and what they're being paid to do. One measure of their performance, and hence a measure of a company's profitability, is return on equity.

Ratios in General

Merriam-Webster defines a ratio as, "The relationship in quantity, amount or size between two or more things." In other words, one thing is divided by another where the units of measure are the same. Although there are many types of ratios used in fundamental analysis, the two we are most interested in are profitability ratios and valuation ratios. Profitability ratios will give us clues as we look for a wonderful company and valuation ratios will give us clues on whether it is a good investment or not. But you need to take care when using ratios.

(1)   Ratios are relative measures. They need to be compared to something else in order to have value, such as to the same ratio for another company within the same sector-industry or to the same ratio for the market.

(2)   While a single comparison might be interesting, the value of ratios is realized when calculated over a period of time. Trends can then be easily seen.

(3)   Several different ratios are needed to get a more accurate picture of a company. Looking at only one ratio could be very misleading.

(4)   Ratios are calculated using historical data. Thus, they should be used with caution because there is no guarantee that the past will repeat itself.

(5)   Care must be taken when comparing the ratio of one company with that of another when they are in different industries. A company that produces computer games is significantly different from one that produces steel.

Profitability Ratios

When viewed over a period of time, profitability ratios can tell you how well the company has been run. As an investor, you would like to see these ratios increasing over time or at the minimum remaining the same. With profitability ratios, at least one of the variables is net income or one of the forms of profitability I discussed above.

Return on assets (ROA)

ROA equals net income divided by average total assets. This ratio measures how effectively a company uses its assets to generate profit. Why is this important? Assets – buildings and equipment – are expensive to buy and own, and in a well-run company they must produce sufficient profit or they are a waste of money. But assets also include cash, accounts receivable, inventory, trademarks, and patents. These too must pay for their keep, either by being kept to a minimum or by providing a return.

Return on equity (ROE)

ROE equals net income divided by average shareowners' equity. This ratio measures the return on shareowners' equity. As you learned earlier, this is the company's book value. In an accounting sense, book value is the shareowners' stake in the company after liabilities have been deducted from assets. It is one of the key ratios that tells you how good of a job management is doing on your behalf – and is why later in this chapter I have devoted an entire section to it.

Profit margin (PM)

PM equals net income divided by sales, where sales exclude returns and refunds. This ratio measures how much profit a company earns from each dollar of sales (or revenue). Clearly, this is a very important ratio and I will discuss it in depth later in the discussion of ROE.

Gross profitability-to-assets (GPA)

GPA equals revenues minus cost of goods sold divided by total assets. This ratio is similar to ROA except it excludes many of the expenses that were included in the calculation of net income and focuses on only the cost of goods sold. These are the costs that are directly related to the production of the goods or services. It would include such things as direct labor costs, material costs, and factory overhead costs. Instead of relating gross profitability to sales (or revenue), as in profit margin, the calculation relates it to something that is ultimately under the control of management, the company's assets.

The Importance of a Company's Management

The board of directors and senior managers sometimes are thought of as being captains of the ship. They are charged with the responsibility of navigating the company through competitive business waters. How good a job they do clearly has a profound impact on the company's stakeholders: its employees, its shareowners, and the community. While senior management sets the company's culture, direction, and profitability, they can't do it alone. It requires a team effort from all the people working in the company pulling together.

Challenges facing management

These can be viewed as components of non-market risk that I discussed in Chapter 7.

> *Strategic risk:* the decisions associated with how to position the company for the expected future environment. This is of vital concern for long-term stock investors.

> *Business risk:* the decisions associated with the business the company is in. Companies that make cars face different kinds of risk than those that supply electricity.

> *Operational risk:* the decisions associated with the day-to-day running of the company. A well-run company tries to keep expenses low while trying to increase revenues. The tricky part is how to do that without impacting quality or unit sales.

> *Financial risk:* the decisions associated with how much debt to have in the company. Although some debt tends to increase earnings, too much increases the risk of bankruptcy.

> *Currency risk:* the decisions associated with fluctuating foreign exchange rates. Many companies have international operations, and changes in the value of foreign currencies can have a major impact on earnings.

> *Reputational risk:* the decisions associated with maintaining or increasing the public's favorable opinion of the company as a valued member of the community is extremely important.

Building a moat

How management handles these risks will ultimately determine whether a company expands, declines, or goes bankrupt. There is a lot riding on the outcome for the stakeholders. Ideally, the goal for management would be to position the company in a manner that excludes easy entry of competitors into the company's market space, perhaps by developing proprietary products and encouraging brand loyalty. Then, by keeping expenses low, innovating, and increasing revenues while being sensible about the use of debt and maintaining an excellent reputation, the company can increase the size and stability of profits over the long term, thus allowing the company to pay ever-increasing dividends.

But a word of caution. Like moats around the castles of old, new technologies can rapidly change the dynamics. Many of the new challengers, which are called disruptors, can quickly devastate a well-crafted strategy of a stable, growing revenue base. Look at Uber® and other transportation-on-demand companies. Taxi companies in some cities thought they had a well-crafted moat around their business by selling a limited number of medallions to cab drivers and thus creating a steady revenue source by controlling the supply of taxies. Uber® and Lyft® upended that business model within a few months.

Assessing the Quality of Management

Making an assessment is difficult for an individual investor who doesn't have access to higher management. Difficult, but not impossible. First, I've already mentioned the value of reading the CEO's and the chairman of the board's reports over a period of years. Do they articulate a clear, sound strategic plan for the future? From what you read, are they honest with shareowners as to failures and mistakes? Are they attempting to follow the crowd? Has ROE been increasing? Is management trying to give the company a clear advantage over the competition?

Second, if you already own the stock, you are entitled to attend the annual meeting and ask your questions in person. Sometimes those meetings are in distant cities, which makes it impossible for you to attend, but often they are accessible via podcasts. Third, the company or a broker often will arrange a conference call around the time the company reports earnings. You can listen in over the internet. You can get the date, time, and how to connect directly from the company or your stockbroker. Analysts often ask pointed questions and management's answers can be a source of insight. But be forewarned: company managers can be excellent used car salespersons, so expect some spin.

Before you go that route, however, you might want to go the indirect route first, and that involves doing your homework. First, look at the products or services the company is producing. Do you like them? Are you, your friends, or your parents buying them? Does the company have a history of bringing out new and exciting products or services? Have sales been increasing over time? A key indicator of good management is a company that consistently provides the public with goods and services customers want at a price they are willing to pay. Second, it's nice to see that a company is still being run by the founder if that founder has produced good products in the past. Founders have a reputation to maintain. Finally, analyze various ratios I outlined earlier and those that I will outline later in this chapter.

All of these ideas have flaws, so don't rely on just one. But together they might give you an impression of the quality of a company's management.

How Management Can Influence Return on Equity

Return on equity (ROE) is an important tool used to measure a management's effectiveness. The analysis described below was used or made popular by the DuPont Company decades ago (see Figure 14-1). Assets and shareowners' equity are normally averaged for the period under study. There is an extended version of this type of analysis that introduces taxes and interest payments; the one below, however, is the most straightforward.

$$ROE = \frac{Net\ Income}{Shareowners'\ Equity}$$

$$ROE = \frac{Net\ Income}{Sales} \times \frac{Sales}{Assets} \times \frac{Assets}{Shareowners'\ Equity}$$

$$ROE = \frac{Profit}{Margin} \times \frac{Asset}{Turnover} \times \frac{Leverage}{Factor}$$

Figure 14-1

Profit margin equals net income divided by sales

This ratio measures how much profit a company makes from its sales. Different pricing strategies as well as other factors can cause profit margin to vary from company to company, as well as from industry to industry. For example, a company might be able to command a higher price (and hence a high profit margin) for its products or services because of its high quality, innovation, brand-name recognition, expensive-to-replicate factories, efficient distribution networks, or patents, just to name a few.

On the other hand, some companies can't command a higher price for their goods or service but make up for it by selling lots of product. An example would be a supermarket, where the profit margin is low but the sales volume is high. In these types of businesses, management will try to differentiate themselves from the competition so that they can charge more. For example, a supermarket might offer organic food in an attempt to increase its profit margins.

Since profit margin varies among companies and within industries, you need to be careful when you do comparisons to make sure the companies have somewhat similar lines of business.

Asset turnover equals sales divided by assets

This ratio gives an investor an indication of how effective the company is at using its assets to generate sales. Assets cost money to buy, own, and maintain and they must be used efficiently. An increasing ratio is desirable, but an ultra-high ratio is unlikely in some industries – for example, Ford Motor Company or a steel company. They require a huge amount of assets to produce sales.

Leverage factor equals assets divided by shareowners' equity

This ratio goes by several different names, one of which is "equity multiplier" and is intended to show how much of the company's assets are financed with debt. In other words, how leveraged the company is. Consistent with prudent risk, ROE can be increased via an increase in debt, all else held constant.

Using the DuPont Analysis

You should have an idea what is driving any change in ROE. This is where the DuPont framework is helpful. Consider the following four scenarios.

Scenario #1 – ROE has increased

On the surface, this is good for investors because management is earning more on shareowners' equity. But what caused the increase? An increase in either profit margin or asset turnover is a good thing. In the first case, the company is making more money from each dollar of sales than before. In the second case, it means the company is making more efficient use of its assets. However, if ROE increased because of an increase in leverage, that may or may not be good. Too much leverage, which means too much debt, may cause trouble for the company in the future if earnings turn down.

Scenario #2 – ROE remains the same

On the surface that may be okay. But, using our DuPont analysis, you may discover concerns. Perhaps to offset a decline in profit margin, management decided to increase leverage.

Scenario #3 – ROE is declining

If the cause is a decline in profit margin or in asset turnover, that's not a good thing. It might mean sales are declining or the assets at the company's disposal are not being used in an optimal way. However, if it's due to a decline in leverage, that might be good move by management. In any case, knowing which of the three might be causing the decline, you can focus your analysis there to see if the company is facing only a temporary setback in ROE or has a long-term problem.

Scenario #4 – Two companies have the same ROE

On the surface, they seem comparable. But looking at the elements that make up ROE may show a different story.

How to Make Earnings Look Better Than They Are

Digging further into the complexity of management decisions, let's see how management can make earnings look better than they really are. Why am I bringing this up? To reinforce the need for you to pay attention to changes in the company's financials.

Fudging the numbers

I already mentioned the wiggle room within the generally accepted accounting principles. Earnings can be nudged in one direction or another. Most of this you might not see. However, by reading the footnotes you might pick up some of what is going on.

Reducing strategic spending

Management can increase earnings by reducing how much is spent on such things as repair and maintenance, research and development, information technology, and labor costs. Although short-term earnings improve, by taking these actions a company might be hurting its ability to achieve long-term growth.

Incurring debt

Management can also boost earnings by incurring debt and that, in turn, can increase its financial risk. Here's a simple example. Let's say XYZ wants to expand and can build a new factory for $2,000,000, the products of which are expected to generate $300,000 in net profit each year. If the company finances the project with internally generated cash, their return will be the $300,000 in net profit divided by $2,000,000, or 15%, which is not too bad. But instead, someone in management thinks the company can do better if it borrows $1,500,000 at a 10% interest rate. The investment in the factory will then be $500,000. The factory is expected to generate $300,000 in net income, and if the $150,000 in interest payments is deducted, $150,000 in net profit will be left. The return on investment will then be $150,000 divided by $500,000, or 30% – twice what it was in the first scenario. Thus, the increase in debt will increase return.

On the surface, this sounds like a good idea. A return of 30% is better than 15%. But the introduction of debt cuts both ways. If XYZ's factory does not generate the $300,000 per year because consumer tastes have changed, the company will suffer. Say the factory now generates only $100,000 in net profit, but the company is committed to pay $150,000 in interest payments, so there is a shortfall of -$50,000. If that shortfall can't be made up somewhere else, the holder of the debt can demand payment in full and, if the company can't pay, can start bankruptcy proceedings.

Some debt might be acceptable depending on the size and stability of earnings, but too much might be harmful. Analysts like to use something called the company's "debt ratio" to measure the amount of debt a company has. This ratio is calculated by dividing total liabilities by total assets – information you can find in the company's balance sheet. Aristotle's "golden mean" – not too much, not too little – seems to be the best approach for most companies when it comes to debt.

Buying back shares

Another way a company can increase earnings is through buying back its own shares. Although there are good reasons to buy back shares (see

Chapter 3), some companies might do it simply to increase earnings. Here's how it's done:

	BEFORE BUYBACK	AFTER BUYBACK
INCOME	$50,000	$50,000
MINUS COST	-40,000	-40,000
EARNINGS	$10,000	$10,000
NUMBER OF SHARES	500	250
EPS	$20.00	$40.00

Figure 14-2

Notice the revenues, costs, and earnings did not change. The only thing that did change was a reduction in the number of shares outstanding from 500 to 250. Thus, there were fewer shares in which to spread a fixed amount of earnings, causing the EPS to increase. In other words, financial engineering caused the increase in EPS, not all the other things investors like to see such as an increase in sales and a reduction in expenses. Also, beware, buybacks tend to increase the company's debt ratio and thus might increase financial risk.

Clues to a Company's Future Prospects?

I showed you some ways a company's management can fiddle with earnings. Now let's look at some signals management, intentionally or unintentionally, might be sending to shareowners about the future prospects for the company. Do your homework first and exercise caution with these "signals."

Using dividends as a signal

Paying a cash dividend requires having – you guessed it – cash on hand. Cash is generated from what's left over from sales after costs have been deducted. When a company increases its cash dividend, especially by a significant amount and coupled with an increase in earnings, management is indicating that future earnings should be great enough to continue making those increased cash dividend payments in the foreseeable future. And since the company's management is closest to knowing how well earnings are likely to be in the future, an increase in dividends generally is a signal that the future is bright.

Companies are very careful when they increase dividends. They want to make sure future earnings will be sufficient to maintain that increase, since a reduction is generally accepted as a sign that sales aren't going well or expenses are getting out of hand, and thus there is less cash available to make the cash payment. If a company reduces or eliminates a dividend, especially if they have been paying it for a number of years, generally the stock's price will take a big hit. As an investor, you might want to pay attention to changes in a company's payout ratio, which is annual dividends divided by EPS. An increase in that ratio might be a cause for further evaluation on your part.

Using stock splits as a signal

A stock split is seen by some as a signal that the company earnings will continue to grow as least as fast as they did before split. After all, it was that growth rate that necessitated the split in the first place.

In addition, when a stock splits, the share price goes down by the amount of the split. That might induce other investors who couldn't afford the higher price to buy the stock. Tim Cook, CEO of Apple, said as much in April 2014 when Apple split its stock 7 for 1: "We're taking this action to make Apple stock more accessible to a larger number of investors."

Using stock purchases and sales by management as a signal

It's illegal for insiders to trade on information that has not been made public first. However, laws have been established by which a company's senior executives, directors, and others can buy and sell their company's stock if, and it is a big *if*, they follow the government rules. If they don't, they go to jail. And they should. However, most people would agree that senior executives, directors and others should have a stake in the company's results and therefore should own their company's stock.

Since an insider must report trading activity in a timely fashion, and since some think that insiders are in the best position to know what's going on within the company, some investors like to follow their lead – buy when they buy and sell when they sell. If you want to go this route it makes sense to pay attention to who is doing the trading and how much is being traded and how often. The chief executive officer and the chief financial officer seem to be the best people to watch, buys are better than sells, and many trades of size are better than small infrequent ones. There are plenty of internet-based websites that are more than willing to provide you with their analysis for a fee. Just realize there can be a long time-lag between when senior management made their trades and when you get the data.

Now we move into the second part of this chapter – a discussion of valuation models.

The Hunt for Intrinsic Value

When you strip everything away, active stock selection is pretty straightforward, at least conceptually. Being successful at it? Well, that's another matter. *All* you have to do is find a wonderful company whose stock is a "bargain" and then wait until everyone else realizes it and they start buying, thus driving the price higher. Then, when that "bargain" stock become overpriced, you sell and pocket the rewards. In other words, "buy low, sell high."

While buying low and selling high is something all active investors strive to achieve, what is low and what is high, and over what time frame should they be measured? High and low are relative terms. Consider tall and short, also relative terms. A six-foot football player is tall relative to a five-foot soccer player but short relative to a seven-foot basketball player. High and low also depend on the time frame. An acorn is "low" relative to a bush, but after several years the oak tree will tower over the bush.

Therefore, we need a standard against which to measure stocks if we want to know if they are cheap or expensive. Enter intrinsic value. The Merriam-Webster dictionary defines intrinsic as, "Belonging to the essential nature of a thing." For example, if your next-door neighbor is selling his old computer for $100, you look at it and think, "I could sell the parts for $200." To you, the intrinsic value (in other words, the essential value) of that old computer is $200. But someone else might think the intrinsic value of the parts is only $75 and that they will be worth even less as time goes by. Who's right? Only time will tell.

Therefore, the intrinsic value of a company and, by extension, its stock is often in the eye of the beholder and depends on the length of time the investment is to be held. Sure, we might be able to look at all kinds of historical financial reports and that will give us a clue as to intrinsic value. That's great. But because the stock market is always forward looking, we must consider the future, and that involves a host of intangibles such as the skill of the company's management, the staying power of the company's brand-name recognition in a changing environment, and the lifespan of the company's proprietary technology – to name a few things.

It's a challenging endeavor, but that does not stop people from looking for profitable trades. Active managers and other investors have developed an almost endless number of methods or valuation models to estimate their perception of intrinsic value. Although these models range from the very sophisticated to the most straightforward, many use the results of fundamental analysis (the things I discussed in the first half of this chapter) as input in their hunt for intrinsic value.

A straightforward model

A straightforward model involves a three-step process: (1) forecast a stock's EPS; (2) forecast the stock's price-earnings ratio (PE); and (3) multiply the two together. The resulting number is an estimate of value that is then compared to the stock's current price in order to make buy, hold, and sell decisions.

Sounds easy, but it's not. A wide variety of tools can be used to forecast EPS, from the simplest, such as trend-lining EPS (drawing a line through a plot of historical EPSs to forecast the future), to the more complex, such as assessing

> *"Just when you think you've discovered the key to the market, some S.O.B. comes along and changes the lock." – G. M. Loeb*

the company's future earnings using the tools and methods I described in the first part of this chapter. Similarly, a wide variety of tools can also be used to forecast the PE ratio from the simplest, such as using an historical average, to the more complex, such as using behavioral theory (how investors feel about the prospect for the future growth of EPS).

A multitude of books and many, many theories have been offered about how to determine the inputs to this straightforward model. One book that is a classic and discusses the subject, and another good book to add to your investment library, is entitled *The Intelligent Investor: The Definitive Book on Value Investing* by Benjamin Graham, revised edition.

Dividend discount valuation model

The logic of this model is captured in an old Wall Street saying: "A chicken for its eggs; a stock for its dividends." I know it sounds silly, but stop and think about it. What is the main thing to consider when assessing the intrinsic value of a live chicken if not its future production of eggs? What is the main thing to consider when assessing the intrinsic value of a stock if not for its future dividends?

Let me explain. Presumably Investor A buys a stock for its future dividends and the chance of price appreciation. Figure 14-3 is a diagram showing the investor's thought process. An up arrow is the money the investor pays for the stock and the down arrows are the dividends the investor receives and the money from an eventual sale.

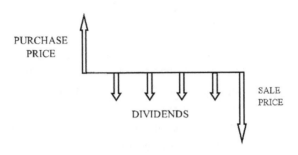

Figure 14-3

After holding the stock for a while, Investor A sells it to investor B who in turn eventually sells it to investor C and so on. The sale price could have resulted in a profit or a loss. In this example, it doesn't matter (see Figure 14-4).

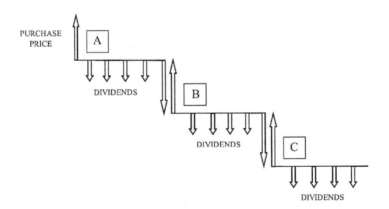

Figure 14-4

Ignoring transaction costs, the sale prices are equal to the purchase prices, and thus cancel each other out. Therefore, we can represent the purchase of a stock as a long line of future dividends (see Figure 14-5).

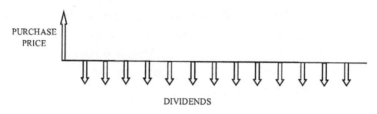

Figure 14-5

If we can forecast that future stream of dividends, we can apply mathematical time value of money concepts to calculate the stock's intrinsic value. I covered compounding in Chapter 1, but now I am going apply that concept in reverse. But to recap first, compounding involves earning interest on your money and interest on your interest. For example, you loan the bank $1,000 and in return they have promised to pay you 9% each year for the use of your money. As you saw in Figure 1-1, and again in Figure 14-6, the $1,000 grew to $5,604.41 in 20 years. In other words, the $5,604.41 is the future value of $1,000 invested for 20 years at a 9% interest rate.

YEAR	BEGINNING OF THE YEAR (A)	ANNUAL INTEREST EARNED (B)=(A)x9%	ACCUMULATED INTEREST (C)=SUM OF (B)	END OF YEAR (D)=(A) = (B)
1	1000.00	90.00	90.00	1090.00
2	1090.00	98.10	188.10	1188.10
3	1188.10	106.93	295.03	1295.03
4	1295.03	116.55	411.58	1411.58
5	1411.58	127.04	538.62	1538.62
10	2171.89	195.47	1367.36	2367.36
15	3341.73	300.76	2642.48	3642.48
20	5141.66	462.75	4604.41	5604.41

Figure 14-6

The present value of money concept is the reverse. That is, the present value of $5,604.41 in 20 years at a 9% discount rate is $1,000.00. When we try to find the present value, instead of using the term "interest rate," we use the term "discount rate" since we are bringing a future amount of money back to its present value. We are "discounting" the future value to a present value at a given discount rate.

Our task then is to bring all those future cash dividends you saw in Figure 14-5 back to a present value. Then, when we add them all up, we will have the intrinsic value of that stock. It's not easy to forecast those dividend payments, so let's simplify the problem. Let's assume the cash dividend doesn't change and is $5 all those years. Now, let's look at the discount rate. In Chapter 7 we discussed risk, that is, we need to be compensated if we are taking a greater risk. One way to reflect that in this example is to assume a higher discount rate for riskier investments and a lower discount rate for less risky investments. We do our analysis and find 10% is a reasonable rate that will compensate us for the risk we are taking with this particular stock investment. We'll also assume the rate is fixed for the entire time period.

With those assumptions, we can discount those dividends to a present value and add them all up to get our estimate of intrinsic value. Mathematically that translates into the simple formula shown in Figure 14-7.

$$\text{Intrinsic Value} = \frac{\text{Dividend}}{\text{Discount Rate}}$$

Figure 14-7

Plugging in our assumptions and completing the calculations, the intrinsic value of our stock is $50.00 (see Figure 14-8).

Given:

Dividend $=$ $5.00

Discount Rate $=$ 10%

Therefore:

$$\text{Intrinsic Value} = \frac{\$5.00}{.10}$$

$$\text{Intrinsic Value} = \$50.00$$

Figure 14-8

If we see the stock is currently selling for, say $60.00 per share, and if we were confident in our assumptions that resulted in an intrinsic value of $50, we would not buy the stock. It's too highly priced.

Now let's change our assumptions and assume dividends will grow 5% every year. So for the first year the dividend is $5.00. The next year it grows 5%, so it is $5.25. The next year it grows another 5% and becomes $5.51, and so forth. Fortunately, we have a formula that will translate all this for us (see Figure 14-9).

$$\text{Intrinsic Value} = \frac{\text{Dividend}}{\text{Discount Rate} - \text{Growth Rate in Dividends}}$$

Figure 14-9

Plugging in our assumptions and completing the calculations, the intrinsic value of our stock is $100.00 (see Figure 14-10).

Given:

Dividend = $5.00

Discount Rate = 10%

Expected Growth Rate = 5%

Therefore:

$$\text{Intrinsic Value} = \frac{\$5.00}{.10 - .05}$$

$$\text{Intrinsic Value} = \$100.00$$

NOTE: The discount rate needs to be higher than the expected growth rate in dividends or the results are meaningless.

Figure 14-10

Now, if we were confident in our assumptions that resulted in an intrinsic value of $100, we might consider buying the stock. The stock is cheaper than what we calculated its intrinsic value to be.

So, what is the stock really worth, $50 or $100? It depends on our assumptions. However, I think you would agree that dividends probably won't grow at a constant rate and neither will the discount rate remain the same through the years. Now

> *Always build a margin of safety into your forecasts.*

what do you do? Forecast the best you can and calculate the present value year by year out to wherever you feel comfortable, then estimate a terminal value for the stock (a sales price) and bring all that back to the present value. The calculations aren't hard now that you have the framework, and a computer will do all the work. The hardest part is making all the estimates of dividends and the discount rate, and small changes in these values can have a major impact on the results.

Some like to conduct an evaluation using different scenarios such as using the yield to maturity curve (see Chapter 24) plus a risk factor for insights into the discount rate and then using earnings projections and payout rates for the size of the future dividends. Other investment managers have different techniques. Your stock broker's database might even have its a version of the results of its own dividend discount model.

Valuation Ratios

Earlier in the chapter I covered profitability ratios. Now is the time to look at valuation ratios. You can easily identify valuation ratios because one of the two variables will be the stock's price. The same cautions about ratios that I outlined earlier also apply here. All the terms are expressed on a per share basis.

Price-to-earnings ratio (PE)

PE equals the stock's price divided by earnings. If the earnings for two companies are similar, this ratio will tell you how enthusiastic investors are about the future earnings prospect of each. The larger the PE the more enthusiasm and the higher the stock's price. Be careful, however, because investor enthusiasm can deflate as quickly as it can expand. Like all ratios, this one should not be viewed in isolation.

PE-to-growth ratio (PEG)

PEG equals the stock's PE ratio divided by the stock's expected earnings growth rate. This ratio's purpose is to see if the enthusiasm reflected in the PE ratio is supported by future earnings expectations. In other words, whether the enthusiasm is warranted. If the ratio is greater than one, investor's might be too enthusiastic and the stock might be overvalued. Less than one, perhaps investors are not enthusiastic enough and the stock might be undervalued. At least that's the theory.

A variation of the PEG ratio is called the Dividend-Adjusted PEG ratio. For this ratio, the stock's divided yield is added to the expected earnings growth rate (dividend yield is the stock's annual dividend divided by the stock's price). This is done to put dividend-paying stocks on an equivalent basis with stocks that pay little or no dividends.

Both PEG ratios are often calibrated to the market's PEG ratio thus becoming a relative measure.

Price-to-sales ratio (PS)

PS equals the stock's price divided by sales. This is a measure of how highly investors value a company's sales. It is a go-to ratio when earnings are negative. A declining PS ratio might be an indication of a stock that is becoming increasingly cheaper or a company whose sales are about to drop. Thus, it is important to understand what is driving sales. To gain further insight, some investors like to conduct a price-to-sales analysis using the number of units sold instead of dollars.

Price-to-book ratio (PB)

PB equals the stock's price divided by its book value. A value below one might indicate an undervalued stock. But that's not always the case, because investors may value the stocks in one sector-industry group differently than the stocks in another sector-industry group. That is why you should compare the PB ratio for a stock not only to its history but also to its sector or industry group.

Dividend-to-price ratio (DP)

DP equals the stock's annual dividend divided by the stock's price. Often investors like to compare this rate to alternative investments such as bonds. A sudden and large increase in this ratio that is caused by a decline in the stock's price might be a signal the company is ready to cut dividends. Also, as with all ratios, be sure you measure the results of this ratio against similar stocks and industries.

Selling

The decision to sell is often one of the most stressful decisions investors faces. Although I advocate investing for the long term, things can change; a company's fundamentals might be deteriorating or it might be losing its competitive edge. But sell decisions are often filled with emotions that tend to stop or delay an investor from acting. Since emotions play such a major role in investment decisions, I have devoted Chapter 22 to the topic.

> *"Price is what you pay; value is what you get." – Warren Buffett*

APPENDIX A

BALANCE SHEET			
	As of September 30, 2017	September 24, 2016	CHANGE
ASSETS:			
Current assets:			
Cash and cash equivalents	20,289	20,484	
Short-term marketable securities	53,892	46,671	
Accounts receivable	17,874	15,754	
Inventories	4,855	2,132	
Other current assets	31,735	21,828	
Total current assets	128,645	106,869	20.4%
Long-term marketable securities	194,714	170,430	14.2%
Property, plant and equipment, net	33,783	27,010	25.1%
Goodwill	5,717	5,414	
Other non-current assets	12,460	11,963	
Total assets	375,319	321,686	16.7%
LIABILITIES			
Current liabilities:			
Accounts payable	49,049	37,294	
Accrued expenses	25,744	22,027	
Other current liabilities	26,021	19,685	
Total current liabilities	100,814	79,006	27.6%
Long-term debt	97,207	75,427	28.9%
Other non-current liabilities	43,251	39,004	10.9%
Total liabilities	241,272	193,437	24.7%
SHAREHOLDERS' EQUITY:			
Common stock and additional paid-in capital	35,867	31,251	14.8%
Retained earnings	98,330	96,364	2.0%
Accumulated other comprehensive income	(150)	634	
Total shareholders' equity	134,047	128,249	4.5%
	======	======	
Total liabilities and shareholders' equity	375,319	321,686	16.7%

APPENDIX B

INCOME STATEMENT

For the entire year ending	September 30, 2017		September 24, 2016		Change
Net sales	229,234		215,639		6.3%
Cost of sales	(141,048)		(131,376)		
Gross margin		88,186		84,263	4.7%
Operating expenses:					
Research and development	11,581		10,045		
Selling, general and admin.	15,261		14,194		
Total operating expenses		(26,842)		(24,239)	
Operating income		**61,344**		**60,024**	2.2%
Other income/(expense), net	2,745		1,348		
Income before income taxes		64,089		61,372	
Provision for income taxes	(15,738)		15,685		
Net income		**48,351**		**45,687**	5.8%
Earnings per share:					
Basic		9.27		8.35	11.0%
Diluted		9.21		8.31	10.8%
Cash dividends per share		2.40		2.18	10.1%

APPENDIX C

CASH FLOW		
For the entire year ending	Sept. 30, 2017	Sept. 24, 2016
OPERATING ACTIVITIES:		
Net income	48,351	45,687
Adjustments:		
Depreciation and amortization	10,157	10,505
Share-based compensation expense	4,840	4,210
Deferred income tax expense	5,966	4,938
Other	(166)	486
Changes in operating assets and liabilities:		
Accounts receivable, net	(2,093)	527
Inventories	(2,723)	217
Vendor non-trade receivables	(4,254)	(51)
Other current and non-current assets	(5,318)	1,055
Accounts payable	9,618	1,837
Deferred revenue	(626)	(1,554)
Other current and non-current liabilities	(154)	(2,033)
Cash generated by operating activities	63,598	65,824
INVESTING ACTIVITIES:		
Purchases of marketable securities	(159,486)	(142,428)
Proceeds from maturities of marketable securities	31,775	21,258
Proceeds from sales of marketable securities	94,564	90,536
Payments made in business acquisitions, net	(329)	(297)
Payments to acquire property, plant, and equipment	(12,451)	(12,734)
Payments to acquire intangible assets	(344)	(814)
Payments for strategic investments, net	(395)	(1,388)
Other	220	(110)
Cash used in investing activities	(46,446)	(45,977)
FINANCING ACTIVITES:		
Proceeds from issuance of common stock	555	495
Excess tax benefits from equity awards	627	407
Payments for taxes settlement of equity awards	(1,874)	(1,570)
Payments for dividends and dividend equivalents	(12,769)	(12,150)
Repurchases of common stock	(32,900)	(29,722)
Proceeds from issuance of term debt, net	28,662	24,954
Repayments of term debt	(3,500)	(2,500)
Change in commercial paper, net	3,852	(397)
Cash used in financing activities	(17,347)	(20,483)
Increase/(Decrease) in cash and cash equivalents	(195)	(636)
Cash and cash equivalents, end of the year	20,289	20,484

CHAPTER 15

Passive Management

You won't see a large staff or much activity inside a passive management firm. The stocks and their quantities have been determined by an outside committee and much of the work to maintain an index fund has been computerized. This is one of many reasons these firms can charge so little for their services, in some cases nearly zero.

In this chapter I will define tracking error, outline how an index fund manager attempts to minimize it, and go through the mathematics of creating a capitalization-weighted index fund.

Not all index funds are created and managed the way outlined in this chapter. But at least this will give you an overview of what is going on inside many passive investment management firms.

Managing an Index Fund

It's your job to pick the index, and it's the investment manager's job to minimize the index fund's tracking error. As defined in Chapter 12, tracking error is the difference between the performance of the paper index created by a committee and the performance of the portfolio of stocks assembled by an investment manager. Tracking error can come from the construction of the index itself, committee activity, uninvested cash, fees and expenses, and poor investment management decisions.

Construction of the index itself

The frequency of rebalancing, and the accompanying drag on performance because of transactions costs, is often driven by how the index is constructed. For example, a capitalization-weighted index, such as the S&P 500, is relatively self-balancing despite changes in the market price of the stocks in the index as well as the occurrence of such corporate events as stock splits or reverse splits. This is because the stock's weight in an index fund changes automatically with the stock's weight in the paper index. Other things might cause minor rebalancing, but still, this relatively self-balancing feature is why many index funds are capitalization weighted. Other weighting schemes can require frequent rebalancing and hence can incur substantial transaction costs and therefore greater tracking error.

Committee activity

From time to time a committee will drop a company from the index and add a new one and that activity will require the index fund to rebalance. For example, in 2018 General Electric was dropped from the DJIA and was replaced by the Walgreen Company. General Electric had been in the index for 110 years, but in the past few years has fallen on hard times. Many index funds held stock in GE – some thousands of shares and others hundreds of thousands of shares. Thus, the simultaneous sale of the dropped company and the purchase of the added name by these index funds can have a dramatic impact on tracking error. Generally, an index committee will make some accommodations through various means to mitigate the impact.

Uninvested cash

Because the paper index does not hold cash, any cash that is held for any reason in an index fund can either help or hurt tracking error. This is called "cash drag," because excess cash can drag performance down when the stocks are going up, or can bolster (or drag up) performance up when stocks are going down. This is due to the stable value of cash as opposed to ever changing stock prices. Most passive managers will do whatever they can to avoid holding cash, but sometimes it is unavoidable.

Cashflows in an index fund come from two main sources – receipt of cash dividends and investor activity.

Dividends: A delay in the reinvestment of cash dividends can be a major cause of cash drag. Fortunately, as noted in Chapter 3, the size of a dividend is known days in advance of its receipt thus passive managers can plan for their almost instantaneous reinvestment. But the dividend cash inflows still need to be invested and thus incur transaction costs.

Investor activity: The timing of cash inflows from new investors and the outflows from existing investors who wish to leave the index fund are largely out of the control of the passive manager. The greater the in/out activity, the greater the possibility of cash drag if, on a daily basis, the inflows and outflows don't offset each other. If they don't, transaction costs will be incurred either by having to buy additional shares when the flow is positive or having to sell shares when the flow is negative. These costs are somewhat mitigated thorough the use of futures, a topic for someone else's book.

Fees and expenses

There are administrative expenses, custodial fees, licensing fees, and especially management fees that are also deducted from the performance of the portfolio and thus contribute to tracking error.

Poor investment management decisions

All investment managers are not the same. Some are outstanding, others excellent, and still others only fair. Although much of passive management is determined by an outside committee and is computerized, investment managers still make decisions that can impact tracking error.

How an Index Fund Is Created

In Chapter 5, I covered the construction of indices that were designed to measure the performance of the stock market. Passive management then takes that information one step further and creates a portfolio of stocks that is designed to track that index. If you are mathematically inclined, here's how you create a four-stock index fund from a paper index that is capitalization-weighted.

> **Step one:** Compute the market-cap for each stock in the paper index by multiplying the stock's price by the number of shares outstanding,
>
> **Step two:** Add all the market-caps,
>
> **Step three:** Divide each individual market-cap by the total to find their percentage of the total,
>
> **Step four:** Multiply a stock's percentage of the total by the money that is to be invested, and finally,
>
> **Step five:** Divide the money allocated to each stock by that stock's market price to determine how many shares to buy.

Voila, you have just created an index fund – a portfolio of stock designed to track the risk and return characteristics of the paper index (see Figure 15-1). Now you have to minimize tracking error going forward.

COMPANY	PRICE PER SHARE	SHARES OUTSTANDING	MARKET-CAP	PERCENT OF TOTAL	DOLLARS TO INVEST	SHARES TO BUY
(A)	(B)	(C)	(D)=(B)x(C)	(E)=(D)÷(1)	(F)=(1)x(2)	(G)=(F)÷(B)
A	50	1000	50000	25.97	25974.03	519
B	15	1500	22500	11.69	11688.30	779
C	45	2000	90000	46.75	46753.25	1039
D	10	3000	30000	15.58	15584.42	1558
			192500	100.00	100000.00	

(1) TOTAL MARKET CAPTIALIZATION
(2) DOLLARS TO INVEST = $100,000

Figure 15-1

Managing an index fund is not difficult; picking the appropriate one to invest in is.

CHAPTER 16

Factor-Based Management

Rather than search for the intrinsic value of an individual stock, the "factor people" are searching for groups of stocks that possess a common factor that, if assembled into in a portfolio, would provide greater than a market return. But how are the searches conducted? I will discuss that in this chapter. Then I'll finish with a discussion of the most popular factors – value, profitability, quality, size, momentum, reversal, and low volatility.

How Factors are Identified?

Let's assume that you want to become a factor-based investment manager. Here's how you might go about your search for a money-making factor.

State a theory

You need to identify and state a theory that this factor, if emphasized in a portfolio of stocks, will outperform another portfolio of stock that doesn't emphasize that factor. The theory should be one that makes intuitive sense.

Identify a proxy

Because it is often impossible to capture the factor directly across many different types of companies, you need to identify a proxy – something that represents the characteristic of the factor that is to be evaluated. For example, if your theory is that the stocks of small companies outperform the stocks of large companies, then the most obvious choice for a proxy (but not the only one) is market capitalization. But what if your theory involves sorting companies by vague terms such as "value or quality?" Then how a factor is defined becomes an issue.

A logical place for you to look for a proxy is in the company's financial reports. These reports are published periodically and are captured by various computer databases. Because of generally accepted accounting principles, the terms used in these financial statements are similar across companies. Clearly, the numbers are different, but the terms are similar. The studies that use historical data, and their results, are often called data-driven.

Select a universe

You need to decide what universe of stocks to use in your study. It could be the 500 stocks in the S&P 500 index or the over 4,000 stocks in the marketplace, or anything else in between. Generally, financial stocks and other stocks are excluded for various reasons.

Since your study will span many decades, your results could be biased if the study focused on only those companies that survived and didn't include the negative impact of those that went bankrupt along the way. You need to include them if you want to avoid what is called survivorship bias.

Decide on a study time frame

You need to decide how far back in time your study should go. Clearly, the limiting factor is how far back you have reliable data. But there are other considerations as well. For example, some might argue that the environment has changed dramatically over time and therefore you shouldn't go too far back. Others might argue that you should go back as far as you can, because if the factor holds over all these different environments, it is more likely to hold over whatever the future may bring. The study time frame you pick will have a huge impact on your results and has the potential of turning a "profitable" factor into a loser, or vice versa.

Conduct the study

You begin this step by calculating the proxy value for each company in the study universe followed by ranking the results beginning with the stock that had the most exposure to the proxy first and continuing down the list to the stock that had the least exposure. The proxy numbers would then be standardized and the list divided into quartiles, quintiles, deciles, or some other division signifying the different degrees of exposure to the factor.

Now you need to create portfolios of stocks from each of those divisions and to compute the performance of each portfolio. In computing performance, you need to decide how to weight the performance of each stock in each portfolio. You could average the individual stock's returns, capitalization-weight them, or use some other weighting method I outlined in Chapter 5. The method you use is very important because it, like the selection of the universe and the study time frame, can dramatically change the results.

Since your study spans years and perhaps decades, and since stock prices and financial data changes over that time period, you must periodically rebalance the portfolios so they remain true to your theory and your study criteria. Some financial data is available quarterly and others annually, and that often determines the interval of rebalancing. It is wise to have the financial data lag a certain period of time to avoid look-ahead bias (using data that were not known or readily available to market participants at the time).

It is at these rebalancing intervals that stocks can move between portfolios and quantities held can change. Therefore, your study should account for transaction costs as a "drag" on performance. If you don't account for all transaction costs you might have a factor that provided great paper returns only to find out it fails dramatically in the real world when they are included.

The performance after transaction costs for each portfolio during each interval would be calculated and linked to give a study period return for each quartile, quintile, decile, or other division that was used to signifying the different degrees of exposure to the factor.

You now need to make sure the performance truly isolates the effect of the studied factor and doesn't reflect aggregate market movements. There are several ways to do this that I will leave to you to explore. Then you would subtract the return of the portfolio that had the least exposure to the factor from the return of the portfolio that had the greatest exposure and apply some statistical measures to the results. That difference is the return from the factor. But you're not finished.

Confirm results

Sure, you have some study results, but did they come from data mining, and therefore are just fool's gold? One way to convince yourself that it isn't is to test your theory using data that weren't used in the study. The academics call this out-of-sample testing. This might be data from a different time period or data from international markets. This testing makes the results more rigorous, but remember you're still using historical data that may or may not hold in the future. Regardless how rigorous the results might be, you will still need to exercise caution and not place too much faith in the money-making ability of your newly discovered factor.

Whew! That's a lot of weeds to go through, but I hope it gives you a general idea how these studies are conducted. You need to know this so you can ask intelligent questions about how the factor was identified before you invest in it.

Below are some factors that have found their way into stock portfolios. Many studies have been conducted, some that contradict others. Rather than going through every one with their pros and cons, I will just cut to the chase and give you my opinion based on my own less-than-perfect observations. If you want to explore the ins and outs, contradictory theories, or other details, you can do so by searching the internet for the specific factor.

Value Factor

Theory: Value stocks outperform growth stocks over the long term.

A value stock has been defined as one whose share price is low relative to some financial measure such as price-earnings ratio, book value, dividends, and/or sales. Something has happened to the company to make its stock sell at what seems to be a depressed price when compared to the financial measure – bad luck, questionable management, a temporary decline in the demand for the company's products, or irregular earnings, to name a few. In other words, the stock's price is cheap because the company is perceived to be in distress, its future earnings are in doubt, and investors are looking elsewhere. Often the stock's price becomes even cheaper because of the irrationality of investors who dump the stock regardless of the price.

The question is: Who would want to buy the stock of a company that looks like it's going down the tubes? The answer might surprise you. Me – if I thought the things that caused the decline had a chance of turning around. If the company's prospects improve, I would have bought a stock at a price that would be recognized later as a bargain. The people who buy these types of stocks are called "value investors."

To get a complete view of the value factor, however, we have to discuss their opposite, the so-called growth stocks or, as some like to call them, glamour stocks. These stocks are the darlings of the market. Their share prices are high relative to earnings, book value, and sales. Frequently these stocks do not pay dividends and prefer instead to reinvest the money they earned back into the business so it can grow even faster with better products or services. They command higher prices for a variety of reasons – good luck, great management decisions, increased demand for the company's product line, and increased earnings.

So, who would buy a growth stock? Me – if I was confident that the company had a good chance at becoming even bigger and better in the future and I could buy it at a fair price.

The problem is that some of these growth companies could be way overpriced as some investors might be engaged in the "greater fool" theory. The logic of the greater fool theory is, "I'm buying this growth stock even though I think these prices are too high because I expect there will be another person who will buy it at an even higher price – the greater fool." People bid up prices higher and higher because they believe the good times will continue to roll and they overestimate the growth prospects, and that sets the stock up for a sharp decline when reality sets in (see Figure 16-1).

Figure 16-1

To test the theory that value stocks outperformed growth stocks, a proxy was needed. Many were tested, and the one that was used in many studies was the price-to-book ratio. As we learned in Chapter 14, the book portion of the ratio is also known as shareowners' equity, which in turn is simply the difference between a company's assets and its liabilities. Share price is then divided by the book value per share to get the ratio, price-to-book (see Figure 16-2).

$$\frac{\text{Price to}}{\text{Book}} = \frac{\text{Share Price}}{\text{Book Value per Share}}$$

Figure 16-2

If the price-to-book ratio for a company was below 1.0, the stock would be considered a value stock candidate. If the number was above 1.0, the stock would be considered to be a growth stock candidate.

So how much extra money can you get by investing in a portfolio of value stocks instead of a portfolio of growth stocks when using the price-to-book ratio as a proxy for value? Easy question to ask, not so easy to answer.

It depends on the study time frame and the methods used in the study. But at least over certain periods, especially very long periods of time, the place to be was in value stocks, not growth stocks. But if you were looking for a sure thing with the value factor, or any of the other factors, you'll be disappointed. Over the past decade or so value stocks have had a rough time. Does that mean value investing is dead? Some say no, it's just the environment we were in with low interest rates and a slow economy that favored growth stocks. The worrying aspect however, is the bandwagon effect I discussed earlier. A lot of money has been allocated to the value factor, thus possibly diminishing its prospects for a higher than growth stock returns.

Profitability Factor

Theory: Highly profitable companies outperform other companies over the long term.

Doesn't every investor want to buy the stock of a company that is profitable or likely to be and whose current stock price doesn't fully reflect that fact? But how does one identify these types of companies? In other words, what proxy should we use in our analysis to measure profitability?

As you recall in Chapter 14, when we started our search for a company's "true" profitability, we had to scrape the barnacles off reported earnings. That is, any items such as income from pension assets, litigation expenses and settlements, and asset sales – anything that was not directly related to the company's money-making ability – was subtracted from net income. This was the approach used by many to come up with a proxy for profitability. Others tried using cash flow as a proxy. Some took a different tack and combined items from both the income statement and the balance sheet.

Many proxies were tested, but one that seemed to work well was identified by Professor Robert Novy-Marx, University of Rochester. It is called the gross profitability-to-assets ratio. It is revenues minus the cost of goods sold divided by assets (see Figure 16-3). The results of his work can be easily found on the internet.

$$\text{Gross Profitability to Assets} = \frac{\text{Revenues - Cost of Goods}}{\text{Assets}}$$

Figure 16-3)

Notice this proxy does not include share price. Rather, it is a measure of how well a company maximizes the return on its assets. If a company is successful at doing this, it is said to be a profitable one and, so the reasoning goes, that should lead to higher stock prices.

His study results showed that, over time, the stock of companies with the highest gross profitability-to-assets ratio outperformed those with the lowest ratio. As a bonus, further research indicated that you can achieve even better returns when you combine the profitability factor with the value factor. The idea was that although the price-to-book ratio tells you how cheaply you can buy assets, profitability tells you how productive those assets were.

Was the money tree discovered? If it was, it might be gone by now. This information is in the public domain and other investment managers undoubtedly hopped on the bandwagon and might have driven any extra returns to zero. But who knows? Time will tell.

Quality Factor

Theory: High quality companies outperform other companies over the long term.

Buying the shares of quality companies and holding them for the long-term has always been the goal of many active investors. Warren Buffett: "It's far better to buy a wonderful company at a fair price than a fair company at a wonderful price." In other words, buy and hold quality. But the problem for academics has been how to identify quality companies whose stock is selling at a reasonable price using financial data. It's a thorny area that is open to data mining.

Professor Robert Novy-Marx appears to have a reasonable answer with his mixture of two factors, value and profitability. Value provides a reasonable price and profitability a quality company.

But others think quality is a combination of a company's profitability, financial safety, and quality of earnings. Here are some of the financial measures that apply to these three areas. For profitability, some measures are gross profitability divided by assets, ROA, ROE, and operating profits. For financial safety, some measures are debt to assets, current assets to current liabilities, and interest coverage. For quality of earnings, some measures are volatility of ROA, volatility of earnings, and size of cash flow. Identifying these variables is the easy part; combining them into a portfolio of stocks is the difficult part. For example, how much weight should be given to their alleged individual importance. Some say that because of all the alternatives (I've listed ten here and there are many more), the search for quality using financial data is open to data mining. Moreover, just changing the weight given to one of these variables changes the results.

Depending on the variables used and the study time period selected, excess return from quality has had extended periods of poor performance. A common-sense reason for these fluctuations in performance is that investors engage in a flight to quality when the economy is in a downturn and market conditions are bleak (risk off). When the economy is booming and market conditions look bright, investors seek riskier stocks (risk on).

Size Factor

Theory: Small-cap companies outperform large-cap companies over the long term.

What do Facebook, Starbucks, and Apple have in common – or for that matter, Microsoft, and Wal-Mart? Answer: They all started out as small companies.

Small-cap companies have a great story to tell. Because of their size, they have a much greater opportunity to grow at a faster pace than larger companies. For example, a 25% increase in earnings seems more doable for a small company than for a large one, and that faster growth rate attracts investors who are hoping it will translate into faster increases in stock prices. At least that's the allure. But like everything else in investing, there are risks. Because of their lack of financial muscle and staying power, many small companies go bankrupt during hard times or become part of the living dead.

Earlier academic studies suggested that small-cap stocks outperformed large-cap stocks by a significant amount over the long-term. So far so good. But, to have any investment value, those academic study results have to be translatable into a portfolio of actual small-cap stocks, and here's where those studies ran into trouble. Although the research itself was not called into question, the ability to be translated into an actual portfolio of stocks was. You see, the best performing group was in very small-cap stocks – stocks in the $2 million to $5 million cap size – and these really small companies trade only a few thousand shares a day, if they even trade on a daily basis at all. To get any reasonable liquidity you have to move up to larger companies and, when you do, the return from the small-cap factor might go down.

So, what to do? A number of investment managers simply dropped the smallest-cap stocks from the study universe and re-ran the study. Others used sampling techniques in an attempt to capture the ultra-small-cap return. While these changes were a departure from the initial study, investment managers who are currently managing small-cap portfolios still believe returns are sufficient enough to exceed the returns from large-cap stocks.

Others have combined factors to increase returns. You can't look at a set of managers without seeing some other factor combined with small-cap stocks. The more popular combinations are small-cap value and small-cap growth. You might think that the combination of small-cap and value is a sure-fire winning combination. Often it is, but not always. A few years ago, the performance resulting from a combination of small-cap and growth far exceeded the performance of a combination of small-cap and value, because small-cap growth contained a large number of biotech stocks that performed exceptionally well at the time.

The bottom line is small-cap investing does seem to add some value. But, remember, many investment managers are now seeking out small-cap stocks, and that tends to drive prices up so we might end up with a self-fulfilling prophecy: small-cap stocks are popular, and that popularity drives prices higher which, in turn, increases their popularity, until the greater fool theory kicks in and eventually a sharp decline occurs.

Momentum Factor

*Theory: Stocks with strong price trends outperform stocks
with weak price trends over the long term.*

Momentum investing is like a surfer riding a wave. The surfer watches for a wave to build, hops on, and rides its momentum for as long as the wave lasts. While most momentum investors use increasing stock prices over a period of time as the wave they ride, others use earning growth, earnings surprises, sales growth, and relative price strength as their measures.

Before I dig into the nitty-gritty, a point of clarification. Academic researchers like to make a distinction between trend following and momentum. Trend following, which I will cover in Chapter 23, is a form of technical analysis and is a measure of *absolute* performance. To the academics, momentum is a measure of *relative* performance. In other words, all stocks might be declining, but a stock that is going down at a slowed pace is considered to have positive momentum. Likewise, all stocks might be going up, but one that is going up at a faster pace is considered to have positive momentum.

Many studies have been conducted on the price momentum. They all seem to have different ideas of which universe of stocks to use (S&P 500, total market, or in between), how to divide them up into groups (quartiles, quintiles, or deciles), and how long an investor should wait before hopping on the wave (3, 6, or 12 months). Many skip last month's return and calculate the return for the previous eleven months in their studies to avoid look-ahead bias. And how long should you stay on the wave? Here again, studies vary. Some say the momentum stalls after two months; others say six or more months. Therefore, establishing a trading rule to capture this factor can be elusive.

Given these variations, the best that can be said is that momentum appears to exist and can be profitable over the long term if the stock has something else going for it and if transaction costs can be minimized, because this factor requires a lot of buying and selling and, as we know, high turnover is a drag on performance. Finally, and this is especially important if you're trying to select one stock, when momentum reverses it can do so quickly and brutally. Therefore, investing in the momentum factor in a turbulent market might not be such a good idea. Best to wait until volatility is low, which has led some to use a volatility index (VIX) as a timing device (see in Chapter 24).

Reversal Factor

Theory: Stock prices revert to the mean over the long term.

This factor is similar to the momentum factor, but the time horizon is longer, perhaps years before a reversal occurs. Generally, something triggers the start of an upward-trend reversal such as a change in management. But even then, the turnaround does not occur quickly. It takes time before the actions of the company's new management team begin to result in higher earnings growth and then higher stock prices.

The studies of the reversal factor often do not consider the company's fundamentals – book value, earnings, sales, and dividends – but rather concentrate only on the stock's price action. The study results are all over the place with respect to when the reversal occurs, but it appears that a group of stocks that have had very low relative returns over a previous three- to five-year period tend to outperform a group of stocks that have had very high returns over the same time period. The outperformance of the laggards tends to last about three years.

Many like to explain this factor as another example of the concept of reversion to the mean. As it applies to individual stocks, that concept says high-flying stocks don't stay that way forever, or as some investment managers like to say: "Trees don't grow to the sky." At some point, the price of a high-flying stock slows down, declines, and reverts to the average return for the market. With respect to many poor performing stocks however, they may not turn around and move higher to the average market return. They might just keep declining as the company continues its downward slide into bankruptcy. This is where including a company's fundamentals might help.

Low Volatility Factor
Theory: Less risky stocks outperform all other stocks over the long term.

One of the latest rages among academics and investment managers has been the low volatility factor. Basically, it says you can have your cake and eat it too – less risk and higher return. This is heresy to those who believe higher returns can only be had by taking greater risks. But some studies have shown that, yes, you can have higher returns with less risk. As you might expect, lots of money has been flowing into this promise, and it is only a promise since this factor has not been tested over many market conditions in real time.

The low volatility factor calls for assembling a group of stocks that don't go up or down as much as the market, hence the name low volatility. The terms factor managers use in explaining their approaches are captures rates (what percentage of a market gain the low volatility group captures) and participation rates (what percentage of a market decline the low volatility group participates in).

Here's an example. Say the market historically has gone up 30% and down 30% and we have assembled a portfolio of low volatility stocks, we'll call LV, that captures 70% of the market's performance when the market is going up and participates in 60% of the market's decline when the market is going down. In other words, when the market is up 30%, LV is up only 21% and when the market is down -30%, LV is down only -18%. The high volatility group we'll call HV and it fully captures and participates in the market's movement, that is, when the market goes up 30% it goes up 30% and when the market goes do 30% it too goes down 30%.

Let's go further and assume the market is up 30% in year one, down 30% in year two, up 30% in year three, and up again 30% in year four, and we have $100 to invest in both LV and HV portfolios. If you work through the numbers you will find that the LV portfolio was worth $121.00 at the end of year one, $99.22 at the end of year two, $120.06 at the end of year three, and $145.27 at the end of year four. This compares with the HV portfolio that had the following results: $130.00, $91.00, $118.30, and $153.79 respectively for each of the years. So, LV was a winner in years two and three and HV was a winner in years one and four.

So, what does that prove? If we are thinking critically, we could surmise that in a strong long-term up market (my example had three up years and only one down year), the high volatility portfolio probably has the advantage, and in a market that fluctuates, the low volatility portfolio probably has the advantage. In a long-term down market, both would lose with the low volatility portfolio losing the least.

But market direction is not the only thing you have to consider when evaluating this factor. Again, thinking critically, you would realize that participation and capture rates play a critical role in performance results. Vary those rates slightly and the results will change.

Next, you would consider the stocks that were invested in. Some low volatility studies resulted in a concentration in big financial, consumer staples, and health care stocks. Other studies tried to spread sector exposure over a larger number of industries with varying results. Still others found they were overweighed in high dividend-paying stocks, which makes the results sensitive to changes in interest rates.

Continuing with our critical thinking, you would need to know how volatility was defined in these studies. Some used standard deviation of a stock's returns over a previous 12-month period, others used beta. But what about other measures? Should they have been used instead?

Finally, some argued that low volatility is a new-found factor, while others think it is just a combination of the value and size factors. Does that make a difference? Yes, because you have to think about the implications of value and size.

Other Factors

There are many, many other so-called factors left for you to explore. The numbers range in the hundreds. Some of them are: the presidential election cycle effect, January effect, leverage effect, high moat effect, high-dividend yield effect, and earning variability effect. You only need to google the internet.

> *When it comes to factor investing you need to critically evaluate the assumptions that are being made.*

SECTION 5
Delivery Systems

In Sections 2, 3, and 4, I covered active, passive, and factor-based investment approaches in increasing depth. From the chapters on active management, you realized that you could make all the buy, hold, and sell decisions by yourself or you could hire someone to make them for you. With both passive and factor-based approaches you have no such choice. You have to hire an investment manager. There are simply too many stocks to buy and hold.

I have also suggested to you that your investment strategy does not have to be all-or-nothing, but that you should consider one of the approaches – active, passive, or factor-based – to be the focal point. Moreover, by now you should realize that if you don't have the time or the inclination, the passive approach might be best for you.

In this section I am going to give you a detailed look at two delivery systems should you want to hire someone. The two choices are mutual funds and exchange traded funds (ETFs). Both have hundreds of alternatives for you to pick from that cover the range of active, passive, and factor-based investing. I purposely used the words "delivery system" because these systems are not your strategy, but rather a way of implementing your strategy.

CHAPTER 17

Mutual Funds

A mutual fund is like buying a pizza when you don't have enough money to buy one for yourself. You and your friends get together and pool your money. Each person is entitled to as much of the pizza as money they put in. And if you have lots of people contributing, you'll have the money to buy many different varieties. You can place your order any time you want but can only pick up the pizza and pay for it in the late afternoon when the pizzeria is open.

Same thing with a common stock mutual fund. You pool your money with lots of other people and together there is enough money to buy stock in a number of different companies and to hire someone to do the selecting and trading for you. Your share of the profits, as well as the losses and expenses, are based on how much money you put in. You can place an order during the trading day, but it will be priced and delivered only at the end of the trading day.

There are plenty of mutual funds that can be used to implement any of the investment strategies we discussed earlier – active, passive, and factor-based. However, the greatest number are actively managed. So, if your strategy calls for an active manager, this is the place for you to start your search.

In this chapter I will start with an explanation of how mutual funds are created and then I will list the benefits and risks of investing in them. We'll then look at the many ways you can buy a mutual fund and we'll get into the nitty-gritty of how net asset value is calculated. Finally, there will be a discussion of closed-end mutual funds that will lead us to the next chapter on exchange traded funds. But before we leave this chapter, in Appendix A, I will provide you with a list of questions you might consider asking yourself and the mutual fund manager before making an investment.

How Are Mutual Funds Created?

Anyone can start a mutual fund – even you, once you're no longer a minor. All you have to do is meet the regulatory requirements and pay the costs to get started. Sure, the paperwork might appear daunting, but there are firms to help you with that. If you don't want to handle all the back-office work, including accounting, trading, governmental compliance, and client reporting, there are outside firms that can do that for you too. If you don't want to do the marketing, there are firms that will help you with that as well. They will brand your business, create a web presence, and even develop a marketing campaign for you. If all you want to do is select stocks and build a portfolio from your selections, you might become a subadvisor to a pre-established mutual fund. All the alternatives are there if someday you want to start your own mutual fund business – all you need is the money, perseverance, and, of course, talent.

The point I'm making, besides showing you a career opportunity, is entering the mutual fund business is relatively easy. Therefore, you need to do a thorough job of research before you invest in one.

What Are the Benefits of Investing in a Mutual Fund?

Here are the highlights for a typical mutual fund. For specific details you must read the prospectus that the mutual fund manager is required to offer you. The prospectus comes in two forms – statutory and summary. Get both.

Limited involvement in investment decisions

With a mutual fund you'll get a team of people who will do the research and make the buy, sell, and hold decisions on your behalf based on their perception of the opportunities in the ever-changing market environment. I said "limited involvement" because you'll still have to search through the hundreds of funds to find the one whose investment philosophy matches your investment strategy and risk tolerance.

> *"Equity mutual funds are the perfect solution for people who want to own stock without doing their own research." – Peter Lynch*

Exposure to many companies

By investing in a mutual fund you'll have exposure to a lot of different companies consistent with the investment strategy you selected. If you choose active, your exposure will be across those companies the active manager believes have intrinsic value. If you choose passive, your exposure will be across hundreds or perhaps thousands of companies that are in the selected index. If you choose factor-based, it will be across the selected factor's benchmark.

Investment flexibility

You can invest a specific dollar amount and the mutual fund will convert it into units or shares depending on what the particular mutual fund calls them. In this book I will use "units" to distinguish mutual fund investments from common stock investments. When you invest dollars, you will probably end up with fractional units. But that's okay. It won't present a problem when it comes time to redeem them. They call it "redeem" rather than "sell" because you must go to the mutual fund company to execute the transaction.

Truer pricing

Because mutual funds are priced at the end of the trading day, they can use closing prices in the calculation of the price of a unit. Therefore, there are no bid-ask spreads to contend with, nor any premiums and discounts to consider as there would be with an exchange traded fund.

Convenience

Once you've met the minimum required deposit amount, which can be substantial, you can often subsequently invest as little or as much as you like. It is even possible that the minimum required deposit might be waived. If not offered, ask. It can't hurt. With some mutual funds you can also arrange for automatic withdrawals from a checking account and for automatic reinvestment of dividends and capital gains distributions.

Record-keeping and administrative services

The mutual fund will keep track of all purchases and redemptions that were made as well as any dividends that might be received or capital gains earned. They will communicate all of this to you via periodic reports, including end-of-year statements that will help you prepare your income tax returns if you have to file one.

What Are the Risks of Investing in a Mutual Fund?

Not all mutual funds are exposed to the following risks. What I have outlined below are some of the things you should look for when you are reading a mutual fund prospectus.

Restricted time of trading

You can only trade a mutual fund at the end of the trading day when a price has been determined. If you haven't placed your order in a timely fashion, you'll have to wait until the end of the next trading day when a new price is determined. Make sure you check the prospectus for the exact cut-off time for purchases or redemptions. It can vary from mutual fund to mutual fund.

Potentially high acquisition costs

Not all of these fees apply to every mutual fund. You must check the mutual fund's prospectus to see which ones apply to the specific mutual fund you are interested in.

Front-end load: This is a sales commission that gets deducted from the money that you thought would go into your account. For example, if the front-end load is 5% and you hand over $1,000, $50 of that amount (5%) goes to the investment advisor who suggested this mutual fund to you and $950 to goes into your account. Since 5% is taken right off the top, that means the $950 that actually gets invested must earn at least 5.3% for you to break even.

Public offering price (POP): This is a front-end load by another name. It's a fee that is added to the net asset value of the cost of a unit, which then becomes the unit's selling price. Instead of the money going to a salesperson like a regular front-end load, this fee normally goes to the mutual fund and less money finds its way into your account.

Back-end load: This is a fee that you might incur when you redeem your units. The fee has many names – back-end load, redemption fee, or deferred commission. But once again it means money out of your pocket. Often the fee will get reduced each year you remain invested in the mutual fund. For example, if the back-end load is 3% to start, the following year it might be reduced to 2%, then 1% and by the end of the third year it might be zero.

Brokerage commission: If you trade through your broker, a commission might be charged as well. Often the commission is higher than what you would have paid to trade a common stock.

Those on the receiving end of these fees would argue they are justified in charging them: Front-end load compensates the investment advisor for services rendered, public offering price compensates the mutual fund for additional administrative expenses that would have been be borne by existing unit holders, back-end load discourages the cost of in/out trading that would have been borne by the unit holders who do not engage in such activity, and broker commissions compensate the brokerage firm for their work. Perhaps they have a point. But you can avoid some of them by choosing a mutual fund where they don't apply.

Potentially high ongoing annual costs

Management expense ratio: This is what you owe the mutual fund for investment management services and for various administrative expenses. Although the fee is quoted as an annual percentage, it is normally prorated and applied on a daily basis to the value of your investment and is automatically deducted from your account at the end of each day.

Since the fee is calculated as a percentage of the money that is in your account, mutual fund managers like to say: "We make money only if you make money." That sounds nice and comforting, but it's only half true. As the value of the fund goes up, yes, they get paid more. But when the value of the fund goes down, they still make money, albeit less, while you are losing yours. I don't object to the mutual fund making money; they have to in order to stay in business. I object to the half-truth of a marketing phrase.

For an active manager the expense ratio could be between 1% to 2%, whereas for a passive manager the expense ratio could be .04% or less. Why is there such a big difference? Part of the reason is because of higher staffing costs for active management. But that's not the only reason. Some others are competition and product differentiation. Many passive managers offer similar products to the investing public such as S&P 500 index funds. And if the products are similar, one way for managers to differentiate themselves from the others is by having the lowest price, thus a pricing war ensues with one manager lowering its price only to be followed by the other. On the other hand, active managers present their product as being unique and as such believe they can charge more. Active managers are not immune from free market capitalism however. As more investors move away from their product to passive management, they too are being forced to lower their fees.

The 12B-1 fee: This fee is named after the section in government regulations that allows it to be charged. It's to help pay for the fund's advertising expenses, promotional material, and some shareholder services.

Yes, you read that right. If your mutual fund has a 12B-1 fee you are paying for some of their advertising expenses.

The fee's original intent was a way to increase the mutual fund's assets through advertising, and that, in turn, was supposed to benefit existing mutual fund investors because expenses could then be spread over many more investors.

Small account fee: Some mutual funds will charge a fee to cover the cost to administer small accounts.

Fees matter. A lot. They add up over time. But they have to be measured in light of the mutual fund's performance. If a mutual fund is beating a comparable market index, net of fees and consistent with your risk tolerances, pay the fees and be happy. If the mutual fund isn't, it's time to fire the mutual fund and transfer your money to another investment alternative.

Potentially higher income taxes

The law requires mutual funds to distribute to you any capital gains or dividends that were derived from the mutual fund's investment activities. Generally, the capital gains distribution is done at the end of the year and the dividend distribution is done quarterly. The tax implications of these distributions depend on your circumstances, that is, the type of account the investment was made from, the time of the distributions, and your tax status. You should consult with your custodian, parents, and a tax expert for an opinion as to your specific situation.

How Can I Invest in a Mutual Fund?

If you are a minor, you can't. Your custodian has to do it for you until you come of age. Here are the routes your custodian can take, or you can when you are of age. Check the exact procedures with the firms involved.

Directly from the mutual fund company

Contact the investment company either online or by phone. An application needs to be filled out and returned along with the required minimum deposit for the mutual fund you are interested in.

Through your stockbroker

Your stockbroker might be able to act as the go-between in the transaction. That is, your money goes to the broker, who then transfers it to the mutual fund on your behalf. The broker might charge a commission and it will probably be higher than what they charge for a stock trade. However, if the broker is sponsoring a mutual fund, the commission might be reduced or waived.

Through an investment advisor

An investment advisor might help you sort through the large number of mutual funds. For that help, you can expect to pay a fee, either a flat fee, a percentage of the money you want to invest, or an indirect fee such as a load. Remember, any fees you pay will reduce your investment returns, so find out how much this is going to cost you before you engage the services of an investment advisor – and don't be embarrassed to ask. It's your money.

How Is the Price of a Mutual Fund Determined?

There is a lot of activity that occurs during the trading day. The prices of the stocks in the mutual fund are continuously changing, sometimes dramatically. Cash is received from dividend payments. Expenses to run the fund are being incurred. And sometimes stocks split and mergers and acquisitions occur. It is for these and other reasons mutual funds wait until the end of the trading day when things settle down a bit to determine how much the fund is worth – its net asset value (NAV).

The calculations are complex but generally go like this. The closing market price for each stock in the fund is multiplied by the number of shares held. Those numbers are then totaled and added to the cash on hand. Accrued income and receivables are added. Subtracted from the total are any accrued expenses, such as licensing fees, wages, operational expenses, administrative expenses, custodial costs, etc. The result is then divided by the number of units in the fund and becomes the NAV of each unit. The NAV is normally the price you will pay per unit when buying and the price you will receive when redeeming – absent any commissions, fees, or expenses.

What Are Closed-End Mutual Funds?

I saved this for last because it is a perfect lead into the next chapter on exchange traded funds.

So far, I have been discussing open-end mutual funds. As the name implies, the doors are open to all investors to enter at the end of every trading day to buy or redeem units. Thus, the number of units in an open-end mutual fund expands or contracts based on investor demand. Closed-end mutual funds, however, are, as the name implies, closed. When a sufficient amount of money has been raised the fund closes and the units are distributed to the investors. The investors cannot redeem their units. Rather, they need to sell them to someone else who is willing to buy them in the open market, usually on an exchange

Why are closed-end funds constructed so differently than an open-ended mutual fund? Say an investment manager sees an opportunity to invest in the stock of very small companies. Being small, the company's stock probably doesn't trade all that frequently. It might be hours or even days before the next trade occurs, and when it does there might be a big difference in price. If this was an open-end mutual fund, investors could come and go as they pleased, and this would play havoc with the fund's NAV and create an impossible situation for existing or future investors. Its price would not be driven by perceptions of intrinsic value, but rather by investor in/out activity. It's better to close the fund and let any trading of the units be done outside the fund.

The quirky thing about closed-end mutual funds is that their shares often trade at a price that is widely different than their NAV. Enter exchange traded funds.

> *It's important to like, trust, and have confidence in the mutual fund's management team.*

APPENDIX A
Some Questions to Consider

(1)   Is the manager's philosophy consistent with your investment strategy?

(2)   Is the philosophy likely to be profitable in the future?

(3)   What is the size of the mutual fund?

(4)   What is the background of the manager and key investment personnel?

(5)   How are investment ideas generated?

(6)   How are stocks selected from the ideas that were generated?

(7)   What criteria determines how much of a particular stock will be held?

(8)   How are sell decisions made?

(9)   What is the mutual fund's turnover ratio?

(10)   How long are stocks held?

(11)   How is the management expense ratio determined?

(12)   What are the acquisition costs you are required to pay?

(13)   What are the annual ongoing costs you are required to pay?

(14)   Does the manager attempt to time the market?

(15)   What were three- and five-year returns and what drove the results?

(16)   What are the returns over a market cycle and what drove the results?

NOTE: The reason for these questions has been covered at various places in this book.

CHAPTER 18

Exchange Traded Funds

An exchange traded fund (ETF) is like buying pizza by the slice. You walk up to the window, select the slice you want, pay for it, and go. You can buy a slice any time during the day when the establishment is open. Your choices could range from plain mozzarella to unbelievably exotic flavors.

Same thing with exchange traded funds. You can buy a slice of a stock portfolio whenever the stock exchange is open. Your choices range from a plain vanilla S&P 500 index fund to an exotic ETF. If you don't like your ETF slice you can sell it to someone else.

There are plenty of ETFs that can be used to implement any of the investment strategies we discussed earlier – active, passive, and especially factor-based, which represents the bulk of ETF offerings. So, if your strategy calls for a factor-based manager, this is the place for you to start your search. You won't find many active managers here because of the amount of disclosure that is required. Active managers like to keep their secret sauce secret. But that's changing as more and more active mutual fund managers are adapting and migrating to ETFs to capture the inflow of investor money into this space.

In order to truly understand ETFs, I will to take you deep into the details to give you an overview of how they are created. This is important because some of their greatest risks lies within their creation. Then I will list the benefits and risks of buying an ETF followed by some thoughts on how to organize them so you can make some sense of the space. Next, I'll discuss leverage and inverse ETFs and conclude the chapter with a discussion of the ETF industry itself. But before we leave this chapter, in Appendix A, I will provide you with a list of questions you might consider asking yourself and the ETF manager before making an investment.

How Are ETFs Created?

It starts with an idea

For example, say you're the Sponsor of a prospective ETF and your research has shown companies whose CEOs are under the age of 40 outperform those companies whose CEOs are over the age of 40. You believe these companies are more dynamic and thus more profitable than all the others. You've identified the specific companies you want in your portfolio and decided to cap-weight their exposure. In other words, you have created a paper benchmark that you will attempt to replicate with a portfolio of stock.

You seek approval and assemble a team

To turn your idea into reality, you must first go to the Securities and Exchange Commission to ask permission. If approved, the next step is to assemble the stocks that will track the benchmark you created. To do that you need to involve market makers, dealers, and/or specialists who have quick access to the stocks in the quantities you need for your portfolio, and that's where an Authorized Participant (AP) comes in.

An AP will act as sort of a go-between between you and the market makers, dealers, and specialists. Some of the better-known APs are Goldman Sachs, JP Morgan, and Morgan Stanley. An AP can be a market maker, dealer, or specialist as well. You can have one or many APs, and others may join you after the ETF has been created and on the market for a while. APs do not receive any pay from you; instead, they are compensated from actions they take in their market-making activities and from other fees that are associated with your ETF. Some or all of those APs who are involved with your ETF can drop out any time they want.

You create the ETFs

With the AP's help, the underlying portfolio of stocks you need to replicate your paper benchmark can be purchased on a stock exchange but are often borrowed from other investment managers. The assembled stock is called the underlying portfolio because it underlies or supports the ETFs that will be created. Once acquired, the stocks will be placed in a trust account under the protection of a Trustee. In exchange, a number of ETFs will be created and will be available directly or indirectly to those who have supplied the stock, or to others. But before that happens, you need to decide the number of ETF shares you initially want to create. Let's say the stocks in the underlying portfolio have a total market value of $10 million and you decided to have an initial price of $20 for each ETF share. That means 500,000 ETFs will be created ($10 million divided by $20 equals 500,000 shares). Another way to look at this is in terms of the net asset value (NAV) of an ETF share. For example, by issuing 500,000 shares you are creating an ETF that has a NAV of $20 ($10 million divided by 500,000 shares = $20).

You market the ETF

You need to market your ETF to the investing public. This is obviously a very important element to the success of your venture. Many Sponsors sell ETFs based on the results of their research. You probably will do the same. As Sponsor, however, you have also made an implicit promise to the investing public to keep the market price of your ETF roughly equal to the ETF's NAV.

Ongoing Management

As time goes by the market price of the shares in the underlying portfolio will change and as a result so will the market value of the underlying portfolio. When that happens the NAV of each ETF share will also change. If the market price of an ETF is above its NAV, the ETF is said to be selling at a premium. If the market price is below its NAV, the ETF is selling at a discount.

But what about that implicit promise you made to keep the market price of the ETF roughly equal to its NAV? How are you going to do that? Through the beauty of arbitrage. Merriam-Webster defines arbitrage as, "The nearly simultaneous purchase and sale of securities … in order to profit from price discrepancies." The potential existence of an arbitrage profit is what you are counting on to keep the market price of the ETF roughly equal to its NAV.

The basic concept is that a bundle of ETFs priced at the market can be exchanged for a bundle of stock in the underlying portfolio priced at NAV – and vice versa. The difference in price between the market price of the ETF and its NAV is what generates the profit-making arbitrage opportunity for the APs and others. For example, if the ETF is selling at a premium, the underlying stock can be acquired and presented to the Sponsor/Trustee and, in exchange, a bundle of ETFs will be received that can then be sold in the market for a profit. The difference between what the shares of stock cost and the proceeds from the sale of the ETFs is the profit from arbitraging the transaction. The sale of ETFs, possibly along with the purchase of the stock, should tend to move the ETF's market price and its NAV closer together. At least that's the idea.

The reverse is true as well. If the ETF is selling at a discount, a bundle of ETFs can be purchased in the market and presented to the Sponsor/Trustee, and in exchange a bundle of underlying stock will be received that can then be sold for a profit. The increased purchase of ETFs, possibly along with the sale of the stock received, should tend to move the ETF's market price and its NAV closer together.

This was a straightforward explanation of how ETFs are created and how their market price and NAV are kept roughly equal by exchanging bundles of ETFs for bundles of stocks in the underlying portfolio, and vice versa. In order for this to happen, the marketplace needs to know what's in the underlying portfolio, that is, what stocks and in what quantities (more about implications of this later).

How ETFs are created and maintained can create serious risks for investors and that is why I took the time to take you through the process. But before I list those risks, I want to present some of the benefits first.

What Are the Benefits of Buying an ETF?

Here are the highlights for a typical ETF. For specific details you must read the prospectus that the ETF manager is required to offer you. The prospectus comes in two forms – statutory and summary. Get both.

Extensive involvement in investment decisions

An ETF manager creates a benchmark – these stocks in these quantities – and then builds a portfolio to track that benchmark. When you look at the prospectus, you'll see the benchmark, and if you buy that ETF you will have agreed that you too want these stocks (no others) and you too want them to be held in these quantitates (no other quantities). Thus, when picking an ETF, you are in effect making stock-selection decisions as well as how much of each to hold. This is neither good nor bad. Just understand the implied decisions you are making when you buy an ETF and look beyond just the name of the ETF to see what you are actually investing in.

Exposure to many companies

By investing in an ETF you'll have exposure to a lot of different companies consistent with the benchmark you selected. If you choose active, your exposure will be

> *Look beyond the name of the ETF to see what you're actually investing in.*

across those companies the active manager believes have intrinsic value. If you choose passive, your exposure will be across hundreds or perhaps thousands of companies that are in the selected index. If you choose factor-based, your exposure will be across the selected factor.

Trading flexibility

ETFs trade during the day when the stock exchange is open, just like stocks. And, like stocks, you can place the same types of orders – market, limit, stop-limit or trailing stop – and if you are trading from a taxable account and are no longer a minor, you can buy ETFs on margin or sell them short if you like.

Favorable tax treatment

Favorable, that is, compared to mutual funds. You still have to pay your taxes. As attributed to Ben Franklin, "…in this world nothing can be said to be certain except death and taxes." As attributed to Will Rogers, "The only difference between death and taxes is that death doesn't get worse every time Congress meets." As a teenager, these truths might be lost on you. But just wait.

Most tax experts think that if you measure the taxes paid from the time when you buy, hold, and then sell an ETF and compare that time frame to a similar one for a mutual fund, the ETF comes out with a lower tax bill. How much lower? That depends on many things. However, a better approach might be to delay or avoid taxes altogether and invest from a Roth account.

Relatively low ongoing expenses

ETFs follow a cookie-cutter strategy. Once the recipe (the benchmark) is finalized, each cookie produced looks just like the last one. That's a cheaper business model than creating a new recipe every time. You don't need a staff of chefs (as with a mutual fund) providing a new menu every time the market changes (as with active management), so those savings can be passed on in the form of lower fees, at least in most cases.

Investment size flexibility

You can buy one or as many ETF shares as you like. There is no minimum requirement. However, the frequent buying or selling of small amounts might not be desirable, since accompanying transaction costs can eat into profits or compound losses.

Record-keeping and administrative services

Your brokerage firm will provide you with the same information as if you had purchased a stock.

What Are the Risks of Buying an ETF?

Here are some very important risks that simply come from the way ETFs are created and maintained.

An ETF could trade as a closed-end fund

The APs are not obligated to use their magic to narrow a discount or premium. Their willingness depends on the arbitrage profit they can make given the risk they perceive they are taking. There might even be situations where the APs decide to step aside, such as in times of severe market stress, or really for any reason. If every AP steps aside, the ETF will trade as a closed-end mutual fund whose price could vary widely, and wildly, from its NAV, possibly to your disadvantage and loss. The ETF can continue like that until an AP decides to step back in.

Depending on the ETF, you can expect the premium or discount to be small. But when the market is under stress, as it was on August 24, 2015, the discount could be huge. Within the first five minutes of trading that morning the DJIA dropped roughly 1,100 points, some say as a reaction to the day-before events in the Asian markets. Regardless of what caused the drop, the effect on some ETFs was dramatic. One crashed 22% while its underlying portfolio did not drop as much, thus causing a huge discount. This disconnect between price and NAV can happen at any time, perhaps not as dramatically as my example, but it can happen and at any time. Some will say the possibility of a huge discount is remote. Only time will tell.

The role and importance of liquidity

As you may recall from Chapter 4, liquidity is the ability to buy or sell shares of a stock with little or no price impact. The liquidity of the ETF shares is one thing for you to consider, but not the only thing. You must also be concerned with the liquidity of the shares in the underlying portfolio. Why? If they're liquid, the ETF is likely to have more APs (and the market makers, dealers, and specialists) engaged in arbitrage and that, in turn, will tend to keep the discount or premium to a minimum.

However, if liquidity of the underlying portfolio is a problem, fewer APs might be interested in the ETF. Hence, the ETF's premium or discount is likely to be larger. This might occur for the more exotic ETFs, those that are invested in ultra small-cap stocks, or those in which sampling techniques are used to track a benchmark. In these situations, the ETF's discount or premium can be large and persistent.

What does this mean to you as an ETF investor?

To minimize your risk, you need to do some more homework. You need to look under the hood and see how many APs are servicing the ETF. The more the better, because the competition between them should keep the ETF's market price roughly equal to the ETF's NAV. The APs should also be financially strong and have been doing this for a while. Equally important, you should check the liquidity of the stocks in the underlying portfolio. As I pointed out in Chapter 4, a quick way to judge liquidity is to look at daily trading volume and the bid-ask spread. The greater the liquidity in the underlying portfolio the better.

Are There Any More Risks?

The downside of trading flexibility

With the ease of trading during the day comes the temptation to trade too often. If you do, you might be doing what is called "trading the noise." Day-to-day or even week-to-week ETF prices can bounce around a lot. Often that short-term volatility is simply noise that hides a longer-term trend. Emotionally driven noise traders lose money, if not from poor decisions then from accumulated transaction costs (see Chapter 22).

Performance considerations

Since the benchmark is of the ETF's manager's choice, and often of the manager's creation, the ETF should closely match its established benchmark. In other words, there should be little tracking error.

Of course, there is always the possibility that you thought the ETF was going to track a certain benchmark only to discover later when there is a large tracking error that you skipped over these words in the fine print of the prospectus: The ETF's "... performance will deviate from the ... benchmark ... [and] the Fund will invest in the companies ... on a conviction basis." Again, you must read the prospectus.

Similar names, different strategies

Money management is a competitive business. If one ETF manager sees another making money selling a particular product to the investing public, that manager might create and sell a similar product. For example, consider biotechnology, an industry in the health care sector. The word "biotechnology" is included in the title of at least six ETFs. To the causal investor they might all seem similar but a closer look will prove otherwise.

I am using these ETFs for *illustrative purposes only*. The iShares Nasdaq Biotechnology ETF (ticker IBB) tracks the cap-weighted Nasdaq Biotechnology Benchmark. In addition to biotech companies, the benchmark includes pharmaceutical companies, medical equipment companies, and other related companies that trade on the Nasdaq exchange. It was created on February 5, 2001 and contains over 150 companies. At last count IBB was over $9 billion in size and had an average daily trading volume of about two million shares. Its expense ratio was 0.47%.

At the other extreme is the Virtus LifeSci Biotech Clinical Trials ETF (ticker BBC). It too has biotech in its name. However, it focuses on small companies with products in various stages of clinical trials. It's an equally weighted benchmark that was developed by the manager. It was created on December 16, 2014 and contains about 100 companies. At last count BBC was about $50 million in size and had an average daily trading volume of about 27,000 shares. Its expense ratio was 0.79%.

The performance difference between these biotech ETFs could be huge. To reinforce the point, consider ETFs that have large-, medium-, or small-cap in their title. As I said earlier large and small are relative terms. Large in comparison to what? Small in comparison to what? In Chapter 3, I gave you an arbitrary ranking of companies by size. That may or may not be what the ETF manager is using. Small might be the companies in the S&P 500 index or the companies in the Nasdaq Composite Index, two wildly different indices. Or small might be the byproduct of a factor study I described in Chapter 16 where the researcher divided the universe by quartiles, quintiles, deciles, or some other division. Read the prospectus so you know what you are really investing in, especially if the ETF titles seem similar.

Trial balloons

Clothing stores are constantly changing their fashion lineup. They will display a style and drop it just as quickly if it doesn't sell. Some ETF Sponsors will do exactly the same thing. If a newly created ETF catches on, they'll keep it. If not, they'll close it down. My favorite example was NASH, an ETF that tracked the companies that were headquartered in fast-growing Nashville, Tennessee – closed in February 2018.

About 100 ETFs of all types close shop for various reasons every year causing a hassle for holders of those ETF shares. If you don't get out early and are caught in a shut-down, you should get most of your money back depending on the NAV of the ETF shares, less any premium you paid together with what you paid in transaction costs and related expenses. Often it is wise to stick with the better-known and better-financed Sponsors and APs, at least until the new ETF proves itself in the marketplace.

Same stocks in multiple ETFs

Some large-cap stocks such as Apple, Netflix, Amazon, and others find themselves as large-percentage holdings in the underlying portfolios of several ETFs. This entwining of ETFs sets up a potential domino effect when one ETF sells a slice of its underlying portfolio to maintain equality between its NAV and the price of its ETF. That selling could trigger other ETFs to sell slices of their underlying portfolio and down we go as the selling accelerates. Surprisingly, it doesn't take much to get the selling started especially if those dominant stocks appear overvalued and economic conditions are dicey. The result of this concentration is increased volatility for those ETFs who hold these stocks.

How Much Does It Cost to Buy and Hold an ETF?

Cost to buy

Acquisitions costs for an EFT generally involve (1) paying a brokerage commission; (2) incurring the bid-ask spread; (3) incurring the premium and discount variation; and, if you so choose; (4) paying an investment advisor to help with the selection. I covered all of this in earlier chapters in this book.

Cost to hold

An ETF charges you an ongoing fee called an expense ratio for its services. The fee is quoted as an annual percentage that is applied to the ETF's NAV and deducted from it on a pro-rata basis. The fees can range from 0.04% for large passive ETFs based on the S&P 500 index, to 1.38% for a long-short ETF based on large-cap stocks.[13] There might be other expenses and charges so, again, read the prospectus.

---

[13] Source: ETFdb.com, author search

How Does Anyone Make Sense of the Different ETFs?

Trying to get a handle on the ETF marketplace is like trying to pick up Jell-O®. The only way I deal with this confusion is to sort, as best as I can, the ETFs into the investment strategies I discussed earlier – active, passive, and factor-based. Within these groupings are sub categories.

Below are the categories and examples of the ETFs I think should be in each. Understand, however, I am not making any ETF recommendations. The ones I cited below are for *illustrative purposes only*. I'm going to start with passive.

Passive

Market ETFs: In this category I would place ETFs that use indices that were used to measure market performance as I described in Chapter 5. These include ETFs that track the S&P 500, Nasdaq, and the DJIA indices. Mutual funds also have similar alternatives offered at very competitive rates. To be considered in this category the ETF should be identical to the pre-established indices.

Sector–industry benchmark ETFs: Some of these indices have been around a long time and were used to measure the temperature of the economy. You can find several ETFs for each sector or industry group. To be in this category the ETF should also be identical to the pre-established indices. But, remember, there is a large risk associated with putting your money into a sector or an industry fund. If you think it has long-term potential and you're willing to hold tight while it goes through its ups and downs, it might turn into a great investment. But realize that some of these sectors, and especially industries, have wide swings in performance.

Factor-based

Single-factor ETFs: This category of ETFs brings one of those factors discussed in Chapter 16 into the portfolio. A straightforward example is taking a market index and tilting it towards a factor like smallness. This can be done by simply changing the weighting scheme of the S&P 500 from cap-weighted to equal-weighted. When you do that you get an S&P equal-weighted ETF.

But it doesn't stop with changing the weighting scheme. It could involve keeping the names of the S&P 500, or any other index, and tilting the portfolio to emphasize the value factor. Then you have an S&P 500 value-tilted ETF or an S&P 500 growth-tilted ETF. If the factor was momentum, you could get an S&P 500 momentum-tilted ETF. Another possible focus is on S&P 500 high-dividend yielding stocks.

Single-factor sector-industry ETFs: Beyond a single-factor market you could also have a single-factor sector–industry ETF. For example, in this subcategory you might find a biotechnology fund that focuses on companies that have positive momentum.

Many-factor ETFs: If one factor is good, several must be better. The theory comes in two forms: a combination that is supposed to increase return or a combination that is supposed to reduce risk through negative correlation (see Chapter 7).

Active

Finally, we have active, niche, or exotic ETFs. They can be something as straightforward as one that specializes in companies that buy back their own shares, ETFs that focuses on stocks in companies that are deemed to have a competitive advantage, ETFs that directly or indirectly supports the ETF industry, ETFs that select companies based on social criteria, or even ETFs that invests in other ETFs. And the list goes on and on.

Some even go further and select, and then often weight, the ETF's exposure to specific factors based on market conditions and complex algorithms. As the input data changes, so does the benchmark.

Leverage and Inverse ETFs

Another major area for ETFs is leveraged and inverse funds. Often, they are referred to as Ultra, Ultra-Pro, Ultra-Short, Enhanced, and Bull and Bear. A leveraged ETF offers the opportunity to provide many times the daily return of the benchmark that the ETF is tracking. For example, if the ETF benchmark goes up 10%, a return of 20%, or 30% is expected depending on the degree of leverage offered by the ETF. However, if the market goes down 10%, the leverage will work against you and expected returns are -20% or -30%.

The key words here are *daily* and *expected return*. Will you double or triple the return if you hold those leveraged ETF over a week, a month, or a year? Unlikely. If you read the fine print, what is being offered is two or three times over a one-day time period. You might think that a series of days can be strung together to get the desired result.

An inverse ETF works the opposite way. That is, if you bought a double inverse ETF and the market goes down 10%, the value of your holdings is expected to go up 20%. If you bought the triple times inverse ETF and the market goes down 10%, your holdings are expected to go up 30%. These inverse funds also focus on expected daily returns.

The ETF Industry

An entire industry of purveyors of ETF stock-selection models and portfolio-weighting schemes has developed not only in the U.S. but globally as well. This used to be the domain of academic researchers who would come up with an idea that was supported by their reputation and personal research, and they would publish their findings in prestigious analytical journals. The investment management community would read the journals, implement the ideas, and sell them to the investing public. Often the academics would receive some sort of a consulting assignment or ownership position with the newly established investment management firm.

But all that has changed. Some researchers have banded together and have started their own firms to license the fruit of their research to others. They charge a licensing fee and leave the nitty-gritty of the investment management business to others.

Some firms have created the software for investment managers to use so the managers can develop their own ETF benchmarks. The software allows the investment manager to create a benchmark from a combination of factors. Pick your combination of factors, pick your weighting scheme, and market the heck out of your ETF. It reminds me of the gold rush in California, where the people who made the most money were those who sold the picks and shovels.

Make sure you understand what you are investing in, and that means understanding the assumptions that were made in the development of the ETF.

APPENDIX A
Some Questions to Consider

(1)   Is the ETF's theory consistent with your investment strategy?

(2)   Does the theory make intuitive sense and likely to hold in the future?

(3)   Did the manager conduct a rigorous study?

(4)   To what degree does the underlying portfolio emphasize the factor?

(5)   Is the factor in an optimal spot in its performance cycle?

(6)   How many APs are there?

(7)   Who are the APs and how financially sound are they?

(8)   How liquid are the stocks in the underlying portfolio?

(9)   How many ETF shares trade daily and monthly?

(10) How frequent is the underlying portfolio rebalanced?

(11) How closely does the ETF's market price track the ETF's NAV?

(12) How long has the ETF been in existence?

(13) How large is the ETF's underlying portfolio?

(14) How many and what stocks constitute the top 25% of the underlying portfolio?

(15) How many of the top stocks are also in other ETFs?

(16) How is the management expense ratio determined?

(17) What are the acquisition costs you are required to pay?

(18) What are the annual ongoing costs you are required to pay?

(19) What were the one-, three-, and five-year returns and what drove the results?

(20) What are the returns over a market cycle and what drove the results?

(21) How do the returns compare with active and passive managers?

NOTE: The reason for these questions has been covered at various places in this book.

CHAPTER 19

Mutual Funds vs. ETFs

In the last two chapters I covered mutual funds and ETFs in detail. In this chapter, I will highlight only the differences as I see them. Each has its advantages and disadvantages, and to help in the decision-making process, I'll put the two side-by-side.

Your Involvement in the Investment Process

Mutual funds

You are selecting an investment *philosophy* and then allowing its implementation to be executed by the manager as the manager sees fit. While you are initially deeply involved in selecting a mutual fund, critical decisions on which stocks to buy, hold, sell, when, and in what quantities will be made by the manager. You will find out only after the fact what stocks have been purchased or sold and in what quantities, as well as the return that has been achieved.

ETFs

You are selecting a *benchmark* and then allowing its implementation to be executed by the manager, not as the manager sees fit, but only to create a portfolio of stocks that will closely track the stated benchmark. As such you are deeply involved in the investment process, because, by picking this benchmark from all the other alternatives, you have agreed that these are the stocks you want and in these quantities. Moreover, if the ETF has been in existence for a while, you'll know the results of the benchmark and how closely the manager has tracked it.

Comments

Often this different degree of involvement is lost in the marketing hype. In both cases, implementation is turned over to a manager. However, in one case you do so with only general instructions and in the other case with specific instructions. Your choice depends on how much confidence you have in your ability to make stock-selection decisions as well as how much of each stock to hold.

Although the discussion above applies to active and factor-based strategies, even in the case of a passive strategy you cannot avoid involvement in the investment process because you must pick the index, that is, these stocks and in these quantities. But there is a distinction. A passive strategy is not trying to pick the best stock or the best factor, but rather to replicate a long-standing market-based index created to inform the public of the stock market's activity. In other words, you're not trying to improve on that performance, only accept it as the best that can be achieved.

Trading

Mutual funds

You can only trade mutual fund units at the close of the trading day. If you miss the trading window you have to wait until the close of the next trading day. However, an advantage of trading at the end of the trading day is that the mutual fund can use closing prices in the calculation of NAV (no bid-ask spread), and if you are trading directly with the mutual fund company there is no brokerage commission. You have to pick your mutual fund wisely, however, so that it does not have a load or any other extra transaction fees. A disadvantage, however, is that you might be required to initially deposit a considerable sum of money to open an account. But, once satisfied, you generally can deposit any additional amount you want.

ETFs

You can trade ETF shares any time the market is open. The advantage is that you can trade right away in the quantities you can afford – one share or many. There is no minimum initial deposit. The disadvantages are that you will incur the bid-ask spread, be exposed to price premiums or discounts to NAV, and, in all likelihood, will be charged a brokerage commission. Also remember with the ease of trading that an ETF offers, there might be the temptation of trading too often.

Comments

If you need the flexibility of day trading, then an ETF is your only alternative. However, if you're planning to invest small amounts over an extended period of time, you might want to consider a no-load mutual fund that has an objective similar to the ETF you were considering. Why? Because the cumulative cost of trading will add up. Unless it's waived you will incur a brokerage commission every time you place an order. Yes, brokerage commissions can be $4.95 per trade or lower at some of the larger online brokerage firms, and this many not seem like much. But if you are planning to invest small amounts over an extended time, these costs, as well as others I discussed earlier, will add up and could seriously impact your returns. For example, a $4.95 commission on a $100 investment means your investment must increase by about 4.7% just to recoup that cost.

Taxes

Mutual funds

Depending on how well the mutual fund performs, you might have a taxable capital gains distribution at year end and taxable dividends paid during the year. Those events might complicate your tax bill, if you have one coming. Capital gains distributions in themselves are not necessarily bad. In fact, they might indicate that the mutual fund you selected is doing its job, that is, making wise investment decisions that generate capital gains. If you reinvest the capital gains and the dividends you receive, your tax basis will change, thus possibly lowering a small part of your future tax bill.

ETFs

You avoid many of the distribution tax issues that plague mutual funds. Most people who are familiar with the tax code give the advantage to ETFs.

Comments

Both mutual funds and ETFs will have taxable events when you redeem your units or sell you shares. However, chances are, as a teenager, you won't have much, if any, tax liability. If you do, and since tax experts claim ETFs are more tax efficient than mutual funds, the nod goes to ETFs.

Performance Comparisons

Mutual funds

You generally would compare the mutual fund manager's performance with a group of mutual funds that have a similar philosophy or with a market index over some period of time such as one-, two-, five-years, or over a full market cycle.

ETFs

You generally would compare the ETF's performance against its predetermined benchmark. Since the manager selected the benchmark and, in some cases, even created it, you would not expect the ETF's performance to deviate widely from the performance of the benchmark.

How well the benchmark performs as compared to the other alternatives is a different story. For example, comparing the performance of one ETF's benchmark with another becomes tricky, even if the ETFs are playing in the same segment of the market. As pointed out in Chapter 18, there are six ETFs that have the word "biotechnology" in their name, each having widely different performance results. Even more problems arise when comparing the performance of an ETF's benchmark with a market index. Many ETF managers claim their benchmark works because their studies show it does. But those results are based on historical data analyzed over very long-time frames, often much longer than what is given to mutual fund managers to prove their worth.

Comments

A comparison between a mutual fund and an ETF is valid if the mutual fund's philosophy is comparable to the ETF's benchmark. In that case, you are measuring the mutual fund's flexibility to pick and choose among the stocks in the ETF's benchmark, a valid performance comparison.

When comparing the performance of a mutual fund with an ETF when both have an equivalent strategy, such as an S&P 500 index, generally the mutual fund has lower investor transaction costs, but the ETF has better tax treatment. If you do not have any tax concerns, the mutual fund gets the nod for this little performance edge. If you do have tax concerns, the nod goes to ETFs.

There is a psychological aspect to performance measurement to be considered as well. If the mutual fund manager did well and beat the market index, you might pat yourself on the back for the good job you did in picking the manager. If the manager did poorly, you might blame the manager, fire that one, and hire another. You were faultless. It was that bad mutual fund manager who messed up.

No such luck with an ETF. All the ETF manager promised was to closely track the benchmark, not to beat other ETFs or for that matter to beat a market index in the short run. If the manager did well against the benchmark but the benchmark did poorly against other ETFs or a market index, well, that's on you. You picked the benchmark you wanted the manager to track. The ETF did its part, it tracked the benchmark. Psychologically it might be difficult for someone to admit to a mistake and thus he or she would be inclined to stay longer with a failing ETF than with a failing mutual fund.

Management Fees

Mutual funds

Apart from passive index funds, where mutual funds and ETFs strategies are comparable, mutual funds generally charge more than ETFs. This is because the investment decisions require more high-cost personnel, which results in higher payroll expenses that need to be recouped through management fees. This added expense is in addition to increasing costs from more frequent turnovers, producing customer reports, and handling customer contacts.

ETFs

ETFs generally have the advantage because they don't need the large staffs, and much of the reporting and customer contact is handled by the brokerage firm as part of normal business.

Comments

How much an investment manager charges an investor depends on the cost to (1) make the investment decisions, (2) execute those decisions, (3) keep the accounting records, and (4) produce reports for the customers. But there are other considerations in determining a fee such as (a) what the competition is charging, (b) what the investment manager thinks potential customers are willing to pay, and (c) what the owners believe is a reasonable profit for starting the firm in the first place. Knowing the elements that make up the fee can help you in head-to-head comparisons of mutual funds and ETFs that operate in similar areas of the market.

Acquisition Costs

Mutual funds

As I mentioned earlier, with a mutual fund you have to deposit a minimum amount in order to open an account and, depending on the fund, it could be a lot of money. Once that minimum amount is met, however, generally there are no additional restrictions on the amount you can invest. Some mutual funds will even waive the minimum for small investors, but be aware that there might be a small account fee assessed every quarter.

What affects mutual fund acquisition costs is all the people taking their cut in between you and those who are actually making the buy, sell, and hold decisions. If it's a load fund you'll be paying the salesperson a fee. If you're quoted a public offering price (POP), you'll be paying a fee to the mutual fund. If you buy through your stock broker and they are not sponsoring the mutual fund, often you'll be paying a larger brokerage commission than if you had bought a stock. Whether any of these apply or not depends on the mutual fund and your willingness to dig into the prospectus before you invest. In other words, it's up to you to determine whether you incur these costs or not.

ETFs

Since you can buy and sell an ETF like a stock, you probably will incur a brokerage commission for the trade. I said probably because some brokerage firms will waive the commission if the ETF is sponsored by their firm. An acquisition cost that you cannot avoid, however, is the bid-ask spread. The spread can be small for an actively traded ETF, and large for one that is not actively traded. Then there is the cost associated with whether the ETF is trading at a premium or a discount to NAV that, at times of market stress, can be very large indeed.

Comments

You need more information before you can decide whether a mutual fund unit or an ETF share is cheaper to acquire. Because their costs can add up over time, it's important to determine that based on the specifics of the mutual fund or ETF you selected.

In-Out Trading by Others

Mutual funds

Some investors use mutual funds as trading vehicles rather than long-term investments. They would think nothing of buying units and selling them again within a short period. All of this in-out trading places a cost burden on the remaining unit holders. The source of this cost burden comes from three areas. First, the mutual fund might hold cash in order to accommodate those who want to sell their units. Cash can be a negative drag on performance. Second, the mutual fund might have to sell stock to accommodate those who want out. Selling stock incurs transaction costs, which might not be borne by the seller, but by you and all the other remaining unit holders. Finally, if the stocks sold result in a gain, you, as a unit holder, will be responsible for the income tax on that gain unless the mutual fund can offset it with the sale of losers it holds in the fund.

ETFs

ETF holders do not incur the costs that are generated by the in-out trade activity except to the extent that the market creates a premium or discount that must be close.

Comments

In-out trading activity is often the reason given by mutual funds for the extra fees they charge investors to buy or sell units. Although these extra charges might discourage in-out trading, those who have no desire to trade the mutual fund's units also incur them.

Mutual Funds vs. ETFs

The choice of which one to select is up to you based on your investment strategy and risk tolerance. No one writing a book can look into you mind and tell you which one you should select. But I can offer a few comments.

First, when you're well into a mutual fund or ETF search, it's easy to become enamored of a specific one and forget about your investment strategy and risk tolerance. That would be a mistake. Your strategy is based on your goals. If you forget your strategy, you'll be ignoring your goals and thus diminishing the likelihood of achieving them. And if you ignore your risk tolerance, you may encounter increased emotional stress in times of market turmoil, and that might lead to poor decisions.

Second, make sure the mutual fund or ETF's approach makes intuitive sense and, importantly, has been around for a while and thus has been tested in the marketplace. The market does not treat dumb ideas kindly and generally finds a way to drive either the mutual fund or the ETF out of business.

Finally, read and reread the prospectus. More mistakes have been made by investors who only skim through them. Know what you are investing in. That is more important than whether it is a mutual fund or an ETF.

SECTION 6
Market Timing

Ever since the beginning of the stock market investors have tried to catch the ups and avoid the downs. So why aren't all market timers unbelievably wealthy? Answer: the market won't cooperate. It's too busy interpreting and then reacting to incoming information. If that wasn't bad enough, to be successful you need to get two decisions right: when to get out and when to get back in. Try that with a moving target. But there are some techniques that can be used to judge the market's condition that may help keep you out of trouble.

CHAPTER 20

Phases of a Market Cycle

A complete market cycle consists of an upward movement called a bull market and a downward movement called a bear market. However, many market timers believe knowledge of where the market is at within these major movements is important for picking stocks, industries, and factors. Therefore, they like to divide bull and bear markets further into these phases: expansion and exuberance (bullish phases), and decline and disillusionment (bearish phases). I'll define them here and give you my opinion of what is going on emotionally during each of the phases (see Figure 20-1).

Expansion

After a major decline, time passes and the market seems to level off as panic sellers who just want to get out at any price are met with ready buyers who are looking for bargains. Slowly at first, then gradually, the market starts to move upward with fewer and fewer major set-backs. Soon each weekly low is higher than the previous week's low.

Then, as the market continues to move higher, hope and eventually optimism enter the marketplace. Business conditions improve, earnings increase, and strong economic data are being reported. As even more time passes (perhaps several months or even years) memories of the previous decline fades.

As the market moves higher and higher, excitement and finally greed enter the marketplace and the greater fool theory kicks in. Speculative high-risk stocks move substantially higher. TV newscasts of market action are positive and cheerful. More and more people are talking about the stock market and asking which stock to invest in because, "I want to make some money."

Unlike the decline, which was quick and brutal, the rise in the market is slow and marked by some minor declines. This expansion phase is the longest in duration and has the largest price movement.

Exuberance

Optimism and enthusiasm turn to euphoria and the market increases rapidly in a very short period of time in what is called a "buying climax." Stock prices have moved so high that eventually sellers come in and buyers slack off, causing stocks to trade within a range. The trend is generally choppy with small ups and downs, but with little direction. Some stocks continue their rise while others show signs of weakness or even decline.

Then the market drops off sharply. Many investors can't believe it. Some think this is a buying opportunity, especially those who missed out on the expansion phase. With this renewed buying, the market moves up but never exceeds its previous high. This is often called a "bear trap."

Decline

The market then continues its downward momentum. Some investors are in denial. After the market was so great how can it turn down so fast? But the decline is rapid and accelerating and soon fear enters, which drives the market down even faster. Stock prices gap lower and margin calls force people to sell. TV news covers the decline on the nightly news. At some point, investors who hung on can't take any more and panic. Desperation and indiscriminate selling take over, and the market moves down sharply with very heavy volume in what is called a "selling climax."

Disillusionment

This phase is called disillusionment because many investors feel let down, depressed, and defeated. It occurs after a major market decline and investors' stocks and expectations for wealth have just taken a huge hit. It wasn't supposed to be this way and investors don't know if more losses are coming. News reports are all gloomy. It is a period of great uncertainty and volatility. Investors are angry and many swear they will never invest in the stock market again.

Eventually, time goes by and a new cycle starts.

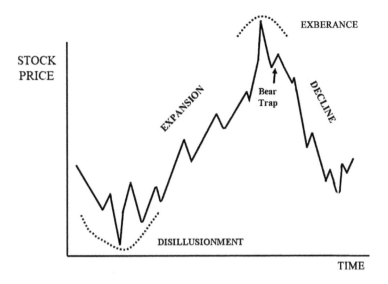

Figure 20-1

These phases are easy to see in retrospect. In real time the emotions of fear, hope, and greed cloud thinking. Now that you know the phases, watch for them to unfold during your investment career. They may take months, perhaps even years, but unfold they will. Count on it.

CHAPTER 21

Avoiding Market Timing

If the market has its ups and downs but somehow seems to rise higher in the end, why not just ignore trying to time the market and use a strategy called buy-and-hold? Or, if you have some money to invest, why not just spread the amount over a period of time instead of trying to determine the best time to invest all of it. That strategy is called dollar cost averaging. Yet another strategy to avoid market timing is to turn your money over to a computer program and allow it to make the decisions for you. This strategy is called robo-investing.

In this chapter we will take a critical look at these strategies.

Buy-and-Hold

An explanation of how the buy-and-hold strategy works should not be a big surprise. You buy and then hold your stock investment for some length of time. Your success, however, depends on three things: what you bought, when you bought it, and how long you held it.

What to buy?

The list of alternatives is long, so it's best to group them by the strategies we discussed – active, passive, and factor-based. Within each group there are many different types of investments from which to select.

Active: This involves investing in individual companies or in actively managed mutual funds or ETFs. If the choice is individual companies, they can be identified through your own unique insight, from lists of stocks that other successful investors have invested in, from computer screens, or ... the list goes on and on. The do-it-yourself approach might seem overwhelming, but there are ideas to help you in Chapters 11 and 14. If you decide not to buy the stock of an individual company, but still want active management, there are plenty of mutual funds and ETFs to pick from.

Passive: This involves investing in an index fund such as the S&P 500, DJIA, Nasdaq, or similar type market-based indices. These give broad-based exposure to the market. There are plenty of passive mutual funds or ETFs for you to pick from.

Factor-based: This involves investing in factor-based funds such as those that focus on value, small-cap, high-yield, or ... the list also goes on and on. These give you exposure to a particular benchmark that has been designed to capture the expected return of the factor. The variety of choices is huge, and there are plenty of mutual funds and ETFs from which to pick.

When to buy?

You can improve your odds of a successful outcome if you make your purchase when the market is down. But when we talk about the market being down (or up), we're really talking about market timing. It seems timing is still an important consideration even in a buy-and-hold strategy.

How long to hold?

This presents the biggest test of the buy-and-hold strategy. Sure, buy-and-hold feels great when the market is going up, but what happens when it's going down seemingly without end? Do you have the fortitude to hold fast when your account is down 40% or more and the emotional demons come a calling? Unless you're like Spock from *Star Trek*, studies show most people crack under the strain of substantial losses and sell at the bottom.

Which is the most important?

Hard to tell. You might have bought something at the top of the market, but if you held onto it long enough it still might turn into a good investment. That favorable outcome depends on what you bought and how long you held it. On the other hand, when you bought could have been perfect, but what you bought was simply destined for bankruptcy or to become part of the living dead, so no amount of time could turn those investments into winners. In other words, all three – when, what, and for how long – should click.

Does buy-and-hold work?

For the 20 years from 1998 to 2017 the S&P 500 index provided an average annual return of 7.20%. But if you missed the 10 best up days during that period your return would have been 3.53%; and if you missed the 20 best up days, it would have been a dismal 1.15%. That's the argument for buy-and-hold – don't miss the up days.

But what would have happened if you had avoided the 10 worst down days during the same time period? If you did, your average annual return would have been 11.31%. And if you missed the 20 worst down days, your annualized return would have been 14.23%.[14] The reason down days have such a greater impact on return than the up days is that it is difficult to make up for losses.

Studies such as these can be very misleading – after all we're talking about being smart enough to be in or out of the market for 10 or 30 days scattered over nearly 3800 trading days over a 15-year period. Complicating the up-and-downs is that many of the spectacular down days are often quickly followed by spectacular up days. One has to be extremely nimble to profit form that degree of volatility. Good luck. However, there is still a valid point to be made for avoiding the down days. It's critically important to preserve your capital when a major decline occurs. Making up for a loss is very difficult because there is less money on which to earn (see Appendix A for the math). Setting trailing stops might be a good idea.

Does buy-and-hold work? It depends on what you buy, when you buy it, and how long you hold it. The safest approach seems to be to invest in a broad-based passive index fund such as the S&P 500. With an index like that you are investing in the growth of the economy, and, if you believe in free market capitalism, that's a reasonable long-term approach especially if you add to your investment on a regular basis. But it's not the only approach, and which path you take depends on your risk tolerance and the amount of time and effort you put into the market.

Dollar Cost Averaging

This strategy is billed by some as the answer to market timing when you have a lump sum of money to invest. With this method, you divide your money into equal amounts and invest them at equal intervals over a period of time. The theory is you will buy more shares at a lower price when the market is down and fewer shares at a higher price when the market is up, but at the

---

[14] ifa.com, Index Fund Advisors: Missing the Best and Worst Days

end of your purchases the average cost of the shares you bought should be lower than the market price, and therefore you will have a profit and you would have avoided the risk of buying at the wrong time. At least that's the theory.

It sounds easy, but does it work? Well, that depends on what you bought, the size of the equal installments, how long you stretched out the installments, and of course, the direction of the market.

If your investment choice is destined to go down, neither investing your money all at once nor dollar cost averaging will work. You'll lose money faster if you invested the lump sum and more slowly by investing in equal amounts over a period of time. In either case you'll lose money. However, if the investment you selected fluctuates over a period of time within a price range, you'll be better off with equal amounts instead of a lump sum. If the trend for the investment you selected is up, then the best thing to do is to invest the lump sum. If the trend is up and fluctuates on an upward trendline, the best thing to do is still invest the lump sum. Thus, sometimes dollar cost averaging works and at other times it doesn't. So, to be successful at dollar cost averaging we're back to market timing: Is the market going down, will it be flat for a while, or is it trending up?

I believe dollar cost averaging is beneficial when an investor has a great deal of anxiety about investing in the stock market in the first place. Not all investors respond to the risk of investing in the stock market in the same way, and dollar cost averaging is a reasonable solution to get some investors off the fence.

One final point before we move on. I don't want to confuse dollar cost averaging with periodic investing over a long time period. As an example, it is important for you to invest as large a portion of your paycheck as you can without concern about the market's direction and probably in a passive index fund to start with. Your investments might be small but over the decades they should add up through the power of compounding.

Robo-investing

Robo-investing is a slang term for an investment service in which a computer algorithm makes the investment decisions for you. There are many versions offered, but an all-inclusive one works like this: The computer asks you risk-related questions and, based on your responses, you are assigned a specific percentage mix of stocks, bonds, and perhaps other investment alternatives. Within your specified mix you are assigned one or several specific ETFs. The service then takes your money and buys the ETFs in the required quantities. As the market values change over time, the investment company's computer program will periodically buy and sell the ETFs to bring the mix back in line with what is currently being specified.

The investment companies that are selling this service have targeted you, a teenager, and your friends as customers. They figure you don't have a lot of money to invest, you lack the skills to invest on your own, and you are comfortable with computer-driven solutions. Because it is computer driven, they say their fees are less than those an investment advisor would charge even if you could find one who would take you as a customer given the small amount you have to invest.

But before you go this route, there are four things you should consider.

Questions asked and responses given

What mix of stocks, bonds, and other investments you get depends on what questions have been asked and your response to them. This is the tricky bit with robo-investing. Often the intent of the questions is to assess your risk tolerance. But as we learned in Chapter 7, the definition of risk is an elusive concept, so how is your tolerance to be measured when the concept itself is so fuzzy? Moreover, can you really answer all the questions? Finally, as any skilled questioner knows, how the questions are asked can bias the results. If you are considering the robo route, you should look long and hard at the questions and the results your answers generated to ensure the asset mix really matches your risk tolerance.

Performance

Trying to get an answer from some of the suppliers of this service is more difficult than getting a nutritionist to agree that Twinkies® are nutritional. The answer you're likely to get will be something like, "We can't tell you because performance varies from person to person based on their individual risk profiles." That's possible, but it's more likely that investors are put into a limited number of pre-established risk categories based on their answers to the questions. If that's the case, then performance of each category can be measured. In my opinion, if you can't get answers to the performance question, I would look elsewhere.

Fees

There are several fees to pay. The robo advisor gets paid a fee, and all the ETFs that have been purchased do too. Robo fees can range from 0.30%

to 0.50%[15] and, as we learned in Chapter 18, ETF fees can range from 0.04% to 1.38%. Finally, you have transaction costs. These are hard to estimate because they depend on how often your asset mix is rebalanced. Adding all these estimated fees altogether, the cost of robo-investing can range from roughly 0.34% to 1.88%. As in all investments, know what the fees are before you invest.

Emotional support

Since major market movements can cause anxiety, somehow a computer-generated voice or an email is not very reassuring. Some robo-advisors have supplemented their approach with some human interaction.

This does not mean that you should reject robo-investing but only that you should look at them, as you would other investment alternative, with a very critical eye.

> *No matter what approaches we develop, we are still subjected to market movements.*

---

[15] Source: AAII, The Robo Report, June 17, 2017

APPENDIX A
Losses Are Hard to Make Up

A 20% loss would take a subsequent 25% rise just to break even. A 50% loss requires a 100% rise to break even. This is because after a loss, you have a lower amount of assets from which to start the hoped-for rise.

Here's the math:

Initial investment	$1,000
20% decline	x .20
Loss	$200
Remaining assets	$800

Knowing you want an ending value of $1,000 at which you will break even, the rate of return can be calculated using this formula:

$$\text{Rate of Return} = \frac{\left[\begin{array}{cc}\text{Ending} & - & \text{Beginning} \\ \text{Value} & & \text{Value}\end{array}\right]}{\text{Beginning Value}} \times 100$$

Given:
 Beginning Value = $800
 Ending Value = $1,000
Solve Formula:

$$\text{Rate of Return} = \frac{\left[\$1,000 - \$800\right]}{\$800} \times 100$$

$$\text{Rate of Return} = 25\%$$

Therefore, a decline of 20% means you must have a subsequent gain of 25% to just break even.

CHAPTER 22

Emotional Market Approach

On October 19, 1987, on what was later called "Black Monday," the DJIA dropped by 22.6%. How could solid, well-performing companies suddenly become 22.6% cheaper in one day? Or what drove Books-a-Million, a dot-com company, to increase from $3 per share to $38.94 and back to $3 two years later?[16] Or how about an obscure company called Xcelera start out at under $1 per share, skyrocket to $111 (split adjusted) in 8 months, and then fell back to obscurity.[17] Or the one-month drop of -29.8% in the S&P 500 starting in late September, 2008. Proponents of the emotional market theory believe these swings were caused by human emotions, and they may have a point.

Like it or not, emotions are built into our DNA and undoubtedly have an impact on our investing decisions. However, there's one small problem. Often it is only in hindsight that we realize market movements appear to be driven by emotions. At the time, everything seemed so rational. During the double-digit drops in 1987 and 2008, the global financial system seemed to be on the verge of collapse and a depression was a real possibility. But even if we believe the market is acting emotionally, how do we profit from it? As Economist John Maynard Keynes once said, "The market can stay irrational longer than you can stay solvent." Perhaps our best bet in this controversy is to understand our own emotions when investing our hard-earned money.

In this chapter I will start with an explanation of the emotional feedback loop. Next, I will give you a brief history of bubbles to show you that they have occurred in the past and will continue to do so in the future. Finally, I'll introduce you to some of the emotional responses that plague investors.

---

[16] Wikipedia
[17] The Motley Fool, November 17, 2004

An Emotional Feedback Loop

Think of an emotional feedback loop as a circle where two people are arguing. One person says something that angers the second person. That person responds and angers the first person more, who responds with even more anger; around and around they go, with each response getting increasingly more heated and less rational. How fast and heated things get depends on the personalities of the individuals and the topic being discussed.

A similar thing can happen in the stock market (see Figure 22-1). Rational expectations can be diverted into a loop of the increasing emotions of greed or fear. Emotions impact liquidity and it is the intensity of those emotions that determines the speed of the change in liquidity and thus changes in stock prices. Once the loop gets going, stock prices move further and further away from intrinsic value (see Figure 22-2). Since fear is a stronger emotion than greed, prices move down faster than they go up.

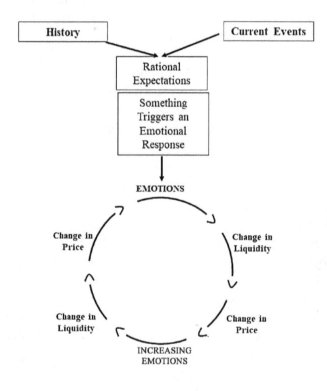

Figure 22-1

For example, at a certain price level, fear creeps silently into the market. Buyers become increasingly reluctant to buy and sellers more willing to sell.

That impacts liquidity and prices move down. The downward movement causes fear to increase and that increases the reluctance of buyers and the eagerness of sellers, which causes liquidity at that price level to evaporate and prices gap down. The process is similar to the Niagara River; slow and meandering at the start, then increasingly turbulent until the river reaches the cliff where the water falls hundreds of feet in seconds. The Niagara Falls effect (maximum fear) in the stock market generally occurs near the end of a down market.

In up markets, greed kicks in but at a slower pace, that is, until the end when an upward spike of buying frenzy (maximum greed) occurs, which generally signals the top of an up market.

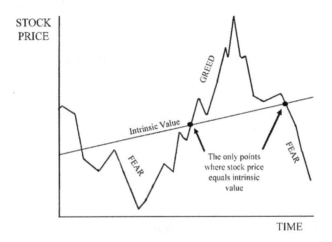

Figure 22-2

There are also several structural issues within the stock market that can contribute to the speed of emotional price changes. First, we have a market system that is geared to the speed of execution rather than the discovery of a fair price. The

> "Be fearful when others are greedy and greedy only when others are fearful." – Warren Buffett

speed of execution is exactly what it sounds like – how quickly a trade can be executed. On the other hand, price discovery is an attempt to find or discover a reasonable price for what is being bought or sold by allowing more time for more participants to analyze and enter the marketplace. Price discovery tends to stabilize the market; speed of execution tends to increase volatility. Thus, the way the trading system is set up can increase the intensity of an emotional reaction.

The second issue is that ETFs have the potential to unintentionally trigger an emotional response. I already discussed ETFs in depth in Chapter 18. But briefly recapping, each ETF represents a portion of an underlying portfolio that contains perhaps hundreds of different stocks. When the price of the ETF varies widely from its NAV, the investment manager must either buy or sell slices of the portfolio in an attempt to bring the market price of the ETF back in line with its NAV. Buying or selling slices of the portfolio that can contain many individual stocks can create a sudden, unexpected change in liquidity in each of those individual stocks and that, in turn, can unwittingly cause an emotional reaction in anyone who owns one of those stocks.

That emotional response is amplified when multiple ETFs hold the same stocks as a large percentage of their holdings. As I stated in Chapter 18, some large-cap stocks such as Apple, Netflix, Amazon, and others find themselves as a large percentage in the underlying portfolios of several ETFs. This entwining of ETFs sets up a potential domino effect when an ETF sells a slice of its underlying portfolio to maintain equality between its NAV and the market price of its ETF. That selling could trigger other ETFs to sell slices of their underlying portfolio and down we go as the selling accelerates. And it might not take much to get the process started.

The third issue is computer driven strategies. For example, in the 1987 crash the strategy was called portfolio insurance, that is, a strategy based on the selling of S&P 500 futures to protect, or insure, a stock portfolio from market declines. The idea is the increase in the value of the shorted futures will compensate for the loss in value of the underlying stock. Once a relatively minor decline began, the computers programs kicked in and started selling S&P 500 futures. That selling caused the market to go down further, which caused the sale of even more S&P 500 futures and so on until no one was willing to buy them. Liquidity dried up until, in the midst of the melt down, someone stepped in with a particular large buy order that reversed the trend. Some suspect that similar automatic computerized strategies intensified the October to December 2018 market decline. As ETFs increase in popularity, more market volatility, both up and down, can be expected.

Bubbles

Think back to when you were younger and you were blowing bubbles at someone's birthday party. The more air you added to the wand, the larger the bubble got. Eventually the bubble burst. It's not too different with the stock market.

In the late 1990s buying stuff on the internet was new and exciting. Investors and speculators started to make huge fortunes in these stocks and, as you might expect, the news media picked up on this. More and more people were drawn in and the emotional feedback loop got started. Stock prices rose and then rose again, and soon the feedback loop accelerated. Stock prices continued to increase, rising so high that commonly accepted valuation measures were considered obsolete. So valuation measures were changed. Rather than earnings per share as the foundation of valuation, it became how many eyeballs visited a particular e-commerce site. More and more air was being pumped into the bubble. The Nasdaq, where many of these new firms were listed, soared from 500 in 1990 to over 5,000 in early 2000. A huge bubble was created in which the price of these stocks far exceeded their intrinsic value.

Then, as always happens with bubbles, it burst. Something small started the process. It could have been a bad earnings report, a particular shaky company failed to raise the money it wanted in an IPO, or interest rates went up – something. For whatever reason, the buying of these stocks leveled off. Then some people began to realize that, yes, these prices really were way out of line, and the selling started. It didn't take long before the selling turned into panic. The feedback loop switched from greed to fear and accelerated, but with greater intensity. The Nasdaq dropped 80% by 2002 and with it the rest of the stock market. Nobody wanted to own stocks.

Gradually the stock market made its way back up, propelled in part by low interest rates. But starting about 2005 and extending to 2008 a new bubble started to form due to the concurrence of two events. The government was encouraging homeownership and investors were seeking higher returns because of the government's low interest rate policy. Since homeowners typically were paying a higher rate for mortgages than what government bonds were offering, mortgages became an alternative way for investors to achieve higher returns. But investors didn't want to invest in individual mortgages. So, Wall Street had the idea of bundling the mortgages and selling them in the form of bonds, hence the birth of mortgage-backed bonds. These bonds had the appearance of being backed by the government. It was a good idea, at least in the beginning.

But then the demand for these bonds increased and that, in turn, created pressure to issue more mortgages and that, in turn, caused lending standards to slip. They slipped so far that anyone, whether they could afford it or not, was allowed to get a mortgage. A good idea was turning bad. Riskier and riskier mortgages were being written to feed the demand for the mortgage-backed bonds. Greed took over. Then even riskier highly leveraged

241

mortgage-backed securities were being sold. Another bubble had formed, this time in mortgage-backed bonds.

Then, one of the firms dealing in these instruments had difficulties and went bankrupt, which set off a chain reaction and the entire mortgage-backed securities market came crashing down and pulled the housing and the stock market with it. Over the course of one month starting in late September 2008 the S&P 500 collapsed 29.8%, and then continued down for the next five months and ultimately hit a low of -44%.

I went through these two bubbles in detail to reinforce one simple point: Bubbles have happened in the past, have different origins, and will happen again, as they have throughout time: the Dutch Tulip Bubble of 1636–1637, the South Sea Bubble of 1715–1720, Japan's Real Estate and Stock Market Bubble of 1985–1990, and the ones we just talked about, the Dot-Com Bubble of the late 1990s–2002 and the Mortgage-Backed Securities Bubble of 2005–2008.

Major markets aren't the only investments susceptible to bubbles. They also occur within segments of the stock market such as industry groups, investment styles, and even individual stocks themselves. The feedback loop starts with money being made, and eventually greed kicks in to push the investment to unheard of heights. Then something happens and prices level off. Then the feedback loop reverses, the selling starts and soon uncontrollable panic takes over. Losses become huge and disillusionment sets in. Then time passes and money is being made again and the cycle repeats itself.

An Individual's Reaction to Uncertainty

Almost every investor's secret wish is to catch a bubble when it is just starting, ride it to the top, and then sell before the crash comes. A bumper-sticker on a California car after the 2008 crash read: "Please God, just one more bubble." But if bubbles are emotionally driven and we don't have a way of predicting when they are going to happen, how large they will become, and how long they will last, how can we make any money? If that is true, then perhaps our best course is to recognize in ourselves our own emotional triggers. By looking inside, perhaps we'll learn when our emotions are getting in the way of making money in the stock market. But before we go there, a little story to reinforce the point.

In Greece, north of Athens on the side of the slopes of Mount Parnassus, there is a place called Delphi. There, an ancient temple complex looks down on a beautiful valley. Although in ruins today, as early as the 7th century BCE ancient kings, rulers, and common folk used to flock to that temple in Delphi to get their questions answered by the oracle. According to legend, the oracle was a priestess who would be (on entering into a trance) in contact with the gods. Her role was to seek an answer from the gods and then deliver the response to a priest, who would then relay it to the questioner. The response would typically be ambiguous or obscure, not unlike the answers investors often get after seeking advice from a Wall Street guru.

But that's not the reason for bring up Delphi. On the walls of the various structures in Delphi were inscribed many important aphorisms such as "Find fault with no one," "Be kind to your friends," and "Respect your parents." These are as true today as they were 2,500 years ago.

What does all this have to do with emotional investing? Also inscribed on the side of a doorway in Delphi is the aphorism "Know thyself." These words of wisdom have echoed throughout time. Even William Shakespeare in his play Hamlet said: "To thine own self be true." What better advice from the ages can you get when you are investing your hard-earned money in an emotionally driven market than to know yourself?

Because of individual behavioral quirks, many investors make huge mistakes that destroy their investment returns – mistakes they don't even realize they are making. For example, they over-rate their investment skills, concentrate their investments in one or two stocks, trade too frequently, invest in stocks that everyone else is investing in, fall in love with a company, hold onto losing positions too long, sell their winners too soon, and think the future will be like the past. It's

> *"Hold the reins of your mind, as you would hold the reins of a restive horse." – The Shvetashvatara Upanishad (c. 400-200 BCE)*

human nature and, I must confess, I've done all of these during my investment career, some many times.

If you can recognize what's going on within yourself emotionally, you'll have a better chance of success in the investment game. The emotional biggies are fear, hope, and greed, but they find outlets in many different ways. As you read on, see if you can identify yourself – and the emotional biggies – in the following detailed discussion.

Loss aversion

Fear of loss is a particularly strong, pervasive emotion that rears its ugly head when investing in common stocks. No one intentionally wants to lose money. We all want to make money, but strangely we fear a loss more than we get pleasure from a gain. That is, if we are faced with a choice of buying a stock that has the chance of increasing $2.00 a share or a chance of a loss of $1.00 a share, we won't buy the stock even though the reward is greater than the risk.

The fear of loss can prevent someone from investing in the stock market in the first place or stop them from investing again after a substantial loss. But consider this. Wayne Gretsky, one of the greatest star hockey player of all time, reportedly said, "You miss 100% of the shots you never take."

Much of the fear of loss comes from looking at stocks as pieces of paper rather than what they really represent – an ownership position in a company. If you selected the stock because of the company, and you believed in the company's management, the short-term ups and downs of the stock's price should not cause you to fear a loss. In fact, if you still believe in the company and have done your homework, the downs might represent a buying opportunity. But if you bought the stock because you wanted to make a short-term profit, then yes, the fear of loss will loom large in your mind when the market is having one of its occasional tantrums.

Regret avoidance

The price of the stock drops and drops yet again, and still we hold on because, if we sell, the loss will become real. We convince ourselves that it is only a paper loss and we think if we just hold on long enough the price will eventually recover and then we'll sell.

We avoid selling to avoid the regret that we bought the stock in the first place, the regret that we should have sold when we had a profit, or the regret that we might feel if the stock goes up after we sell. Sometimes this is why we hire someone else to manage our money. If the manager makes money, we feel good because we selected the manager. If the manager losses money, well, that's the manager's fault not ours and we fire the manager and hire another one.

Self-recrimination

"How could I be so stupid to have bought that stock in the first place?" or, "Why didn't I sell earlier?" But it doesn't have to be a losing stock. It could be the one

> *By focusing on the past, you can lose sight of the future and get caught up in a cul-de-sac of regret.*

that got away. "Darn, that stock has gone up $100. Why didn't I buy it when I had the chance?" I have seen countless investors beating themselves up for not having pre-established rules of when to sell or lamenting over a missed opportunity. The truth is the market doesn't care about how you feel. Sorry.

But by focusing on the past you can lose sight of the future and get caught in a cul-de-sac of regret. The market will always present another opportunity, perhaps an even better one, if you're not mentally beating yourself up about the past. Learn from it and move on.

I remember going to listen to a young man play an oboe as part of his requirement for graduation with a master's degree in music. He had no family in the U.S. and he asked another friend and me to go to his concert. To untrained ears, he played beautifully and was greeted with enthusiastic applause, but when he listened to the audio tape with us later, he pointed out his mistakes. At that point, many people would just castigate themselves, but not him. He said: "I played the very best I could *at the time*." He had no regrets over his performance. Instead he was filled with the anticipation of studying his performance in detail to look for ways of getting better in the future.

Anchoring

When we think of an anchor, we think about the equipment that keeps the boat in one spot. The winds might blow and the sun might shine, but we are anchored to this one spot by a heavy piece of metal. When we buy a stock, or consider buying one, we remember the price we paid or the profit we could have received had we bought it. That price forms a reference point or an anchor from which we tend to base our future decisions and how we react to subsequent price movements with hope, fear, or greed. The influence of an anchor is profound and pervasive. Depending on where that anchor is located, we could be happy and confident in our ability to pick winners and take on more risk, or depressed with fear and self-recrimination and trapped in the quicksand of "shoulda, coulda, woulda." And if we really want to be hard on ourselves, we'll start using the word stupid: "I was stupid for not selling." "I was stupid for buying that stock in the first place." It's human nature.

The important thing to remember, however, is an anchor price has no importance except perhaps at tax time. You might just as well pick any other price out of history, because the price you paid, or at which you could have bought the stock, is in the past. It's gone. Things have changed and you need to change too.

Often professionals at this point will reevaluate the stock with one question in mind: "Would I buy the stock at this price?" If the answer is no, they sell. If yes, they hold. In other words, the price we paid has nothing to do with its current price or its future as an investment.

Forecasting errors

Often, we think the recent trend will continue forever. Clearly trends don't last forever, and trees don't grow to the sky (an old Wall Street saying). Sometimes trends can suddenly reverse and comes crashing down if the recent trend was up, or break out and move higher if the recent trend was down. As humans, we don't like to delve into reams of data or detailed analysis. Instead we like to forecast based on rules of thumb, educated guesses, or stereotyping. Rules of thumb are based in the past and may or may not hold in the future. By the time you find out, however, it might be too late. Educated guesses, often called intuition, can be powerful but, unless you make a career of the stock market, how do you acquire the knowledge to make one? Stereotyping is if one stock in an industry is going up then all stocks in that industry must eventually go up too. We forget there's good management and products and bad ones too. We love short-cuts and hope they will hold true. Often, they don't.

Gambler's fallacy

If the stock's price is below the anchor, a gambler might buy more to reduce the average cost in the hopes of a recovery. Buying more stock as it declines in price is the basis for the dollar cost averaging strategy we covered in Chapter 21. However, as we also learned, buying more stock in a company destined for bankruptcy is not such a good idea. You'll end up with enough stock certificates to paper the walls and little else. If you're going to average down, you better make sure your purchase will be around for a while. Averaging down in a broad-based market index fund where you are diversified across many companies might make sense. With that type of investment, you are betting on the recovery of the economy rather than an individual company.

The gambler's fallacy, together with anchoring, not only influences our decisions on the downside but also on the upside. There is a tendency to think we're brilliant and on a winning streak and that it will continue. We get greedy and start buying more aggressively.

Holding losing stocks and selling winners

Doing that is a bit like pulling out the roses in your garden and keeping the weeds. Quite often the losing position will lose even more before an investor finally sells in disgust at a substantial loss. I heard one investor say "If I never sell, then I'll never have a loss." I couldn't help but think "A declining stock is an indication there is something wrong with that company and, if it goes bankrupt, you'll lose everything." It's far better to do the reverse. Sell your losers and let your winners run.

To avoid this trap, you might consider developing sell rules. Some investors use the percentage-decline rule where if the stock declines a certain percentage from its buy-point, the stock gets sold immediately. You can pick the percentage that suits you, but you might want to give the stock a little leeway because, if the number is too tight, you might find yourself stopped out of a good position. Others like to use technical analysis to help with the sell decision (see Chapter 22). If the stock goes down shortly after you bought it, that might be a signal you made a mistake. Mistakes happen, so you might consider immediately reevaluate the assumptions you made and if you think they are still sound, wait. However, if the percentage-decline rule or the technical analysis indicates sell, you sell, then wait, and possibly reenter in the future, or move on. Finally, although I suggest holding your winners, they can become ridiculously priced. The company's fundamentals and the stock's technicals should be reevaluated and you might consider placing trailing stops.

And, yes, I have seen a stock reverse course and move higher after I sold it. However, with sell rules you are protecting your capital so that you will have the funds to continue investing. More often than not, a small loss will be small when compared to how far that stock could sink.

There's an old saying that you'll never go broke by taking a gain. On the surface that's true. But will you become wealthy by taking short-term gains and holding onto your losers? Perhaps. But I think you're more likely to do better by selling your losers and letting your winners continue to run.

Finally, you should not talk about your stock investments. Doing so sometimes creates a tendency to defend a losing position and diminishes your flexibility.

Following the crowd

Loss aversion, regret avoidance, and self-recrimination might lead us to follow the crowd. We are told that more minds are better than one, so all those people who are investing in a particular stock, industry, sector, factor, or the market itself must be right. We're not sure of ourselves and psychologically it's easier to just go along with the crowd.

Rather than being pulled in with an investment that is increasing in price, we might get pulled in by a good story. After all, everyone loves a good story. Hollywood makes billions of dollars telling stories visually. Novels, rap and folk music, and gossip are all storytelling in one form or another. So why would we expect stocks to be any different? We hear tales of Facebook doing this and Apple doing that. "Have you heard about the new product?" "I made a lot of money in stock X." There is a real temptation to buy the stock without even doing some basic research. We'll just follow the crowd with hope and greed in mind.

Sure, that strategy might work for a while, but soon the crowd will turn, and if you don't turn before everyone else you might get burned, and badly. Sometimes following the crowd is an example of the greater fool theory I discussed earlier. The classical example of this is the tulip bulb mania in Holland in 1637 that I mentioned in the "Bubbles" section of this chapter. Yes, tulip bulbs – the ones you see growing in the spring – centuries ago became an investment bubble. Why tulip bulbs? They were rare, desirable, and a status symbol, but the bubble that was created was because so many people were making money buying and selling them that others decided to follow the crowd. In fact, at the height of the bubble, some tulip bulbs were in such demand that they sold for four times what a skilled craftsman earned in a year. Then the bubble burst.

Becoming extremely negative

This is another trait we should be aware of when the market is going down, especially after it has gone down a lot. Yes, you've lost money, perhaps lots of money. You sell and swear you'll never, ever invest in the stock market again. "The market is fixed." "Only the fat cats can make money." More and more negative thoughts and words come out, and in all that negativity you lose sight of the fact that good investments are always occurring. But you miss them because your brain is in a negative fog.

What helps me in these emotional slumps is faith in our economic system – free market capitalism.

Overconfidence

This is the opposite of inaction and negativity. We are absolutely sure that something will happen. We convince ourselves that this stock will go up. No doubt about it. We're so confident that we decide to put all of our money into the stock and what happens? It goes down.

Now investors need some degree of confidence in themselves and in the future or they will constantly sit on the sidelines replaying the opportunities that passed them by. Although we can study all we want about past performance, we need to remember that that's all in the past. For example, stock prices may seem high relative to history. But does that mean the market will go down? No, the market doesn't work by looking backward. Only forward. We don't know for sure what's going to happen. And neither does the person who says they are 100% confident of a stock's direction. Unforeseen events occur.

Overrating our abilities

Sometimes we think we are so smart when we pick a stock and it goes up that we forget that perhaps we were just lucky. The marketplace is loaded with some really smart people. So not only do you have to be smart, you have to be smarter or luckier than the others who are buying and selling shares as well. Moreover, just because you were successful in one area of your life doesn't mean you'll be successful in the stock market. A little humility goes a long way.

Chasing winners

Much of our society is short-term oriented. We want it and we want it now. That can translate into someone who likes to buy and sell stocks over a very short period of time based on whichever stock is moving up. If the price of one company's stock is not moving, sell it and move on to one that is. Some people can make a lot of money this way, but they may lose it just as fast. In general, however, all they are doing is making their broker rich. Besides, rapid trading negates a teenager's investment advantage, and that is a long investment time horizon. Emotionally driven noise traders lose money, if not from poor decisions, then from accumulated transaction costs.

Falling in love with a company

I've often found myself in this trap: riding the company up, then making excuses for it on the way down. I told myself, "Sales will pick up next quarter and all will be good." This emotion is probably the hardest one for a long-term investor to deal with, that is, when to cut the ties with a company you have come to love. Sorry to say, each company requires a cold-eyed look, and sometimes it's better to dump the stock and put the money into another one.

When Is the Influence the Strongest?

Now that I've pointed out some possible emotional reactions, you might ask when in the investment process are they likely to have the strongest influence? You'll have to decide that for yourself. For me, I've outlined in Appendix A where I feel my emotional stresses are the strongest. Then, when I'm seeking to buy, for example, I'll review the "buy" side of the list to see if I'm being unduly influenced by a subconscious emotion. The same applies when I'm thinking about holding or selling.

APPENDIX A
Strongest Influence

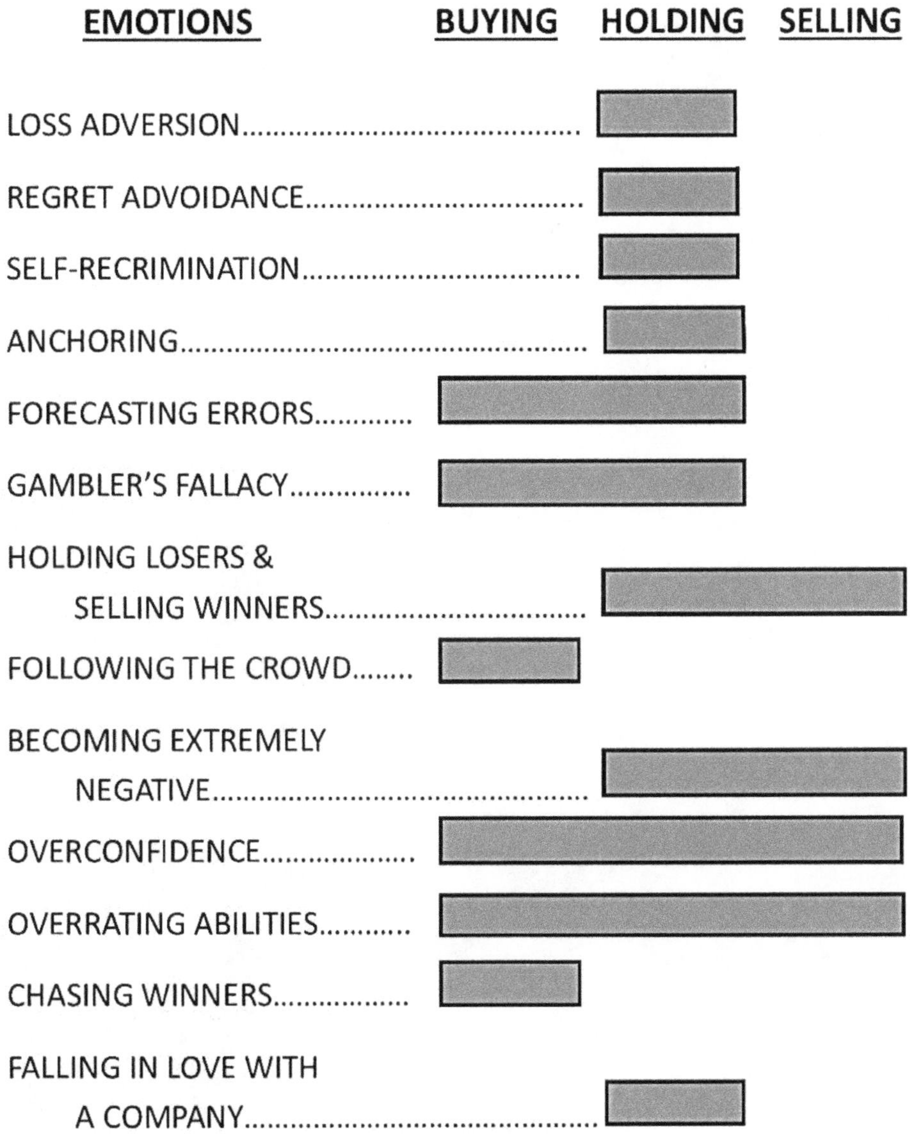
EMOTIONS
BUYING
HOLDING
SELLING
LOSS ADVERSION
REGRET ADVOIDANCE
SELF-RECRIMINATION
ANCHORING
FORECASTING ERRORS
GAMBLER'S FALLACY
HOLDING LOSERS & SELLING WINNERS
FOLLOWING THE CROWD
BECOMING EXTREMELY NEGATIVE
OVERCONFIDENCE
OVERRATING ABILITIES
CHASING WINNERS
FALLING IN LOVE WITH A COMPANY

CHAPTER 23

Technical Market Approach

Pythagoras, a Greek philosopher who died in 495 BCE, is quoted as saying, "All things are numbers." If he were alive today and working on Wall Street, I think he would be working as a "technician." That's the name given to people who believe the future direction of the market is hidden in historical price and volume numbers. A technician would say that if you can identify past trends, you can predict the future.

As you might expect, many, including the academics, make fun of the theory and say it's like reading tea leaves, or, to put it in the terms familiar to Pythagoras' time, like reading the entrails of sacrificial animals. Technicians reply by saying, "Don't be so quick to judge." Technical analysis is based on sound logic and, if properly implemented, can add significant value. Besides, it is a very appealing way to avoid dealing with the complexity of the investment environment. Why read financial reports or worry about what is happening in the economy? Those reports are always changing and often give conflicting signals anyway. Just look at the historical price and volume trends. The answers are there.

In this chapter I will give you the logic behind the technical market approach to market timing. Then, we'll look at the different types of charts that are used to develop trading rules. I'll then discuss charting patterns and trending techniques and what they purport to be saying about the future direction of the market. I will conclude with a list of market breath indicators.

The Logic Behind Technical Analysis

The logic is straightforward and at some level makes sense. Changes in a stock's price are determined by willing buyers and willing sellers operating

253

in a free and open market. What brought them together could be the fundamental analysis of a company, the desire to take advantage of a factor, or maybe they're acting on emotions such as fear, hope, and greed. But according to technicians, the only thing that matters is that a willing buyer and a willing seller met and agreed on a price and a trade was consummated. Therefore, supply and demand determine a stock's price, and the most important thing is what the market is doing now, not what brought the traders together.

If that sounds like the efficient market theory, you'd be right except for one big difference: Technical market theorists also believe stock prices move in long trends and follow certain patterns, whereas the efficient market theorists believe stock prices respond to unforeseen and randomly occurring information. In other words, one believes if you are skillful enough to spot trends and patterns early enough in their development, you can make some money. The other believes that this is nonsense since the historical patterns were actually the result of randomly occurring information and thinking otherwise is a result of a human frailty that assumes the future will be like the past.

Regardless of which side of the debate you take, it is human nature to look at a historical stock chart and see trends and patterns emerging. And after viewing these patterns for different stocks and over different time periods, you're tempted to make a trading rule to capture some profit the next time you believe a similar pattern is starting to occur. The trading rules that are the result of these observations can be straightforward or complex. Some are so complex and subjective that I wonder if they are not the result of data mining.

But technical analysis, in my opinion, does play a role in investment analysis – if not in logic, then in hope. For example, consider value stocks. The premise of a value stock is that it trades below its intrinsic value. Okay, but when do you buy the stock? Perhaps it is cheap now, but maybe it will get even cheaper or perhaps even slide into bankruptcy in the future. So, what should you do: buy now and hope it will appreciate in price soon, or wait and let technical analysis help you make a decision? Most active investors will take any help they can get and will wait until some technical rule tells them it's okay to buy.

Charting

Before we get too technical – no pun intended – technicians rely on charts and as a result are often also called "chartists." A chart is intended to provide visual information about the movement of a stock over some time frame. The chart can be developed from data consisting of the high, low, and closing prices as well as of the volume of trades, or all of them. The plotted data can have happened during the day, week, month, or any other time period. The horizontal axis denotes time, whereas the vertical axis dollar amounts. The data can be plotted as a line, bar, candlestick, or point and figure chart. How detailed you make it is up to you.

The best way to explain these different charting techniques is for you to see what they look like. I'm not going to use actual charts but rather stylized ones so you can understand the concept. Later I will pull it all together with an actual chart.

Line chart

This type of chart just connects the closing prices with a line, hence its name. It is mostly used for very long-time frames, such as years or decades (see Figure 23-1).

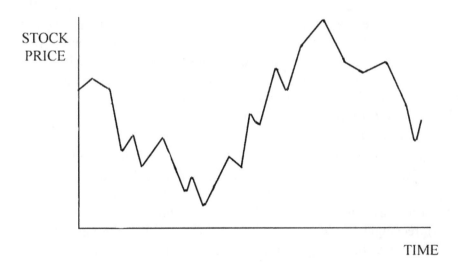

Figure 23-1

Bar chart

This type of chart connects the high and low price that occurred during the time interval with a vertical line. The closing price is then drawn as a small horizontal line as shown in Figure 23-2.

STOCK PRICE

HIGH

CLOSE

LOW

TIME

Figure 23-2

Candlestick chart

Candlestick charting is said to have been developed centuries ago by a Japanese rice trader who was trying to visually display the collective emotions of other traders in the rice market. He started with a bar chart, but then added another small horizontal line for the opening price. He then created a rectangle by connecting the edges of the horizontal lines used to identify opening and closing prices. The rectangle was kept blank (or now is colored green) if the closing price was greater than the opening price and colored black (or now red) if the closing price was below the opening price (see Figure 23-3).

The small vertical line above the rectangles are called wicks and, together with the rectangles, made the figures look like candlesticks, hence the name of this charting technique. A series of long black (or red) rectangles suggest a bearish phase (a declining market) and a series of long blank (or green) rectangles suggest a bullish phase (a rising market). A mixture indicates a possible change in market emotions and thus direction.

The size of the rectangle and the length of the wicks are supposed to communicate information to short-term traders. For example, a short rectangle with longs wicks above and below is called a spinning top and is supposed to indicate a neutral market. A small box at the top of a long wick is called a hanging man and thought to be a warning sign of a reversal in an uptrend. A box at the bottom of a long wick is called a shooting star and is thought to be an unfavorable downward sign. Finally, a box at the top of a long wick with a short top wick is called a hammer and, if found in a down

256

trend, is thought to be a sign of a possible reversal. There are many other characterizations.

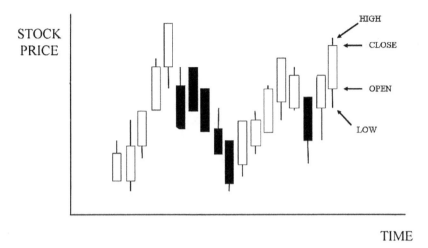

Figure 23-3

The inclusion of volume

The volume of shares traded is also added to some of the charts. Up-volume is when the stock's closing price is higher than it was the day before, and down-volume is when the stock's closing price is lower than it was the day before. A lightly colored (or green) vertical line represents up-volume and a dark (or red) vertical line represents down-volume. Some technicians like to overlay the volume chart with a moving average to highlight significant changes in volume (see Figure 23-4).

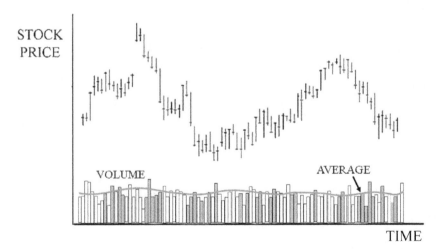

Figure 23-4

Point and figure chart

This type of chart does not have time intervals or volume numbers, since only significant price changes are displayed. As a result, some say it focuses on what is most important in identifying trends – changes in price.

When constructing a point and figure chart, the technician must first decide what constitutes a significant price change. That depends, in part, on whether the technician intends to use the chart for identifying short- or long-term trends. If a short-term trend is desired, smaller price changes would be appropriate; if a long-term trend is desired, larger price changes would be appropriate. Instead of using dollar changes in prices, some prefer to use percentage changes. These price changes are represented by "boxes" and they are placed one on top of another to form a column (see Figure 23-5). A series of X's in a column represents consecutive upward price changes and a series of O's in a column represents consecutive downward price changes.

The second thing for the technician to decide is whether to use closing prices for all measurements or a combination of high, low, and closing prices – high when the stock is in an uptrend, low when the stock is in a downtrend, and closing prices at all other times.

Finally, the technician must decide the reversal amount, that is, what size price change would signal a reversal. Reversals are often talked about in terms of boxes. Some like only a one-box change, others a three-box change before a new column is used.

As an example, say a $1 closing price change in a stock currently selling for $30 a share is considered a significant price change. The technician would draw a grid like you see in Figure 23-5. Each box would represent a $1 change in price. If the stock's price moves up $1 from its $30 starting point and closes in the $31.00 to $31.99 range, the technician would place an X in that box representing an upward change in price. If in the next time period the stock moved up again and closed within the $32.00 to $32.99 range, another X would be placed in the column. If in the following time period the stock closed within the $35.00 to $35.99 range, three more X's would be placed in the column. Assuming we are using a one-box reversal, if the stock moved down the following time period and closed between $34.99 and $34.00, the technician would start a new column and place an O in that box. If in the following time period the stock closed between $32.99 and $32.00, the technician would put two more Os in that column. If the price action did not trigger either an X or an O, no mark would be made. As the process is repeated, the stock's price movements are revealed graphically.

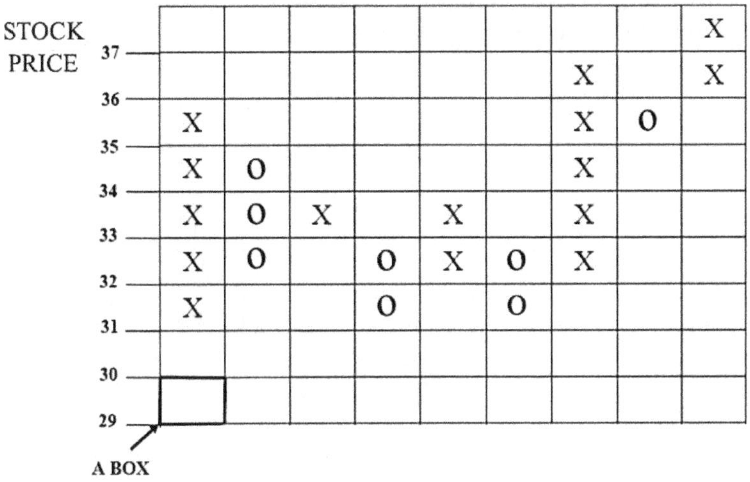

Figure 23-5

Chart Patterns

Once a chart is drawn, technicians like to look for patterns as clues for the future direction of a stock, industry, sector, factor, or market index. Since identifying a pattern is often a visual exercise, it is said to involve more art than science. Artificial intelligence, which is said to be particularly good at pattern recognition, might make the exercise more rigorous. Here are some patterns out of the hundreds that are possible and what they are supposed to be telling us about the future.

Trendlines

When the stock appears to be trending upward, it is useful for technical traders to plot a straight line along key low points. If the up trendline is "broken," some interpret this to mean the start of a downward trend (see Figure 23-6). Conversely, when the market appears to be trending downward, a straight line plotted along key high points helps reveal the trend. In this scenario, if a trendline is broken, it might mean the start of an uptrend (see Figure 23-7).

Up and down trendlines get broken all the time without a change in the original trend. Therefore, some technicians apply another rule saying the trendline must be broken by some dollar or percentage amount before becoming a valid signal.

Finally, you must exercise caution when plotting a trendline. You may get conflicting signals depending on the time frame you use. For example, a month's worth of price movement might indicate a down trend, whereas a year's worth might indicate an uptrend.

Figure 23-6

Figure 23-7

Channels

This does not refer to what you find on your TV set but rather a boundary within which something moves like a boat between the banks of a river. A technician is looking for what happens when the stock bumps against one of the boundaries; perhaps more important, when the stock's price pierces the boundary, because that is often viewed as a signal of a change in market direction. Channels can be constructed by visual observations or mathematically.

Visual observation: A technician would look at a bar chart and draw two trendlines – one that connects significant low points and the other that connects significant high points, thus creating a channel (see Figure 23-8 for an up channel). The same idea applies for a down channel.

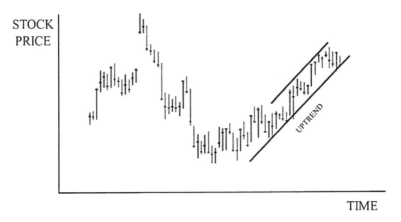

Figure 23-8

Mathematical construction: This technique can be accomplished in many different ways. For example, a moving average might be constructed using the stock's high price and another might be constructed using the stock's low price (more about moving averages later). When both are plotted, they approximate a channel in which the stock has meandered. Another mathematical way is called the Bollinger Band®, which is named after John Bollinger who developed it. I'll let you research how that one is constructed as well as all the other ways channels can be mathematically constructed.

Cup and handle

As you can see from Figure 23-9, the pattern is aptly named. The cup portion generally develops over an extended period of time after the stock has finished an uptrend. The stock price gradually goes down, reverses and gradually goes up until it reaches the previous high thus completing the bowl portion of the cup. As people who bought earlier fear a major decline start selling, a portion of the handle starts to appear. But others recognize this is really a buying opportunity and the price moves above the previous high, at which time a buy signal is supposedly given.

Chartists say for best results, the cup should have a cup-like depth and opening rather than a sharp, deep, and narrow opening like a wine glass.

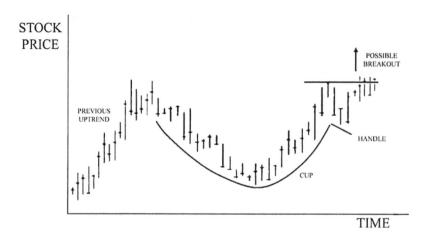

Figure 23-9

Support and resistance

When you look at enough charts you begin to see a repeating pattern where a declining stock, industry, sector, factor, or market index hits a certain level, or "floor," and bounces off it like a rubber ball and, so the theory goes, moves higher. Chartists call these "support levels." The reverse also happens, that is, a rising stock hits a certain level, or "ceiling," and bounces off that before it goes down. Chartists call this a "resistance level." Support and resistance lines are normally horizontal, so they differ from trendlines.

What causes support and resistance levels to occur has been debated without a conclusive answer. The theories range from differing opinions on intrinsic value, to the psychology of anchoring that I discussed in Chapter 22. The simplest explanation, perhaps, is that if enough investors believe support and resistance levels exist, they become a self-fulfilling prophecy until significant new information changes investor opinion and a break out occurs. Figure 23-10 shows what support and resistance lines might look like.

Triangle

This pattern combines the plot of a down trendline with an up trendline where over time the pattern starts to resemble a triangle (or flag depending on its length). As the triangle forms towards a point, pressure builds for a break out of these conflicting opinions of direction. When that occurs, a new trend might be established (see Figure 23-11).

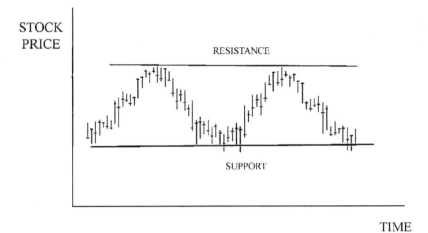

Figure 23-10

Figure 23-11

Other chart patterns

In Figure 23-12 and Figure 23-13 I have shown some other important chart patterns that technicians watch for. One is aptly called "head and shoulders" and the other "double bottom." They are self-explanatory.

Figure 23-12

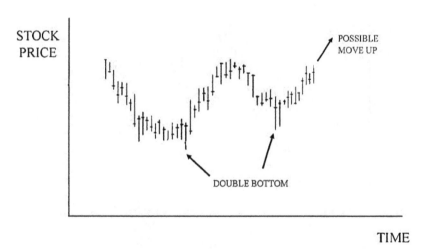

Figure 23-13

Moving Averages

Since a moving average uses historical data, it only provides a picture of the past; since it is an average, it does so with a lag. Technicians like to combine the moving average with other techniques to establish trading rules for when to buy and sell.

A moving average has three parts: (1) the moving aspect of the average; (2) the number of datapoints used to compute the average; and (3) the weight or emphasis given to each data point in the average. For the first element, its moving aspect occurs when a new data point is available, then it is included and the oldest data point is dropped, causing the average to move forward through time.

The second part is the number of datapoints you use to compute the average. For example, you can use 2, 20, 100, or more datapoints – whatever number you think is important. This is often referred to as the length of the average. The fewer datapoints you use the more responsive the moving average will be to newer incoming data but the greater it will be exposed to noise and the possibility of creating a trendline where one doesn't exist. However, the more datapoints you use, the less responsive the moving average will be and thus the more likely you will miss the start of a new trend.

The final part is the weight you give to each data point in the average, and thus its importance in the average. Many technicians give equal weight to each data point, whereas others believe newer incoming data are more relevant and should be given more weight in the calculations. There are many possible weighting schemes. Here are some of them.

Simple moving average (SMA)

This is often called an equal-weighted average since all the datapoints are given an equal value of 1. The weighted datapoints are then totaled and divided by the sum or the weights. Figure 23-14 shows the resulting calculations for a five-period moving average.

FIVE- PERIOD MOVING AVERAGE

DATA POINT (A)	WEIGHTING SCHEME (B)	WEIGHTED DATA POINT (C)=(A)*(B)	SUM OF WEIGHTED DATA POINT (D)=Σ(C)	AVERAGE EQUALS (D) DIVIDED BY SUM OF WEIGHTS
10.00	1	10.00	48.95	9.79
9.65	1	9.65		
7.28	1	7.28		
11.00	1	11.00		
11.05	1	11.05		
10.95				
9.75				
8.65				
9.03				
9.25				
9.65				
10.50				
SUM OF THE WEIGHTS =	5			

Figure 23-14

Weighted moving average (WMA)

This moving average uses a different weighting scheme than the SMA. It could be anything you want. For this example, I will use a progression that starts with a weight of 1 for the oldest data point and then increases the weight by 1 until the most recent data point is reached. Figure 23-15 shows the resulting calculations for a five-period moving average.

FIVE- PERIOD MOVING AVERAGE

DATA POINT (A)	WEIGHTING SCHEME (B)	WEIGHTED DATA POINT (C)=(A)*(B)	SUM OF WEIGHTED DATA POINT (D)=Σ(C)	AVERAGE EQUALS (D) DIVIDED BY SUM OF WEIGHTS
10.00	5	50.00	143.4	9.56
9.65	4	38.60		
7.28	3	21.75		
11.00	2	22.00		
11.05	1	11.05		
10.95				
9.75				
8.65				
9.03				
9.25				
9.65				
10.50				
SUM OF THE WEIGHTS =	15			

Figure 23-15

Exponential moving average (EMA)

This moving average uses a weight scheme that increases exponentially over time. For this scheme you need to first calculate the smoothing factor which is 2/(N+1) where N is equal to the length of the average. The formula then becomes:

$$EMA = \left[\text{Closing Price} - \text{Previous Day's EMA} \right] \times \text{Smoothing Factor} + \text{Previous Day's EMA}$$

Since we don't have a "previous day's EMA" in our example, to get the average started we need to fabricate one. Most technicians use a simple moving average. For our five-period moving average N is equal to 5 thus the smoothing factor is equal to .333 (2 divided by the sum of 5 plus 1) and our five-period moving average is 9.42 (see Figure 23-16). The other EMA numbers are calculated using the above formula.

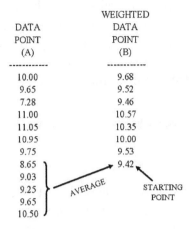

FIVE- PERIOD MOVING AVERAGE

Figure 23-16

Median value moving average (MVMA)

This approach uses the number where, out of a given length and ranking of datapoints, half the numbers are above and half are below that value (see Figure 23-17). This scheme is useful when the datapoints have one or several extreme numbers that if used in an average will distort the results.

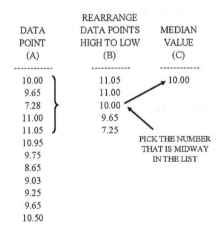

FIVE- PERIOD MOVING AVERAGE

Figure 23-17

The datapoints can be the closing price of a stock, industry, sector, factor, or market index over some time interval such as daily, weekly, or monthly. Some technicians use the high or low price for their moving averages, but most prefer using closing prices. The choice is up to the technician and, as you can now understand, many different trendlines giving different interpretations can be constructed from the same list of datapoints.

Some Ways to Use A Moving Average

Golden cross/death cross

The colorful name gives you an idea of what is going on here. In this strategy, two moving averages are computed, one of a shorter length than the other. The shorter one is considered an early warning signal as it is more responsive to incoming data. When the shorter one crosses the longer one from the bottom moving upward, that crossover is supposed to signal a possible future upward movement of the

> *"One of the funny things about the stock market is that every time one person buys, another sells, and both think they are astute." – William Feather*

market and thus a buying opportunity. It is called the "Golden Cross" for the obvious reason. When the reverse happens and the shorter one crosses the longer one from the top moving downward, that is supposed to signal a possible future downward change and thus a selling opportunity. It's the "Death Cross" portion of the title. Sometimes 50-day and 200-day averages are used. Others like the 12- and 26-week combination. Some prefer a simple weighting scheme while others prefer an exponential one. The choices are up to the technician.

Convergence/divergence oscillator

From a colorful name we go to a technical one. This indicator also uses two moving averages of different lengths and perhaps even different weights. But rather than being concerned with crossover points, this indicator is concerned with how far the moving averages move apart. The idea is that the further apart they move (diverge), the more likely it is that there will be a reversal (they will converge). This idea is based on the theory of reversion to the mean, which states that the further a value moves from its trendline, the more likely it is to reverse course and head back to it. An extreme divergence is said to be an early warning signal of a change in direction. You might see this oscillator referred to as MACD, which stands for Moving Average Convergence Divergence index.

Ribbons

Some technicians like to compute multiple moving averages of different lengths and plot them on a chart to try and tease out buy and sell signals. When these ribbons tend to converge the thought is the uptrend is weakening and a downturn might be coming. On the other hand, when the ribbons are wide and widening the thought is the uptrend is strong. The number of moving averages, and of what length and type, varies from technician to technician.

Combined Chart

I have given you the concepts, so now let's see what a combined chart looks like (see Figure 23-18).

Figure 23-18

Relative Strength

As you learned earlier, the word "relative" can be tricky and we should always ask the question, "Relative to what?" For example, we can compute the strength of a stock's return relative to its past performance, to the market's performance, or to other stocks in a list. We can also compare one industry or sector to another, or one market index to another.

Although point-in-time comparisons of relative strength are interesting, using the raw relative numbers in the construction of trendlines, support and resistance lines, moving averages, and convergence/divergence oscillators might be more useful when making buy, sell, or hold decisions.

Raw numbers

There are many ways to calculate relative strength. One way is to calculate the percent return for one part of the comparison and subtract from it the percent return for the other part using the same time period for the calculation of returns. The time period could be daily, weekly, monthly, or whatever time period you deem important. For example, assume you wanted to compute the relative performance of Apple to the S&P 500 index and you wanted to use changes in weekly prices for the last two years. For last week, assume Apple's price change was +1.50% and the S&P 500's was +0.60%. Thus, the relative performance of Apple for that week was 0.90 (1.50% minus 0.60%). A plus sign means Apple outperformed the S&P 500 and a negative sign it underperformed. You would continue going back in time week by week for the two-year period. As a result, you will have identified the raw relative strength numbers to conduct the studies I outlined earlier.

Another way to calculate the raw relative strength numbers is to divide the ending price by the beginning price for one part of the comparison and divide that by the result of dividing the ending price by the beginning price for the other part of the comparison. For example, assume the ending price for the month for Apple was 214.30 and the beginning of the month's price was 209.88. Dividing the ending stock price by the beginning stock price, we get 1.021. Now do the same for an index fund where its ending price for the month was 293.54 and its beginning price for the month was 294.72. The result is 0.996. Then divide the 1.021 by .996 and our resulting raw relative strength number is 1.025. Above 1.0 means Apple was performing better than the S&P 500. Had the number been below one, it would have meant that Apple was performing worse that the S&P 500.

These approaches could be done for Apple versus Microsoft, the S&P 500 index versus the Nasdaq index, the technology sector versus healthcare, or whatever comparison you deem relevant. Either of the above approaches is fine, just be consistent.

Relative strength as compared to other stocks in a list

The above was for comparing this versus that. But what if you wanted to compare the relative performance of one stock versus a list of other stocks. The list could consist of 10, 100, 500, or more stocks. How would you do that? You would start by determining how many stocks are in your list (in our calculations that number will be referred to as "N"). You would then compute the return for each stock over the same time period and rank the results highest to lowest. Next, you would determine where in the list the target stock is located (in our calculations that number will be referred to as

"R"). Finally, you would divide R by N, subtract the resulting number from 1.0, and multiple that by 100. The result is the percentile of your stock. For example, say the target stock is fifth (R) from the top of a list of 20 (N) performance ranked stocks. R divided by N equals 0.25. Subtracting that number from 1.0 and multiplying the result by 100 results in a value of 75. So, the target stock is the 75th percentile meaning its performance was better than 75 percent of the other stocks in the list.

Again, this is for only one point in time. To add meaning you need to repeat the process for as far back in time as you deem relevant.

Using relative strength

The analysis of relative strength can be used in many ways. For example, some technicians use the results to focus on those stocks that are exhibiting relative strength in expectation that the strength will continue. Others look for relative weakness and use that as a sign of a possible money-making reversal. Still others believe that stocks that decline less than the market when the market is declining are the ones that perform better than the market when the market recovers and moves higher. Some think those stocks that are weaker than the market when the market is rising are often the ones that fall the hardest when the market reverses and declines.

Some use the relative strength of industries or sectors to pick the strongest and then pick the strongest stocks within that industry or sector. Others might use relative strength for market timing. That is, when consumer discretionary and technology stocks are stronger than the market, perhaps the market is becoming more aggressive. On the other hand, if utility, healthcare, and consumer staple stocks are stronger than the market, perhaps the market is becoming more defensive. As you can see, there are many ways to use relative strength. But remember, like all technical analysis it is based on historical data and relative performance should be used in conjunction with other indicators.

Market Breath Indicators

Breath, in this context, is not what your diaphragm and lungs are doing to keep you alive. Rather, if you check the thesaurus, you'll find these synonyms for breath: spirt, vigor, and force. Therefore, market breath means the market's spirit, vigor, or force. Often this is interpreted to mean indicators that compare (1) the number of stocks reaching their 52-week high price versus the number of stocks reaching their 52-week low price; (2) the number of advancing stocks versus the number of declining stocks; and (3) the volume of advancing stocks versus the volume of declining stocks. These different breath indicators can be used alone, but they also find themselves in various combinations in all different kinds of breath indicators. For visual effect the indicators could be plotted on a chart resembling the line chart discussed earlier. Some like to take it one step further and compute a moving average of the values.

On-balance indicator

This indicator keeps a running total of up- and down-volume. When the market closes above the previous close (previous day, week, month, or whatever period the technician decides is important), it is considered to be up-volume and is added to the running total. When the market closes below the previous period, it is considered to be down-volume and is subtracted from the running total.

This indicator was developed by Joseph Granville in the 1960s. The idea behind it is that changes in the direction of the running total precede a change in stock prices.

Accumulation–distribution indicator

This indicator also keeps track of up- and down-volume but in a different way. It takes into consideration where the closing price lies in relationship to the period's high and low values, computes a multiplier from that relationship, and then applies the multiplier to the volume before it is added to the running total. Marc Chaikin developed this indicator. The calculations are shown in Figure 23-19.

$$\text{Value to be Added to the Running Total} = \frac{\left[\text{Close - Low}\right] - \left[\text{High - Close}\right]}{\left[\text{High - Low}\right]} \times \text{Period's Volume}$$

Figure 23-19

The direction of the line is often used as a confirmation of a trendline, or, if the market and the line are moving in opposite directions, an indication of a possible change in the market.

Advance-decline indicator

This indicator keeps a running total of the difference between advancing and declining stocks. As explained earlier, advancing stocks are those whose close is above the previous close and declining stocks are those whose close is below the previous close. Another indicator based on the same idea keeps a running total of the difference between advancing volume and declining volume. Volume is often considered to be the number of shares rather than the dollar volume. The direction of both indicators is considered to be an indication of the strength of the current trend.

TRIN (Trader Index)

This breath indicator was invented by Richard W. Arms, Jr. It combines the number of advancing and declining stocks with volume, volume being number of shares traded. The calculations are shown in Figure 23-20.

$$\text{TRIN} = \frac{\text{Advancing Stocks Divided by Declining Stocks}}{\text{Advancing Volume Divided by Declining Volume}}$$

Figure 23-20

A TRIN above one, is thought to be a bearish signal; if below one, a bullish signal. Some computed TRIN over a period of time as a moving average and look for extreme values as possible reversals of market direction.

Absolute breath index (ABI)

This index was developed by Norman G. Fosback and also combines the number of advancing stocks and declining stocks with volume. The calculations are shown in Figure 23-21.

$$\text{ABI} = \frac{\text{Absolute Value}\left[\text{Advancing Stocks - Declining Stocks}\right]}{\text{Number of Shares Traded}}$$

Figure 23-21

Since this index uses the absolute value, it doesn't show direction, only that volatility is increasing, and this could mean a change in market direction.

Money flow index

This index, created by Gene Quong and Avrum Soudack, attempts to measure the relative amount of money (dollars) that flows into and out of a stock. It's generally thought of as a short-term indicator of investor enthusiasm.

The first thing you need to do is to calculate the "typical" price of the stock you are interested in during the time period that is being measured. Most technicians will approximate it by adding the high, low, and closing prices together and divide the total by three. Next, you would multiple the typical price by the day's volume to get a raw money flow number (see Figure 23-22).

$$\text{Raw Money Flow Number} = \underbrace{\frac{\left[\text{High} + \text{Low} + \text{Close} \right]}{3}}_{\text{Typical Price}} \times \text{Volume}$$

Figure 23-22

Next you will need to identify whether the flow is positive and negative. Positive flow is when today's typical price is above yesterday's typical price; negative flow is when today's typical price is below yesterday's typical price.

Now you have several choices. You could just use those positive and negative flow numbers in the calculation or, better yet, maintain two columns, one for positive flow and another for negative flow. For each column, you could either maintain a running total over a specified length of time (a week, a month, or longer) or you could also calculate a moving average for each column.

Once you have the positive and negative money flow numbers, either the current ones, a running total over some time period, or a moving average, you're ready for the final step (see Figure 23-23).

$$\text{Money Flow Index} = 100 - \frac{100}{1 + \left[\dfrac{\text{Positive Money Flow}}{\text{Negative Money Flow}} \right]}$$

Figure 23-23

A value over 80 often is considered a signal of an overbought condition and under 20 an oversold condition.

Do these market breath indicators always work as intended? Of course not. While they might be useful, they certainly are not definitive – especially when used alone.

> *Technicians believe stock prices move in long trends and follow certain patterns. The difficult part is identifying the trend or pattern early enough in order to make some money.*

CHAPTER 24

Fundamental Market Approach

Investors who follow the fundamental approach to market timing believe there is a solid link between future economic conditions and stock prices. In this chapter I will start by explaining a basic model used in fundamental market timing – earnings times the PE ratio. I will list some of the key economic indicators that are often helpful in making earnings forecasts. Next, we'll look at some sentiment indices that are commonly used to develop a future PE ratio. Finally, we'll look at some future trends in fundamental market timing.

The Basic Model Used by Fundamental Market Timers

Corporate earnings are generally thought to be the main driver of long-term stock returns. And earnings, in turn, largely depend on economic conditions. Thus, if you are going to engage in fundamental market timing you need to develop a personal vision or forecast of future economic conditions and, together with an assessment of the PE ratio, translate that into a market forecast. To do that you will be best served by employing a four-step approach using the S&P 500 index as a proxy for the stock market:

> **Step one:** Using key economic indicators, develop an economic forecast.
> **Step two:** Convert the economic forecast into an S&P 500 earnings forecast.
> **Step three:** Develop a PE ratio forecast for the S&P 500.

Step four: Multiply the earnings forecast by the PE ratio forecast, and the result is your forecast for the S&P 500.

Once you have your forecast for the value of the S&P 500 you can then compare that to its present value, and the outcome of this comparison will drive your buy, sell, and hold decisions. Most people who are engaged in fundamental market timing like to use the earnings forecast for the S&P 500 index as a proxy for the stock market because it simplifies the process. This index represents about 75% of the total capitalization of the U.S. stock market and contains companies that represent large segments of the economy, so it is a reasonable index to use. How do you develop the forecasts mentioned in the steps above?

For the economic forecast: You need to assess the direction of the economic indicators described in this chapter. No single one of these indicators will provide you with an answer, but collectively they will give you a general impression of future trends.

For the earnings forecast: Some like to take an historical trendline of the S&P 500 earnings and nudge their future forecasts one way or another based on their impression of what the economic indicators are saying. Others develop detailed econometric models for their forecasts.

For the PE ratio forecast: Some just use a simple historical average of the PE ratios for the S&P 500. Others use the historical average modified based on the results of the economic indicators or valuation measures. Still others use market sentiment indicators to make a judgment decision because they believe the PE ratio is largely emotionally driven. It's up to the person doing the analysis, and there is much debate about how to go about this.

Once you have made the forecasts, simply multiply the forecasted earnings by the forecasted PE ratio and, voila, you have a forecast for the S&P 500 that you can compare to existing numbers and therefore make market buy, hold, and sell decisions. This approach can be used for any future time period – the next quarter, the next year, or the next decade. It must be recognized, however, that the reliability of any forecast, which probably will be low to begin with, diminishes the more distant the forecast.

All that sounds so easy. It's not. Forecasting the future direction of an economy as complex as ours and translating that into an earnings number, much less forecasting the future PE ratio which is often driven by human emotions, is difficult to say the least. I have outlined in the next section some economic indicators that are often used to assess the future economic environment and therefore earnings. In the final section I have outlined indicators of investor sentiment that can play a role in forecasting the PE ratio.

Economic Indicators

When employing economic indicators, what's important to remember is that there is no one definitive indicator. There is a lot of noise in the data and these indicators often give contradictory signals. Also, there is a variable lead/lag time between changes in these indicators and changes in the economy. So, the best one can do is to take them in their totality and try to make a judgment call about the general future direction of the economy and the likely impact on the S&P 500. The following is a description of some of the most important indicators as well as a brief introduction to the Index of Leading Economic Indicators.

Direction of interest rates

Expectations about changes in interest rates play a huge role in stock valuations and hence in stock market timing. One way to illustrate this is to use a valuation model I discussed in Chapter 14. Referring to Figure 24-1, one of the components of that model is the discount rate. The discount rate has many parts, and one of the most important is interest rates. Thus, as interest rates change the discount rate is likely to do so too. The growth rate in dividends is also influenced by changes in interest rates. How? Changes in interest rates can impact a company's expenses which, in turn, impact earnings, and that in turn impacts the amount of cash available to make dividend payments, and thus, over time, the growth rate in dividends.

As you can see from Figure 24-1, an increase in the discount rate and a decrease in the growth rate in dividends causes the stock's intrinsic value, and, hence, its market price to decrease and, if enough stocks are impacted, a decline in the market results. This is why so many fundamental market timers pay such close attention to interest rates and the Federal Reserve's policies.

$$\text{Intrinsic Value} \Downarrow = \frac{\text{Dividend}}{\text{Discount Rate} \Uparrow - \text{Growth Rate in Dividends} \Downarrow}$$

Figure 24-1

Like the discount rate, interest rates also have many parts such as the time to maturity, credit risk, and, perhaps the largest component, inflation.

As inflation, or its prospects, increases so will interest rates (more about inflation later).

Shape of the yield curve

Another indicator that is closely watched for clues about the direction of the economy is the shape of the yield curve. The shape is determined by the difference between the yield to maturity of short-, medium-, and long-term debt instruments. Yield to maturity is the return you would receive if you held the instrument to maturity. When these datapoints are plotted on a graph you have what is called the yield curve.

Although a yield curve can be prepared for any grouping of debt instruments, many fundamental market timers like to use U.S. Treasury bills, notes, and bonds when constructing this graph. Treasury bills have a maturity of a year or less; notes a maturity of between 2 and 10 years, and bonds a maturity of between 10 and 30 years from when they were issued. If you want the current numbers, go to www.treasury.gov/resource-center on the internet and click "data," then "daily treasury yield curve rates." Your broker's research database may also have the data and might have already drawn the curve for you.

What's important to remember is that the yield curve is not static. Over time it can move up, down, or change shape based on the actions of the Fed and the buyers and sellers of government debt. By comparing the current shape to past historically significant curves, you might be able to glean predictive information. What are those different shapes telling us?

A normal shaped curve: The so-called normal yield curve has long-bond rates higher than short-bond rates. The rationale is that long-term bond investors are demanding greater compensation for investing their money for a longer period of time. A reasonably upward sloping curve is generally an indication of an economy that is growing at a reasonable pace (see Figure 24-7).

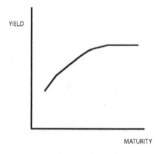

Figure 24-2

A steep curve: With a steep curve, long-term rates are very much higher than short-term rates. The rationale is that the Fed is attempting to lower short-term rates in order to stimulate weak economic growth. However, if the curve is simultaneously steep and is moving up, perhaps it might mean investors believe inflation is a problem (the reason for the entire curve moving up) and long-term bond investors are fearful of losing the value of their currency (the reason for the steepness). A rising and an ever increasingly steep curve is generally not a good sign for the stock market (see Figure 24-3).

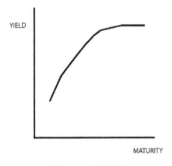

Figure 24-3

An inverted curve: Short-term rates are higher than long-term rates. The Fed might be trying to raise short-term rates because they are concerned about future inflation and want to slow the growth of the economy before inflation becomes a serious problem. In the past, an inverted curve has been an indication that a significant decline in economic activity is likely to occur in the near future, especially when the difference between 3-month and 10-year Treasury bonds is substantial and has been so for some period of time often for a month. This is generally not a good sign for stocks (see Figure 24-4).

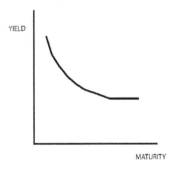

Figure 24-4

A flat curve: This is an indication of a transition in the economy. It can occur before a recession or economic growth (see Figure 24-5).

Figure 24-5

Measures of inflation

The causes of inflation have been hotly debated. Generally, it is thought that it comes from either cost push or demand pull. Cost push means that the cost of goods increases because of increased labor costs and/or raw material prices and that pushes up inflation. Demand pull means the demand for goods and services outstrips their supply and that pulls up inflation. Others have thought inflation is caused by increases in the supply of money, and still others have different ideas. In such a dynamic economy as ours it is unlikely that any single cause can be isolated.

Measuring inflation is not easy either. The U.S. Bureau of Labor Statistics (BLS) reports their Consumer Price Index (CPI) monthly. This index is based on the change in the price of a basket of consumer-related goods and services. Although what's in the basket may not change quickly enough to capture shifting consumer preferences, at least it gives a reasonable measure of the changes in the cost of living. The other monthly index reported by the BLS focuses on the goods-producing sectors of the economy and is called the Producer Price Index (PPI). It too has its faults but also provides a reasonable measure of changes in the costs incurred by businesses. Many market timers focus on the PPI because it tends to lead consumer price changes which, when you stop and think about it, makes sense. The increased cost to produce things often gets translated into higher costs for consumers.

The Fed preference is to use the "personal-consumption expenditures price index (PCE) excluding the more volatile items of food and energy." This is just a real long title for something that is a relatively straightforward measure of what you, me, your parents, and every other consumer spends on good and services in the U.S. economy; since food and energy costs tend to be more volatile, and that volatility can cloud the underlying trend, they are excluded. The index shows how much is spent versus how much is being saved for future consumption. The report is issued monthly by the Bureau of Economic Analysis, which is part of the Department of Commerce. The Bureau's website contains a host of other economic reports and studies.

All of these indices – CPI, PPI, and PCE – are useful but often market timers will either come up with their own measures of inflation or simply use the PPI.

The degree to which inflation impacts individual stock prices depends on the level and speed at which inflation increases and whether companies can pass their higher input costs on to customers. Depending on the industry, some companies can raise prices pretty much in line with inflation after a relatively short time lag so earnings should not suffer as much. When inflation goes down, however, the prices a company charges for its goods or services are more or less sticky, that is, prices remain the same or go down slowly, which tends to help boost company earnings, and that's good for the stocks of those companies. Therefore, declining inflation provides a nice sweet-spot for corporate earnings, but dramatically increasing inflation puts a real crunch on earnings, especially for those companies that can't adjust quickly.

Unemployment

The monthly number of the unemployed is published by the Bureau of Labor Statistics (BLS). The unemployment rate is defined as those individuals who are unemployed but are actively looking for work, divided by the labor force, which is defined as the unemployed plus the employed. The number is then seasonally adjusted to account for the fluctuation due to the seasonality of some jobs.

Changes in the unemployment rate give us clues on the tone of the country's economic environment. Understandably, people get nervous when the unemployment rate goes up because they don't know whether they will be the next to lose their job. As a consequence, spending goes down and therefore the economy gets dragged lower. There are also social implications when the unemployment rate rises that could influence governmental policies, including increases in welfare spending. However, when the unemployment rate goes down people become more confident. They are more willing to spend on big ticket items like cars and houses. They believe they will either remain employed or be able to find another job quickly. As a result, economic activity increases.

But the unemployment rate gives us only part of the picture. What is missing are those people who are neither employed nor actively seeking work but are classified as eligible to work. The BLS approaches this by computing the Labor Force Participation Rate. That is, the number of people who are employed or who are actively seeking work divided by various adjustments to the population over the age of 16. The BLS website has more details if you're interested.

Why is the labor participation rate important? Consider this. The unemployment rate could be going down because more people are working, or it could be going down, at least in part, because fewer people are participating in the work force. At the end of 2016, the unemployment rate was 4.7% and the Labor Participation Rate was 62.7%, which means that 37.3% of people who were eligible to work were not working. That's a lot of people. Some argue the Labor Participation Rate is partly influenced by the number of retirees leaving the work force and young adults staying in school longer. Others say no, it's mostly due to governmental policies that tend to discourage working. Regardless who is right, the size and direction of the Labor Participation Rate has major implications for the economy and policy decision makers. At the end of 2018, and after favorable governmental policy changes starting in 2017, the unemployment rate declined to 3.9% and the Labor Participation Rate increased to 63.2%.

An alternative source of business-related employment data comes from a monthly report issued by a company called Automatic Data Processing, Inc. (ADP). ADP is involved in a wide variety of human resource and data processing activities for companies of various sizes. They survey their customers on employment trends and report the results a few days earlier than the more comprehensive BLS report.

Durable Goods Orders Report

This monthly report, which is released by the U.S. Census Bureau, gives an indication of whether businesses have placed orders to buy new equipment that will be used over a longer period of time – so-called durable goods. The idea is that if businesses are buying this type of equipment they must be doing so because they think there will be future growth. The reported numbers are volatile, so many choose to use a moving average to see if they can identify a trend.

New Residential Construction Report

This monthly report, released by the U.S. Census Bureau and the Department of Housing and Urban Development, is broken down into many different parts; one of the most interesting is the Building Permit Survey. This summary attempts to capture the number of building permits issued for new construction over a given time period. It's an indication of the health of the residential construction industry and all the other companies and businesses that directly and indirectly depend on residential construction. Why is this index so interesting? In addition to giving you a nine-month lead time, the time it typically takes to build a house, it is also an indication of the impact on a whole host of other industries once the house is completed. These involve companies such as those that make furniture and appliances – in other words, everything necessary to make a newly constructed house livable.

A related report is the Existing Home Sales Report issued monthly by the National Association of Realtors. This is based on a seasonally adjusted sampling of the median sales price of residential property. The report also provides data such as the number of properties sold and an indication of the existing inventory of houses still on the market. The seasonal adjustment is necessary because much of the activity occurs during the summer months. These figures provide a clue to the business environment for home improvement retailers such as Home Depot.

Consumer expectations

Since up to two-thirds of the U.S. economy is consumer driven, it pays to have an insight into what consumers are thinking about current and future economic conditions and about their own attitude toward their personal finances. Surveys to capture this are done by many organizations and groups, but the two that are most quoted are the Conference Board, an independent business and research association that also produces the Consumer Confidence Index, and the University of Michigan, which sponsors the Consumer Sentiment Index. These indices purport to be indications of future consumer spending.

There are slight, but important, differences between the two indices. The Consumer Confidence Index is determined monthly by sending out questionnaires to 5,000 households asking their views about current and future business conditions, current and future job market conditions, and family income expectations. Questionnaires are sent to a new group of people each month.

The Consumer Sentiment Index is somewhat similar in terms of the questions they ask, but it is conducted by telephone interviews of 500 people, 60% of whom are new people and 40% represent repeaters. The questions that are asked include consumers' views on the business climate, personal finances, and personal spending.

The Beige Book

Although we'll never know exactly what the Fed is going to do, at least we can look at some reports and data in which we might find some clues. One source is the Summary of Commentary on Current Economic Conditions, which is more commonly known as the Beige Book. This book is issued by the Fed eight times a year prior to a Federal Open Market Committee meeting. It is at these meetings that the Fed sets monetary policy. The book contains anecdotal information collected by each of the 12 Federal Reserve Districts regarding the current economic condition in their district. Clearly the Fed doesn't make its decisions based solely on anecdotal information – at least I hope not – but that book gives them (and us) clues on how the economy is doing across the country.

Index of Leading Economic Indicators

This monthly index is published by the Conference Board, an independent business and research association. It is made up of ten components that tend to lead changes in the economy. They are:

(1) Average weekly hours, manufacturing

(2) Average weekly initial claims for unemployment

(3) Manufacturers' new orders, consumer goods and materials

(4) ISM® Index of New Orders

(5) Manufacturers' new orders, non-defense capital goods excluding aircraft orders

(6) Building permits, new housing units

(7) Stock prices, 500 common stocks

(8) Leading Credit Index™

(9) Interest rates spread, 10-year Treasury bonds minus the federal funds rate

(10) Average consumer expectations for business conditions

Instead of using just the change in the index as a clue to future economic activity, many fundamental market timers analyze the ten individual components and want to see a decline in more than half of them, in addition to using a six-month decline in the index itself, before declaring an economic recession.

Real Gross Domestic Product

This number is issued by the U.S. Bureau of Economic Analysis quarterly. It measures the market value of all goods and services produced in the U.S. during a quarter, but is presented as an annualized number. It's called "real" because the data are adjusted to take inflation into account. This is not a leading indicator but it is watched closely because it gives clues on the current state of the economy and possibly the country's psychological mood as well.

Sentiment Indices

These sentiment indices attempt to codify Warren Buffett's much quoted statement: "Be fearful when others are greedy and greedy when others are fearful," which by itself is good advice. However, putting Mr. Buffett's advice into practice using published sentiment indices might not be such a good idea. The point is that sometimes these indices work and sometimes they don't. Sometimes they are contrary indicators, that is, a bullish reading is actually a time to sell. There isn't any consistency here. Often the index is a lagging indication, not a leading one, and belief in one is simply a behavioral response called an "illusion of validity." That is, people seek out evidence that confirms their own opinion and ignore information that is counter to it. But I felt you should be at least aware of a few of them that are talked about and might be of some use in trying to assess future PE ratios.

CAPE

CAPE stands for Cyclically Adjusted Price to Earnings ratio. This ratio is also known as the Shiller PE and the PE 10. It was developed by Professor Robert Shiller in an attempt to assess undervaluation or overvaluation in the market as represented by the S&P 500 index. It differs from the regular PE ratio in that is uses the average of the last 10 years of inflation (CPI-adjusted earnings) for the earnings portion of the calculation.

Although some have used it as a timing tool, it is not. It's a valuation tool, and as anyone who has attempted to time the market knows, the market can be undervalued or overvalued for very long time periods. Thus, those who want a precise timing tool challenge its usefulness and point out that it doesn't take into account the changes in the accounting for earnings or the lower interest rate environment.

Like all such indices, it's useful, but not perfect. Nothing I know of is.

Investor sentiment indices

There are a lot of opinions floating around the market, and that is what makes the market a market. Some think the market is going down while others think it is going up. Here is a quick survey of some of the sentiment indices. The "Fear and Greed Index" is produced by CNN Money. It tracks seven indicators of investor sentiment – market momentum, put and call options, safe haven demand, stock price breadth, stock price strength, market volatility, and junk bond demand. These indicators are analyzed separately and combined into an index that is then visually communicated by something that resembles a temperature gauge. The readings can go from extreme fear to extreme greed. The American Association of Individual Investors (AAII) has a sentiment index as well. It asks its members to express their opinion on whether they are bullish, bearish, or neutral about the direction of the market. Another sentiment index has been created by TD Ameritrade. It's called the Investor Movement Index®. Its website says that the index is created "…by analyzing and averaging the holdings/positions, trading activity, and other data from real portfolios held by real investors each month …" But often investors use these indices as contrary indications. That is, they are bullish when the indices are negative, and bearish when they are positive.

Others might look for clues in places other than the stock market. For example, the momentum of donations to non-profits, the size of margin debt at brokerage firms, enthusiasm for speculative investments, or even airline bookings and heavy truck sales. The list goes on and on.

Volatility Index (VIX)

Some smart people thought they could get a feel for future market volatility by looking at the volatility that is implied in the price of a basket of S&P 500 put and call options. They thought that if they knew how volatile the market might be, they could express an opinion about the future direction of the market.

I won't go into what puts and calls are, since they are beyond the scope of this book. Rather let's just get to the point. There is a special formula that many believe provides an indication of a fair price for these instruments. One of the input variables in that formula is expected volatility. Therefore, if you accept the current price of the basket, you can reverse engineer the formula and tease out the value for volatility that is implied by the price of the options. Voila, you have a market-based opinion of option traders as to what the future volatility in the S&P 500 index might be.

People like to call the VIX the "fear index" because it is thought that when the VIX increases above some normal range, the likelihood of a bear market also increases. Is that valuable information? Perhaps for short-term investors, but for long-term investors it might just be noise. Others view it as a coincidental indicator reflecting the current emotional state of those who buy and sell options on the S&P 500. The point is that this indicator, like all others, works some of the time.

The thing that got people really interested in the VIX, and perhaps reduced its usefulness as an indicator of future market direction, was its use as insurance policy against market declines. The idea was to buy the VIX when it trades at a low level. Then if the market declines in price the VIX would go up in price, and that increase would offset some or all of the loss.

Therefore, buyers were using the VIX as a means of insurance. That's not a bad idea, but there is one small problem. Because of the way options are priced, a component of the formula causes the option to decline in price over time all by itself independent of what the market does. It is like an ice cube melting on a hot day. Its value diminishes the longer and hotter the day. Thus, every so often you have to buy another insurance policy and destroy whatever predictive value the VIX might have had in the past.

Future Trends in Fundamental Market Timing

Information is a valuable commodity in forecasting the future direction of the stock market. Finding and processing it is not as easy as one might think. However, in the future two areas might help – neural networks and Google Trends®. I couldn't close this chapter without a few words about them.

Neural networks

This has become increasingly popular in forecasting the stock market. Merriam-Webster defines a neural network as, "A computer architecture in which a number of processors are interconnected in a manner suggestive of the connections between neurons in the human brain and which is able to learn by a process of trial and error."

The idea goes something like this. There is a huge amount of data out there, ranging from economic data to stock market data to company data. All of this in some way can explain short-term market movements if we can just figure out how. It's a complex process because it is so interconnected, with one variable affecting another, that affects yet another, that loops around affecting the first variable and so on. A lot of investment people are working on it because there is money to be made if someone identifies the answer.

Neural networks are all part of a larger field called artificial intelligence (AI). This field is evolving rapidly but if you want a brief, easy to understand overview get a copy of the November 2017 edition of *Popular Mechanics.* If you want more detailed information, a good source is *MIT Technology Review* articles.

Google Trends®

One of the many services provided by Google allows you to track the words and phrases used in Google searches. The number of Google queries is huge. Last September 2018, GEO Tribunal estimated the number to be about 63,000 queries a second. That means an astounding 5.6 billion every day. Recording this is like monitoring what a large slice of humanity is curious about.

Given this huge amount of current and historical data and the relative ease of accessing it, some investors and academics decided to see if they could tease out information that would give them a useful insight in forecasting the stock market's direction. Good idea, but the problem was – and remains – deciding what words, phrases, or trends are relevant. Just because two variables tend to move together doesn't make it a good indicator for predicting future movements. For example, just because the occurrence of the word "blue" increases at the same time that the S&P500 increases doesn't make it a good predictor – that is, a correlation without causation. In other words, there is no rationale for the two to move together, and thus the relationship is likely to change at any time.

Some think perhaps one can use Google Trends® to identify economic activity and use that to forecast the stock market. Perhaps. But historically there has been a variable time lag between changes in the economy and the stock market, with the stock market leading economic activity by months. After all, the S&P 500 is a component of the Index of Leading Economic Indicators.

> *"Calling the market is easy. Getting the market to answer is difficult."* – D. L. Upshaw

CHAPTER 25

Forces That Impact Long-Term Investing

Since I have been encouraging you to invest early, often, and for the long term, it is necessary to look at some of the forces that can impact long-term investing.

It's hard to underestimate the impact that demographics have on long-term investing. After all, people are consumers and they consume at different rates and on different things during their lifetime. If you can see those trends coming you can position your investments to take advantage of them. In this chapter I'll spend some time on U.S. demographics. Next, I'll discuss productivity and its impact on earnings. If people aren't productive, goods will cost more, there will fewer of them, and we will have a lower standard of living. Then I'll address a very important topic to long-term growth – the impact government has on the size of the economic pie. Finally, I'll conclude with a brief discussion of economic wave theory.

Demographic Trends

When we talk about demographics, we're talking about sorting people into groups in order to tease out useful information. The U.S. Census Bureau does this by grouping the population by age, race, sex, income levels, and locations, just to name a few of the ways. Their data comes from a requirement in our Constitution that our population be counted every 10 years. Most of the information is gathered by mail and the rest is conducted by door-to-door surveys. The last census, or official counting of our population, was done in 2010. The Census Bureau conducts smaller surveys to modify the official census in order to provide useful information for the in-between years. In addition to current information, the Bureau also makes forecasts on the size and composition of the population decades into the future. One such forecast is shown in Figure 25-1.

Population by Age Groups: 2014 to 2030
Population in thousands
(Source: U.S. Census Bureau)

Age	2014	2020	2030	Change 2014 to 2030
Under 18	73,591	74,128	76,273	3.60%
18 to 24	115,426	120,073	126,588	9.70%
45 to 64	83,477	83,861	82,434	-1.30%
65 & older	46,255	56,441	74,107	60.20%
Total	318,748	334,503	359,402	12.80%

Figure 25-1

When displaying the results in this way it becomes clear that everyone is on the conveyor belt of life. For example, with the passage of time people in the under-18 age group will gradually enter the 18 to 44 age group, then the 45 to 64 age group, and eventually the 65 & older group. Assuming that the Census Bureau is reasonably accurate in estimating births, deaths, and migration patterns (a big assumption, not because of their capabilities but because of the unknowns), we have a pretty good idea of how many people will be in the various age groups in 2020 and 2030.

What does this have to do with investing in common stocks? Here are some general observations. You'll have your own.

The first observation

The population is growing. This has profound implications for long-term investors, especially for investing in those types of quality companies in industries whose products people use throughout their lives regardless of what age group they are in. Simply put, an increasing number of people means an increasing demand for that company's products, and that means increasing profits over time which means increasing dividends and increasing stock prices. The place to start looking for these types of companies are in the ranks of those who have been paying dividends for decades. But you need to convince yourself that the company you identified has staying power, for example, has a competitive edge. Then, when the market has one of its periodic emotional fits and your company's stock is selling at a discount, you buy more shares.

The second observation

Because of the nature of life, each group has different needs, wants, and desires. For example, healthcare is more of a concern and is used more often by those individuals in the 65-&-older group than those in the under-18 group. If the 65-&-older group is expected to increase in the years to come, perhaps positioning your investments in companies that provide goods and services to this group might be a good idea. Digging even further into the reports prepared by the Census Bureau you'll find that the fastest growing subgroup in the 65-&-older group is the young-elderly (70 to 85) and the oldest-old (85+). What are their needs, wants, and desires? Is there an investment opportunity in these expanding groups?

Although the changing distribution by age matters, that's not the only thing to consider. As people move from one group to another, they carry with them vestiges of what happened while they were in the previous groups. For example, the people who lived during the Great Depression of the 1930s in the under-18 age group carried those experiences with them throughout their lives and it colored their choices going forward. In the fullness of time, that group will be replaced by a new group whose experiences are different. Now consider your group (under-18 age group) and your involvement with technology and social media as you age. How will that impact your wants, needs, and desires as you age and move into another group? And what impact will biotechnology and artificial intelligence have on the current 18-to-44 group when they enter into the over-65 group in the future?

The third observation

If you take a comprehensive view you might ask: "What impact do the shifts in population have on the overall stock market?" Consider that the 45-to-64 group is expected to decline by the year 2030. Historically, people in this group have been the largest savers and investors because they have had the extra income to do so. Historically, as people move into the 65-&-older group, they typically become spenders. What implications does the shift from investors to spenders have for the direction of the stock market if the other age groups don't acquire the investing habit?

To summarize, you have changing numbers, lingering vestiges of the past, and the impact of recent events to consider as you plot your strategy to take advantage of demographic trends. It's up to you to put the pieces together. The idea is to take advantage of the knowledge of an increasing population and the movement of people from one group to another and to position your stock investments accordingly.

But before you get all excited about investing based on demographic changes, some warnings. Demographic changes can build at a very slow pace or change very quickly, as in the case of economic collapse, diseases, and war. You have to be careful. But if you can identify a trend, it can be very rewarding indeed to a long-term investor.

Productivity Trends

It's hard to overemphasize the importance productivity has for our economic wellbeing. But what is productivity? In straightforward terms, it is simply the ability to produce more at a lower cost or to produce better quality for the same cost. The key components necessary for increased productivity are innovation, a skilled labor force, good management, and increased capital investment.

The road that productivity travels to arrive at an improved standard of living goes like this. If the cost of goods and services is lowered through increased productivity, those who consume those goods and services have more money left over for other things. Moreover, those who do the producing can receive increased wages without impacting the company's profits. If the quality improves for the same cost, consumers are better off. Lower costs, higher wages, and better products increase our standard of living.

But some will say that producing more at a lower cost just means a continuation of consumers buying stuff they really don't need. For the moment, put aside the arrogance of someone telling you what you can and cannot buy. What about the things you do need and the things you do want? Consider cellphones. In the early days of that remarkable invention, the cost to own one, much less pay for air time, was very high. Few people could afford it. Moreover, the phone resembled a brick and you had to haul around a small suitcase that contained the electronic equipment that made the phone work. Hard to believe now, but true! So, what happened? Innovation, a skilled labor force, good management, and capital investment in factories and equipment kept making the cell phone smaller and smaller and cheaper and cheaper. So instead of buying an expensive inconvenient item, through the magic of productivity and free market capitalism you and millions of others could buy a better phone cheaper, and you could save the difference in cost and still have a better experience. Your standard of living increased.

Productivity is often thought of only in terms of labor output. Sure, that's a large component, but there also is a managerial component to consider as well. With bloated management, decisions have to go through multiple levels of management, which increases costs and stifles productivity. Also, there is capital productivity, which is making capital investments perform in an efficient, productive way. Sometimes that means using capital to build more efficient factories rather than a new office building. In fact, increased productivity through capital investments seems to have a direct impact on a company's future earnings. Finally, the productivity of a country depends on the number of workers who are productive and innovative. That, in turn, depends not only on demographics but heavily on education.

Point-in-time measures for productivity are provided by the Bureau of Labor Statistics, generally on a quarterly basis, for a wide variety of areas in the economy so you can track the direction over time.

Government Actions

It's useful to think of the economy as a pie whose size is measured by the country's Gross Domestic Product (roughly the dollar amount of what our country produces). If that's the case, then our slice of the pie is GDP divided by the size of the population.

Some say the pie is fixed in size and the government needs to decide who gets a slice and how big. I say no. The size of the pie is a function of government actions, changes in productivity, and other factors and, as a result, it can increase or decrease. Moreover, if the pie grows faster than the population, everyone gets a bigger slice and is happy. However, if the pie grows at a slower pace, then the size of the slices gets smaller and everyone is unhappy, especially those who don't even get a slice.

Many things can influence the size of the economic pie. One that has the greatest impact is the policy actions of the government itself. Rather than try to explain how all this intricacy works in words, I did it visually in Figure 25-2. Congress raises money from the right-hand side of the diagram and spends it on the left-hand side. Any short fall is made up by borrowing. The little black circles with a "T" on them are intended to be valves like you would see on a water faucet. Tighten them and less flows through; loosen them and more flows through. Instead of water, the flows are all about money. If Congress tightens the valves on the right side of the figure, less money flows to those people and more initially flows to Congress to spend on the items listed on the left side of the figure. However, if the valves are tightened too tight on the right side, the size of the economic pie will shrink and Congress will get less and less money from the right side. Unless Congress cuts back on spending, borrowing increases as do the interest payments on that debt.

There are literally thousands of boxes on the left side where the government spends money. I narrowed it down to those you see. For decades Congress has spent more than it raised from taxes and the shortfall has been made up by borrowing. Our borrowings have been so great, we now owe over $21 trillion dollars. That's a lot of money – so much it is hard to conceptualize until you put it into a per individual basis, that is, every person in the country, including you and babies and children, owes about $65,000 each.

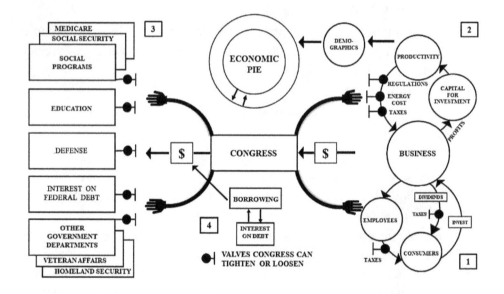

Figure 25-2

To help you understand some of the outcomes of governmental actions, I have divided the figure into areas that I describe below. The areas are identified by the square boxes with numbers in them.

(1)   This area represents the interaction between employees, consumers, investors, and businesses. Congress controls the amount of taxes as represented by the valves. Businesses have employees. Employees are both consumers and investors. The higher the taxes (the tighter the valves are closed), the less after-tax income is

available to employees to spend as consumers or to invest as investors. The higher the taxes on capital gains and the double taxation of dividends, the less there is available to reinvest. The result is consumers will consume less and investors will invest less and both will impact the near- and long-term viability of businesses. That, in turn, will negatively impact employees, consumers, and investors and eventually work its way through the lens of productivity to a decreasing economic pie. Loosen the valves and the opposite effect will occur.

(2)   This area represents the impact taxes have on a business, on capital for investments, and on productivity. The higher the taxes on business, the less money there is available to expand or modernize, to hire new employees, to increase wages, to increase dividends, to increase share buybacks, or to pay down corporate debt. The government also controls the amount of regulations placed on business which, if too tight, reduces the flow of income to the business. All of this reduces productivity and, when filtered through the lens of demographics, reduces the size of the economic pie. Loosen the valves, the opposite effect will occur.

(3)   Congress also controls the valves for spending on defense, social programs, education, and other governmental expenditures. If they are opened too wide, government must tighten the valves on businesses, employees, consumers, and investors in order to raise the money necessary to pay for these expenditures. To meet any shortfall, the government must increase its borrowings. Because of the amount it borrows, government can crowd out businesses from borrowing money to build factories. All of this reduces productivity and, when filtered through the lens of demographics, reduces the size of the economic pie. Tighten the valves on government spending and the opposite effect will occur.

(4)   This area represents the debt that has been incurred by the government spending more on the left side of the diagram than what is coming in from the right side. Since the government borrows the difference, it must pay interest on that amount as well as the interest on all the previous debt that has been incurred. As debt grows so does the

amount paid in interest, and if interest rates increase, the interest payments will accelerate at an increasing rate until they consume a substantial portion of what is coming in from the right side of the diagram. When that happens, economic collapse occurs. To avoid that disaster, the government must stop spending more than what is coming in and work to increase the size of the economic pie.

The lesson from this analysis is if the government cuts taxes, avoids burdensome regulation, becomes more pro-business, and cuts spending the economic pie will increase and our people will be better off.

Do the opposite and the economic pie will shrink. When that happens, the skilled get the jobs and the divide between those who have the skills and those who don't widens and inequality increases. Then there is an increase in social programs, which results in increased taxes and more governmental borrowing. This leads to less capital for businesses and therefore less productivity; this in turn, leads to a lower standard of living which, if the cycle is not broken, leads to a further shrinkage of the economic pie. The country enters into a vicious downward cycle (see Figure 25-3).

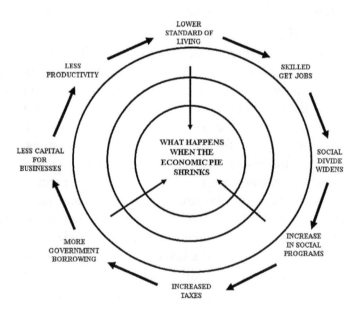

Figure 25-3

I hope these two figures give you at least a feel for the enormous role government plays in increasing or decreasing the size of the economic pie, and therefore your wellbeing and your stock investing opportunities.

Wave Theory

At some point, you may encounter a different method of long-term economic forecasting called the wave theory. One of its earliest proponents was an author who paid with his life for his ideas. His name was Nikolai Kondratieff, and in 1925 he wrote a book entitled *Major Economic Cycles*. His great misfortune was that he lived in Russia and those in power didn't care for his main idea, which was that was all economies periodically go through ups and downs. The policy of the communist party at the time was that capitalism in the West was a flawed system doomed to failure, not one just going through a periodic down period. So off to the Gulag he went, and he was executed in 1938.

His theory was that economies go through major waves of ups and downs that last 50 to 60 years. Within the major waves are smaller one of shorter duration and within these, still smaller ones. He illustrated his idea with ample historical research.

Waves or cycles are part of the historical economic landscape. Economies have seen periods of rapid expansion followed by periods of quiet consolidation or decline. We have also seen bursts of inflation that are often followed by periods of low inflation or even deflation. But the problem has been and remains that only in retrospect can we see the peaks and valleys and when we do, the time period between them is variable. But exist they do.

Our logical mind wants a reasonable explanation for the waves. Although there is no one explanation, the consensus appears to be that the major waves are caused by major technological change such as the steam engine, cotton gin, automobile, telephone, computers, and internet. Again, that makes intuitive sense. However, if that's the case, then the length of the cycles should be shorter given the rapid changes we've seen in the last few decades. International jet travel, for example, is about 60 years old and look what technological changes have happened since then. Or maybe the waves are caused by governmental action. Consider this. If the cycle lasts 50 to 60 years, that's about the time for two generations to pass and this is about the right amount of time for the current generation of political leaders to forget the lessons of the past.

The Last Word

The stock market doesn't care what race, ethnic group, religion, or sexual orientation you claim. It doesn't care what economic group your parents are in or, for that matter, your height, weight, or IQ. The stock market simply is the most inclusive institution in the world. All it asks of you is to believe in yourself, believe in free market capitalism, have a bit of money (not necessarily a lot), and take the time to learn about the stock market and the opportunities it presents to you.

Unlike so many other investment books on the market, I have not given you some get-rich-quick secret formula, and maybe you are disappointed. Don't be. Instead, I gave you something of real value – a comprehensive, organized, and easy-to-understand overview of the stock market so you can make your own investment decisions, based on your own personality and risk tolerances. And when you do make an investment, you'll know what you invested in, why, and what to expect.

By now you should know how to open a brokerage account, how to select the right type of order, and how to evaluate the risk. You learned about corporations and found that they give you the opportunity to acquire serious wealth by participating in the success of their products or services. You learned how the stock market works and how market indices are constructed, as well as what these indices can tell you if you pay attention. You learned how important free market capitalism is to our country's economic success and thus the prosperity it provides our people. You learned our economic system also produces dynamic companies for you to invest in. You learned all that, and much, much more, in the first section of this book.

I went into increasing depth about the major investment strategies you should consider. I started with an overview (Section 2), then a more detailed look (Section 3), and ended with a look inside various investment management firms so you can see how they go about their business (Section 4). As a result, you should know which strategy – active, passive, or factor-based – suits your personality and risk tolerance. In my opinion, one of them should be the center piece of your investment strategy.

But it doesn't have to be an all-or-nothing approach. You can start with a passive strategy and after you have built up your capital (and you have the time and inclination) you can shift some of your money into do-it-yourself active management or into factor-based strategies. Splitting money like this between passive and an alternative is called a core/non-core approach. Core represents the money allocated to passive investments and generally represents the majority of the monies invested, and non-core represents the money allocated to active or factor-based strategies.

Although many investors successfully use the core/non-core approach, it is just one of many combinations available. For example, you may want to have all your money in one strategy or in one or several individual stocks. It's up to you depending on your risk tolerance and how much time you are willing to devote to the market. And you now have the knowledge of where to start and how to go about it.

After you have selected an investment strategy, you need to implement it. I've given you plenty of ideas how to do that from do-it-yourself active management to engaging the services of active, passive, or factor-based mutual funds or ETF managers. With respect to engaging an investment manager, you could conduct the search for one yourself or you could hire an investment advisor to help you. The details on how to make this happen were explained in Section 5.

When it comes to buying and selling, in Section 6, I explained the popular strategies for avoiding market timing and identified their limitations. I also covered in depth the fundamental and technical approaches to market timing and, importantly, explained the major emotions you are likely to encounter when investing in the stock market. If you can recognize what's going on within yourself emotionally, you'll have a better chance of success in the investment game. Finally, I concluded with how demographics can influence investment decisions, the importance of increasing productivity, and the critical role the government plays in long-term investing.

As you can see, a lot of material was covered in this book and to fully understand it you might have to reread it several times. But what has been presented to you should provide you with a solid framework for evaluating investment alternatives and thus a strong foundation for informed decision-making. The next step is up to you.

Just remember, the long-term odds of achieving serious wealth are in your favor if you:

Invest early because "early" provides you with a longer time frame to participate in the power of compounding.

Invest often because "often" increases the amount of money you have invested.

Invest for the long term because "long term" gives the first two, early and often, the time to fulfill their promise of serious wealth.

> *I wish all of you who have taken the time to thoroughly read this book great success, wealth, and happiness.*

INDEX